ASSESSMENT PACK
with Audio CD and Test Generating CD-ROM

3

FOCUS
ON
GRAMMAR

AN INTEGRATED SKILLS APPROACH

THIRD EDITION

JOAN JAMIESON

CAROL A. CHAPELLE

WITH

LESLIE GRANT

BETHANY GRAY

XIANGYING JIANG

HSIN-MIN LIU

KEVIN ZIMMERMAN

D0217965

PEARSON
Longman

Focus on Grammar 3: An Integrated Skills Course
Assessment Pack

Pearson Education, 10 Bank Street, White Plains, NY 10606

Staff credits: The people who made up the *Focus on Grammar 3: An Integrated Skills Course, Assessment Pack* team, representing editorial, production, design, and manufacturing, are listed below:

Rhea Banker
John Barnes
Nancy Blodgett
Elisabeth Carlson
Christine Edmonds
Margot Gramer
Laura Le Dréan
Wendy Long
Michael Mone
Linda Moser
Julie Schmidt

ISBN: 0-13-193140-7

Printed in the United States of America
5 6 7 8 9 10—BAH—10 09 08

Contents

Introduction

The *Focus on Grammar 3 Assessment Pack* includes the following assessment tools to help you determine students' grammar proficiency level and monitor their progress and achievement in the *Focus on Grammar* course.

In addition to the tools listed below, a separately packaged *Focus on Grammar Placement Test* (ISBN 0-13-199437-9) is also available. To obtain a copy of the *Placement Test,* contact your local Longman ELT specialist.

FOG Student Book Assessment Tools

- Part Diagnostic and Achievement Tests
- Unit Achievement Tests
- Audio CD with the listening portions of the Diagnostic and Achievement Tests

Supplementary Assessment Tools

- Two ETS Grammar Proficiency Tests (Levels 4 and 5)
- Test Generating CD-ROM

You can find detailed descriptions of each type of assessment tool, as well as instructions on administering and scoring the tests, in the "General Information" sections that precede the test forms.

About the Authors

Joan Jamieson, Project Director, is a Professor in the Applied Linguistics program in the English Department at Northern Arizona University. She received her Ph.D. from the University of Illinois at Urbana-Champaign. Dr. Jamieson is the author of several publications on English as a Second Language assessment and computer-assisted language learning. She has collaborated with Pearson Longman and Carol Chapelle in the past on several projects, including *Longman English Assessment* and the testing program for *Longman English Interactive.*

Carol A. Chapelle, Project Director, is a Professor of TESL/Applied Linguistics at Iowa State University. She received her Ph.D. from the University of Illinois at Urbana-Champaign. She is the author of *Computer applications in second language acquisition: Foundations for teaching, testing and research* (Cambridge University Press, 2001), *English language learning and technology: Lectures on teaching and research in the age of information and communication technology.* (John Benjamins Publishing, 2003), and *ESOL tests and testing: A resource for teachers and program administrators* (TESOL Publications, 2005). Dr. Chapelle was until recently the editor of *TESOL Quarterly.* She has collaborated with Joan Jamieson and Pearson Longman in the past on several projects, including *Longman English Assessment* and the testing program for *Longman English Interactive.*

Project Staff

The following people worked on the development of the tests under the guidance of Joan Jamieson and Carol Chapelle:

Leslie Grant, Ph.D., Northern Arizona University

Bethany Gray, MA-TESL student, Iowa State University

Xiangying Jiang, Ph.D. student, Northern Arizona University

Hsin-min Liu, MA-TESL, Iowa State University

Kevin Zimmerman, MA-TESL, Brigham Young University

and

Liza Armstrong, MA-TESL, Northern Arizona University

Maja Grgurovic, Ph.D. student, Iowa State University

James McCormick, Ph.D., Michigan State University

Erin Kate Murphy, MA-TESL, Northern Arizona University

Pamela Pearson, MA-TESL student, Iowa State University

Lia Plakans, Ph.D. student, University of Iowa

Kornwipa Poonpon, Ph.D. student, Northern Arizona University

Kerri Quinn, MA-TESL, Northern Arizona University

Betsy Tremmel, MA student, Iowa State University

Part Diagnostic Tests, Unit Achievement Tests, and Part Achievement Tests

General Information

Overview

The *Focus on Grammar* Part Diagnostic, Unit Achievement, and Part Achievement Tests have set a new standard in ELT grammar teaching and testing. Developed under the direction of applied linguists Joan Jamieson and Carol A. Chapelle, these tests

- are manageable in length and easy to administer and score;
- accurately reflect the material presented in the Grammar in Context, Grammar Charts and Notes, and Focused Practice sections of the course;
- offer a sufficient number of items to assess students' knowledge of each grammar point;
- include a wide variety of item types;
- provide a powerful remediation tool.

About the Test Development

These tests have been carefully developed so that the weighting and distribution of test items mirror those of the Student Book content. For example, if 40 percent of the items in a unit practice the simple present and 60 percent of the items practice the present progressive, then the Unit Achievement Test maintains the same balance. The Part Diagnostic and Achievement Tests additionally reflect the distribution of items across the units in a part. For example, if one unit in a part has 110 practice items, and the second unit in the part has 53 practice items, then the Part Diagnostic and Achievement Tests maintain the same balance.

Using the Tests for Remediation Purposes

Codes provided in the Answer Key help you determine what grammar points students might be having difficulty with. In the Unit Achievement Tests, each answer has a code that refers to one or more of the Grammar Notes or to the Grammar Chart. In the Part Diagnostic and Part Achievement Tests, each answer has a code that refers to the unit where the item was presented. By referring to these codes, both you and the student can try to pinpoint grammar points that are causing confusion or proving to be difficult.

> **EXAMPLE:**
>
> Item 5 in Exercise 2 of the Unit 14 Achievement Test has the code **N3**. This means that the item is testing the grammar point associated with Grammar Note 3 in the Student Book: "Use *should* for questions. We do not usually use

ought to or *had better* for questions." If a student answered this item incorrectly, that student may need more help with this grammar point.

NOTE: If a test item has two codes separated by a comma (for example, `N1, N2` or `U1, U2`), that item is testing two grammar points or two units.

Test Purpose and Design

The **Part Diagnostic Tests** help you determine how well students know the material they are about to study in the next part of the Student Book. Since the material they are about to study is usually new, students often score low on these tests.

Each Part Diagnostic Test takes 50 minutes and includes about 60 items. The test begins with a listening exercise, includes several contextualized grammar exercises, and ends with an editing exercise.

The **Unit Achievement Tests** help you assess students' knowledge of the specific grammatical topics presented in the unit. If students have mastered the material presented in the unit, they should answer most of the questions correctly. The codes provided in the Answer Key help you determine what grammar topics students may need to review.

Each Unit Achievement Test takes 30 minutes and includes about 30 items. The test begins with a listening exercise, includes two to three contextualized grammar exercises, and ends with an editing exercise.

The **Part Achievement Tests** help you determine how well students have mastered the material they have studied in that part of the Student Book. If students have mastered the material presented in the part, they should answer most of the questions correctly. The codes provided in the Answer Key help you determine what units students may need to review.

Each Part Achievement Test is identical in structure to the Part Diagnostic Test for the part, including the same number of items and testing the same grammar points with equal balance and weighting. By comparing a student's results on the Part Diagnostic Test and on the Part Achievement Test, you can determine how much students have learned.

Administering the Tests

Before administering a test:

- Make photocopies of the test form.
- Set up your CD player in the testing room and check the volume.
- Check the track list on the inside back cover for which track you will need to play.

The listening section in the Part Diagnostic, Unit Achievement, and Part Achievement Tests is the first section of the test so that it may be administered to all students at the same time without interfering with the other parts of the test. When students are ready to begin the test, play the audio CD and have students listen and answer the questions. You should play each track two times.

After students have completed the listening section, stop the CD and ask students to work on the remaining sections of the test.

Scoring the Tests

To determine a student's score on the tests, add up the number of questions the student answered correctly, using the Answer Key on pages 229–258. You may also wish to subtract the number incorrect from the total number of items. The total number of items for each test is shown on the first page of the test.

To determine the percentage score, first divide the number correct by the total number of items; then, multiply that proportion by 100. (Use the total number of items on the test, not the number of items that a student answered.)

EXAMPLE:

The Part VI Achievement Test includes 60 items.
A student answered 47 items correctly.

$47 \div 60 = .78 \rightarrow .78 \times 100 = 78$

The student's percentage score is 78%.

A scoring box is provided on the first page of each test to record the student's score.

PART I Diagnostic Test

| 60 Items |
| Score: _____ |

1 | LISTENING: GOING OUT

A. 🎧 *Sheila is talking to her roommate Carla. Listen to their conversation. Complete the conversation by writing the words that you hear. You will hear the recording two times.*

CARLA: What ____*are you doing*____ ?
0.

SHEILA: I'm getting ready to go out.

CARLA: Oh, yeah? Where _____ ?
1.

SHEILA: I'm going out to lunch and then to a geography lecture. Hand me my purse, please.

CARLA: Sure. Here you go. So, _____ with?
2.

SHEILA: I'm going with this guy Ray. I met him at Virginia's party last night.

CARLA: _____ he like?
3.

SHEILA: He's really cool. He used to live in Madagascar, just like me. And he speaks French!

CARLA: Wow! Well, let me know how it goes.

SHEILA: OK. I'll tell you _____ I get home.
4.

B. *These sentences are based on the conversation. Circle the correct words or phrases to complete the sentences.*

0. Sheila (is getting) / gets / will get ready to go out.

1. Sheila used to meet / was meeting / met Ray at Virginia's party the night before.

2. Sheila goes / is going / did went out to lunch and then to a lecture.

3. Sheila said, "Please to hand / be handing / hand me my purse."

4. Ray used to live / is used to live / was used to live in Africa.

5. Carla said, "To let / Let / Be letting me know how it goes, OK?"

2 | AFTER THE LECTURE

Ray and Sheila listened to the geography lecture. Now they are talking. Complete the conversation. Use the words in the box.

before	'll give	's raining	used to be
'll buy	going to be	say	used to go
'll call	going to go	showed	~~was~~
don't have	like	speak	won't be
explained	meet	talk	work
get	points out	until	'll work

SHEILA: That _____was_____ a good lecture! I _____ coming to these
0.   **1.**

lectures. They're interesting. But what did the professor say about the rocks in South

America?

RAY: Remember when he _____ the picture of the two rocks? He
2.

_____ that the rocks in the eastern part of South America are similar to
3.

the rocks in Western Africa. He pointed out that this is evidence that South America and

Africa _____ one continent.
4.

SHEILA: Oh, I see now. You know, it's nice that you _____ French. I usually
5.

_____ anyone to speak French with, except once a week at the French
6.

Club. You should come. We _____ on Wednesdays at 6:30. Can you come
7.

next Wednesday?

RAY: No, I'm _____ at work at that time, so I _____ able to go.
8.   **9.**

I _____ on Wednesday evenings. But tomorrow I'm _____
10.   **11.**

hiking. Do you want to go with me, at around two o'clock?

SHEILA: Sure! But call me _____ you come over. I have to work tomorrow
12.

morning, and I'm not sure when I'll be home.

RAY: OK. I _____ you tomorrow when I'm ready. Oh, no . . . it looks like
13.

it _____! I _____ you my umbrella so you don't get wet.
14.   **15.**

PART I

3 | AFTER THE FIRST DATE

Ray is talking to his roommate Leo about his date with Sheila. Complete the conversation. Use the correct forms of the words in parentheses. Some items may have more than one right answer.

LEO: So, _____*how was*_____ your date with Sheila? _____?
                   0. (how / be)   **1. (what / happen)**

RAY: The date was good. We heard Dr. Fina talk.

LEO: _____ Dr. Fina, and _____ about?
           2. (who / be)   **3. (what / he / talk)**

RAY: He's a geography professor. _____ on the history of the earth.
                                    4. (he / lecture)

LEO: So _____ about Sheila. Do you like her?
           5. (tell / me)

RAY: Yeah, she's cool. We have a lot in common. She _____ in
                                           6. (use to / live)

Madagascar too, and _____ French. _____
                         7. (she / know)   **8. (we / be going to / go)**

hiking tomorrow.

LEO: What time are you leaving?

RAY: _____ at 2:00. Then _____ dinner. Why?
      9. (we / leave)   **10. (we / probably / will have)**

LEO: Well, I'm surprised you can go on Friday. _____ Fridays off of
                                      11. (you / never / use to / have)

work.

RAY: But it's a holiday, remember?

LEO: Oh, yeah! Well, _____ how your hike goes.
                       12. (let / me / know)

RAY: OK, I will.

4 | GETTING READY

Sheila is getting ready to go hiking with Ray. Complete the sentences. Use the correct forms of the verbs in the box. Some items may have more than one right answer.

be	~~go~~	love	start	tell	walk
get	have	see	take	think	want
give	leave				

CARLA: Virginia and I ___are going___ skating tonight. Do you want to go?
              0.

SHEILA: Maybe, but I'm not sure when I _____ home. I _____ ready
                                              1.   **2.**

to leave right now. Ray and I _____ hiking this afternoon. I don't know
                                    3.

how long we _____ out. I'll call you from my cell phone when I
                  4.

_____ a better idea of when I'll be back.
      5.

CARLA: Didn't you see Ray last night, too?

SHEILA: Yes, and he was such a gentleman. When we _____ that it was raining,
                                                          6.

he _____ out an umbrella and _____ it to me. I
      7.   **8.**

_____ that was really nice. And it's so great to have someone to talk to
      9.

about Madagascar. While Ray was walking me home in the rain, he _____
                                                                        10.

me about his time there. He _____ the Malagasy people and he
                                  11.

_____ to go back someday.
      12.

CARLA: It seems like you really like him.

SHEILA: I think I do.

5 | EDITING: ON THE HIKE

Read the conversation between Ray and Sheila on their hike. There are thirteen mistakes. The first mistake is already corrected. Find and correct twelve more. Remember to look at punctuation!

SHEILA: I think it's ~~being~~ amazing how much we have in common!

RAY: Me too. I was being glad that you wanted to go to the lecture with me yesterday. I thinked it was interesting.

SHEILA: I did too. It was a very nice evening, and I was having a great time! I told my roommate all about the lecture when I getted home.

RAY: Oh, good. Hey, I brought some sandwiches. Would you like one?

SHEILA: Sure, I'm getting hungry. When you called this afternoon I was eating lunch. But that was four hours ago . . . Mmm. Thanks for the sandwich. It's tasting good.

RAY: This place is reminding me a little bit of Manakara in Madagascar. Were you ever there?

SHEILA: No, I never was there. I spended most of my time in Antananarivo. Do you want to see my pictures sometime?

RAY: Sure.

SHEILA: OK. I'll bringing them when we'll see each other next.

RAY: And I'll to show you my pictures, too.

SHEILA: That sounds great!

Unit 1 Achievement Test

30 Items
Score: _____

1 | LISTENING: QUINTUPLETS

A. 🎧 *Quintuplets are five babies that are born at the same time to the same mother. Listen to this news item about quintuplets from a TV news broadcast. Complete the news item by writing the words that you hear. You will hear the recording two times.*

STEVE: And now some local news. Eileen Hill is at Arkansas General Hospital with an

interesting story. Eileen, what _____*'s happening*_____?
0.

EILEEN: Kevin, I'm standing outside General Hospital, where Mary Griffith just gave birth to five

babies. Mary _____ fine, but doctors are watching the quintuplets
1.

carefully. We've been told that the father, John Griffith, is preparing for a press

conference . . . Wait a minute, it _____ like he's starting to talk now!
2.

JOHN: First, I _____ to thank the nurses and doctors. Mary and I appreciate all
3.

of their hard work. Thanks to them, we believe the five babies will be just fine.

EILEEN: How is Mary doing?

JOHN: Well, she's tired, of course. Right now she _____, but she's doing well.
4.

EILEEN: Do you have all the help that you need?

JOHN: Obviously, we need a lot of help, but fortunately we have some wonderful friends and

neighbors who are helping us. That's all for now. I need to get back to Mary. Thank you.

B. *Reread the news item. Write each verb from the box below in the correct category. An example is given.*

~~'m standing~~	are watching	is preparing
appreciate	need	believe

PRESENT PROGRESSIVE	SIMPLE PRESENT
0. *'m standing*	1. _____
1. _____	2. _____
2. _____	3. _____

2 | AT HOME WITH THE GRIFFITHS

The Griffiths are home from the hospital. Complete the sentences about what is going on in their home a month later. Circle the correct words or phrases.

0. Right now, two of the babies sleeps / (are sleeping) / sleep.

1. Mary is feeding / feeds / feed one of the babies at the moment.

2. It seems like the babies always want / want usually / are sometimes wanting to eat.

3. Mary is making / made / makes 50 bottles every day.

4. She isn't getting much sleep rarely / nowadays / often.

5. She usually feels / is feeling / felt tired.

6. Fortunately, neighbors still came / come / are coming over every day to help.

7. John stayed home for two weeks, but now he is working / works / worked again.

8. He works / work / is working as a computer programmer.

9. Every day after work he hurries / hurried / is hurrying home to help Mary.

3 | A YEAR LATER

Read about the Griffiths a year after the babies were born. Complete the sentences by writing the simple present or present progressive form of each verb.

0. Mary Griffith _____*is getting*_____ more sleep now.
   (get)

1. The babies _____ better these days.
   (sleep)

2. Still, the babies often _____ at night.
   (cry)

3. Fortunately, the Griffiths' neighbors _____ their situation.
   (understand)

4. The Griffiths still _____ in their two-bedroom apartment.
   (live)

5. John Griffith _____ for work at 8:00 in the morning every day.
   (leave)

6. He _____ home at 5:30 in the afternoon.
   (arrive)

7. Right now, John _____ on a big project.
   (work)

8. At the moment, he _____ his newest computer program.
   (test)

4 | EDITING: BEDTIME

Read this paragraph about getting ready for bed. There are five mistakes in the use of the present progressive or simple present. The first mistake is already corrected. Find and correct four more.

        is getting
It's nighttime, and Mary Griffith ~~gets~~ ready for bed. She can hardly believe that the house is

so quiet. At the moment, all five babies sleep, and she wants to sleep too. All five babies rarely

are sleeping at the same time. There usually is at least one baby up or crying. She looks in their

room to make sure they are all OK. They are all sleeping, and they are looking beautiful.

Unit 2 Achievement Test

| 30 Items |
| Score: _____ |

1 | LISTENING: EXERCISE

A. 🎧 *Tracy Powers teaches exercise and diet at a local health gym. She is teaching an exercise class now. Listen to her instructions to the class. Complete the instructions by writing the words that you hear. You will hear the recording two times.*

OK, everybody. _____*Get*_____ ready! First we're going to stretch. We're going to try to
0.

touch our toes. Bend over slowly, and _____ in that position for three counts. One,
1.

two, three, and come up. Good! We'll try it again. Now, as you're stretching, you should feel a

stretch in the back of your legs and in your lower back. _____ your knees, if
2.

possible. If you bend your knees, your muscles won't stretch as much. _____ your
3.

neck so that your head hangs straight down. This will help stretch the muscles in your neck.

Breathe deeply. Your body needs a lot of oxygen, so _____ your breath.
4.

Concentrate on your breathing. One, two, three, and stand up. Exhale. Whoo!

B. *Reread the instructions. Find five verbs in the imperative form. Write them below. (Note: Only use words that are given in the instructions. Do not use any words that you wrote.) An example is given.*

0. _____*Bend*_____

1. _____

2. _____

3. _____

4. _____

5. _____

2 | WHO'S SAYING WHAT?

Read the following instructions and write who is speaking. Use the words in the box.

a boss	a robber	a driving instructor	an exercise instructor
a ~~parent~~	a receptionist	a telephone operator	an airport security officer
a librarian	a police officer	a financial advisor	an employment specialist

0. Come on! Hurry! Don't be late! Don't forget your lunch. Zip up your jacket. Give me a hug. Come home right after school.

   _____ *a parent* _____

1. Drive slowly. Turn right at the corner. Stop at the red light. Now, park the car behind the bus.

   _____

2. Don't move! Follow my instructions! Give me your money and don't ask any questions!

   _____

3. Please deposit 25 cents to make a call.

   _____

4. Please come in. Have a seat and make yourself comfortable. Dr. Park will be with you in just a moment.

   _____

5. Come to work on time. Don't leave so early. Work harder. Show me you really care about your work.

   _____

6. Wear your best clothes to the interview. Tell them all about your work experience. Listen carefully and answer all their questions. Don't talk too much. Be very polite.

   _____

7. Please speak quietly. Don't eat or drink in here. Put the books on the shelf when you're done.

   _____

8. Show me your ticket. Remove anything metal from your body. Walk through the metal detector.

   _____

9. Save at least 10 percent of your income for retirement. Don't buy new cars. Keep some money in the bank for emergencies.

   _____

3 | EDITING: RECIPE FOR CHICKEN CASSEROLE

Tracy Powers is teaching a healthy recipe to her class. Read her instructions. There are thirteen mistakes in the use of the imperative. The first mistake is already corrected. Find and correct twelve more.

     Preheat

~~You preheat~~ the oven to 400° F or 200° C. Spraying a casserole pan with cooking spray. No use butter because butter will burn. You are heating the oil in a large pan until hot. Cooks the onion and garlic for a few minutes. Add the corn, bell peppers, ½ cup of the chicken broth, black pepper, and thyme. Continued cooking until the bell pepper becomes soft. Stir in the other ½ cup of broth, the sour cream, mustard, and cooked rice. To add the chicken. When the chicken is cooked, removes the pan from heat, and mix until everything is well combined. Stirring in ¼ cup of the mozzarella cheese and all the parsley. You transfer the mixture to the casserole dish. Spreads the mixture evenly. Sprinkle the rest of the mozzarella cheese on top and you bake for about 25 minutes. Overcook not. The casserole is ready when it is hot all the way through.

Unit 3 Achievement Test

| 30 Items |
| Score: _____ |

---

1 | LISTENING: CONVERSATION BETWEEN CO-WORKERS

A. 🎧 *Roberto and Lucille are co-workers. Listen to their conversation. Complete the conversation by writing the words that you hear. You will hear the recording two times.*

ROBERTO: When _____*did you arrive*_____ in the United States?
               0.

   LUCILLE: I came two years ago. How about you? When _____ here?
                                                                    1.

ROBERTO: Three years ago.

   LUCILLE: Were you married at that time?

ROBERTO: No, I met my wife Marcela in 2003 at the restaurant where _____. We
                                                                                        2.

               also lived in the same apartment complex, but we didn't realize that until after we

               started dating. We got married two years later.

   LUCILLE: And when _____ an engineer?
                              3.

ROBERTO: Last year. I started my studies in Mexico. That was in 2001. I completed my studies

               here in the States.

   LUCILLE: _____ that you're going to be a father soon?
                   4.

ROBERTO: Well, actually, I already am. I became a father yesterday.

   LUCILLE: Congratulations!

B. *Reread the conversation. Match the events with the times.*

	Event		Time
_c_	**0.** Lucille came to the United States	**a.**	three years ago.
____	**1.** Roberto came to the United States	**b.**	four years ago.
____	**2.** Roberto met his wife	~~c.~~	two years ago.
____	**3.** Roberto became an engineer	**d.**	in 2003.
____	**4.** Roberto started his studies in Mexico	**e.**	last year.
____	**5.** Robert became a father	**f.**	in 2001.
		g.	yesterday.
		h.	last month.

2 | ROBERTO AND MARCELA'S ANNIVERSARY

*Complete the sentences about Roberto and Marcela's anniversary. Circle the correct words
or phrases.*

0. Roberto and Marcela celebrated their anniversary last month. They are leaving / leave /(left)
   their baby with Marcela's parents.

1. They went / go / are going out of town and into the mountains.

2. They are having / have / had a picnic.

3. After lunch, they are going / went / go on a hike.

4. They didn't hike / not hiking / didn't hiked for a long time.

5. They return / returned / are returning home in the late afternoon.

6. In the evening, they didn't watched / are watching / didn't watch a movie they rented. They
   went to bed early.

3 | MARCELA'S BIOGRAPHY

*Complete the biography of Marcela Blanco. Use the simple past form of the verbs in the
box. Some items may have more than one right answer.*

~~be~~	enroll	find	have	meet	walk
catch	feel	get	make	move	work

Marcela Blanco was born on May 6, 1983, in Mexico City. Her mother _____was_____
0.

a dressmaker, and her father _____ shoes. In 2001, Marcela and her family
1.

_____ to California. At first Marcela _____ lonely. Then she
2.   3.

_____ a part-time job as a cook. She _____ in a Mexican restaurant.
4.   5.

She _____ Roberto at work, and they _____ married in 2003. They
6.   7.

_____ a baby last year. A month ago, Marcela _____ at the
8.   9.

community college. Her goal is to own a restaurant someday.

4 | EDITING: SATURDAY

*Read about Roberto and Marcela's Saturday. There are seven mistakes in the use of the
simple past tense. The first mistake is already corrected. Find and correct six more.*

                                    had

Roberto and Marcela ~~did have~~ a good Saturday. In the afternoon, they eated at one of their

favorite Mexican restaurants. They saw some of their friends there. Their friends were happy to

see the new baby. After lunch, they goed shopping. They needed to buy food for the week. After

shopping they return home and put their food away. Then Marcela do laundry while Roberto give

the baby a bath. In the evening, they invited their neighbors over and they play a board game.

Unit 4 Achievement Test

30 Items
Score: _____

---

1 | LISTENING: QUESTIONS ABOUT THE ROBBERY

A. 🎧 *There was a robbery at Arthur's office this morning. A police officer is asking Arthur about his activities. Listen to their conversation. Complete the conversation by writing the words that you hear. You will hear the recording two times.*

OFFICER: <u>Were you sitting</u> at your desk at 10:20, when the robber came into the office?
                0.

ARTHUR: Yes, I was.

OFFICER: What _____?
                          1.

ARTHUR: I was working on a report.

OFFICER: I find it strange that you didn't hear anything. _____ on the telephone?
                                                                              2.

ARTHUR: No, not at that time.

OFFICER: _____ to the radio?
                    3.

ARTHUR: No.

OFFICER: So what were you doing that stopped you from hearing while the robber

_____ through the office?
            4.

ARTHUR: Well, while I was sitting at my desk, I was listening to the news over the Internet.

OFFICER: Why were you listening to the news while you _____?
                                                                            5.

ARTHUR: Well, sometimes the work I do doesn't require much thought. This morning I

_____ numbers into the computer. Listening to the news doesn't distract
            6.

me with that kind of work.

OFFICER: I see.

B. *Reread the conversation. Find four past progressive verb forms. Write them below. (Note: Only use words that are given in the conversation. Do not use any words that you wrote.) An example is given.*

0. _____ *was working* _____

1. _____

2. _____

3. _____

4. _____

2 | EARTHQUAKE

In 1989, a big earthquake struck the San Francisco Bay area of California. At that time, many people were waiting for a World Series baseball game in Candlestick Park to begin. Combine these pairs of sentences about the earthquake. Use the simple past or the past progressive forms of the verbs.

0. The earthquake struck.
   Thousands of people waited for a baseball game to start.

   When the earthquake _____*struck*_____, thousands of people _____*were waiting*_____ for a baseball game to start.

0. The earthquake struck.
   The lights went out.

   When the earthquake _____*struck*_____, the lights _____*went*_____ out.

1. The players got ready to play.
   The earth began to move.

   Players _____ ready to play when the earth _____ to move.

2. Many people watched the game on TV.
   The electricity went out.

   Many people _____ the game on TV when the electricity _____ out.

3. The earth stopped moving.
   The police told the crowd to leave the stadium calmly.

   When the earth _____ moving, the police _____ the crowd to leave the stadium calmly.

4. People got to their cars.
   They turned on their radios.

   When people _____ to their cars, they _____ on their radios.

5. They drove home.
   Some people heard about a collapsed highway.

   While they _____ home, some people _____ about a collapsed highway.

6. They heard the news of the collapsed highway.
   They got out of their cars.

   When they _____ the news of the collapsed highway, they _____ out of their cars.

7. They finally got home.
   Their neighbors stood in the streets.

   When they finally _____ home, their neighbors _____ in the streets.

8. They entered their homes.
   They discovered a lot of damage.

   When they _____ their homes, they _____ a lot of damage.

3 | EDITING: GRACE REMEMBERS THE EARTHQUAKE

Read the conversation between Grace and her friend Cheryl. There are five mistakes in the use of the past progressive and the simple past. The first mistake is already corrected. Find and correct four more. Remember to look at punctuation!

GRACE: Do you remember that big earthquake in 1989?

CHERYL: Of course. How could I forget? What ~~you were~~ *were you* doing that day?

GRACE: Well, when the earthquake hit I was working at the stadium at Candlestick Park.

CHERYL: Really? What you were doing when you first felt it?

GRACE: I sold soda. While the stadium was shake, the sodas were jumping out of my box like

   popcorn! I was OK, but they spilled all over the customers. No one was angry,

   though—everyone was too scared. I remember it took a long time to get home that

   night!

Unit 5 Achievement Test

---

1 | LISTENING: TEENAGERS AND FASHION

A. 🎧 *Leslie and Hillary are talking about strange fashions they liked when they were teenagers. Listen to their conversation. Complete the conversation by writing the words that you hear. You will hear the recording two times.*

LESLIE: Isn't it hard to believe some of the crazy things we _____*used to do*_____ to be cool?
                                                     0.

HILLARY: I know. Just think about jeans. Remember how tight we used to wear them?

LESLIE: I sure do. _____ with your new jeans on in hot bath water to make them
                                1.

        shrink?

HILLARY: No, I never used to do that. I just used to buy jeans that were already too small for me.

LESLIE: Didn't it hurt to wear them?

HILLARY: It did at first, until I got used _____ them.
                                       2.

LESLIE: Why did we use to do that to ourselves?

HILLARY: Because it was cool, I guess.

LESLIE: Oh, and whenever I got new sneakers, I used to get them dirty on purpose.

HILLARY: Me too! _____ I try hard to keep my shoes clean.
                        3.

LESLIE: I know. I'm glad we don't do that _____. But we had fun, didn't we?
                                           4.

HILLARY: We sure did.

B. *Reread the conversation. Find four examples of **used to** + the base form of the verb. Write them below. (Note: Only use words that are given in the conversation. Do not use any words that you wrote.) An example is given.*

0. _____*used to wear*_____

1. _____

2. _____

3. _____

4. _____

2 | FASHION, THEN AND NOW

Read this paragraph from a magazine article. Complete the paragraph with the correct verb forms. Write the letter of the best answer on each line.

Isn't it interesting how fashions change? In many ways, fashion ____*a*____ (a. used to be b. gets
                                                                        0.

used to be c. used to being d. gets used to being) much simpler. Women _____ (a. not used to wear
                                                                          1.

b. didn't used to wear c. didn't use to wear d. didn't used to wearing) pants, and men's clothes _____
                                                                                                     2.

(a. used to never have b. never use to have c. never used to having d. never used to have) such bright colors.

People _____ (a. used to dressing b. use to dress c. used to dress d. were used to dress) in special
       3.

ways for different situations. But in the United States today, you can go to the opera and find

some women in evening gowns while others are in blue jeans.

Even buying blue jeans _____ (a. used to being b. use to be c. was used to be d. used to be) easier.
                       4.

When I _____ (a. was used to buy b. used to buy c. got used to buy d. used to buying) new jeans, they
        5.

were always bright blue and very crisp. Today, teenagers like their jeans "worn and torn."

3 | TIMES HAVE CHANGED

Complete these sentences about how life used to be different. Use the words in parentheses and the correct form of **used to**.

0. Trains were invented in 1826. Before then, there _____*didn't use to be*_____ any way to
                                                            (not / be)

    efficiently transport large things over long distances on land.

1. Introduced in 1873, the first blue jeans were worn as work clothes. People

    _____ them fashionable clothing.
           (not / consider)

2. The first telephone was made in 1876. Before then, people _____
                                                               (write)

    letters to communicate over long distances.

3. The automobile was invented in 1886. Before then, people _____ or
                                                             (walk)

    ride horses.

4. The radio was invented in 1895. Before then, people _____ to live
                                                        (listen)

    musicians or they made music on their own.

5. The first permanent hair waves were given in London in 1909. Before then, women

   _____ their hair to get waves.
   (braid)

6. The first zipper was used on clothing in the early 1900s. Before then, people

   _____ buttons on their clothing.
   (use)

7. Crossword puzzles appeared in an American newspaper for the first time in 1913. My

   grandfather _____ crossword puzzles when he was a boy.
   (love)

8. Women were first allowed to vote in the United States in 1920. Before then, only men

   _____ able to vote.
   (be)

9. The first movie with sound was produced in 1926. Before then, people

   _____ movies with live music.
   (watch)

10. Television was invented in 1927. Before that, people _____ to the
    (listen)

    radio a lot.

---

4 | EDITING: BARRY

*Read this paragraph about Leslie's husband. There are eight mistakes in the use of **used to**. The first mistake is already corrected. Find and correct seven more.*

Leslie's husband, Barry, ~~is~~ used to be really different. He used to have long hair, but now it's

short. Leslie liked his long hair, but she got use to the new style. Barry used to wore colorful

clothes, but now he usually wears a business suit. He didn't like wearing ties at first, but now he

used to it. He used to have a beard, but now he is clean shaven. Barry didn't used to read the

paper, but he does now. He used to listen to rock, but now he listens to classical music. He used

to playing his guitar a lot, but now he doesn't have time because he works full-time. He uses stay

up past midnight, but now he goes to bed at 10:30. He used to going dancing, but he doesn't

anymore.

Unit 6 Achievement Test

1 | LISTENING: THE NEW MALL

A. 🎧 *Tanya and Victor are neighbors. Listen to their conversation. Complete the conversation by writing the words that you hear. You will hear the recording two times.*

TANYA: Did you hear about the new mall they __*'re going to build*__ ? They say it's going to
0.

create a lot of jobs.

VICTOR: Really? I didn't hear anything about it. Where will it be?

TANYA: It'll be right across the street from us.

VICTOR: Oh, no! Is there _____ more traffic?
1.

TANYA: Probably, but now we _____ to drive so far to go shopping.
2.

VICTOR: I suppose, if you shop at malls. But I'm probably _____ shop there.
3.

Everything is too expensive at malls. Hey . . . will our houses decrease in value?

TANYA: That's a good question. I don't know.

VICTOR: When are they starting construction?

TANYA: I think they start soon.

VICTOR: Well, I _____ online. There must be some more information there.
4.

B. *These sentences are based on the conversation. Find five sentences that talk about things in the future. Check (✓) them. An example is given.*

__✓__ They're going to build a new mall in this area.

_____ The new mall will be right across the street from them.

_____ Their houses will probably decrease in value.

_____ I didn't hear anything about it.

_____ When are they starting construction?

_____ I think they start construction soon.

_____ Things are usually very expensive at malls.

_____ The construction of the mall is going to create a lot of new jobs.

2 | PROTESTING THE NEW MALL

Read this paragraph from a website protesting the new mall. Complete the paragraph with the correct verb forms. Write the letter of the best answer on each line.

The mall may provide jobs now, but it ____*a*____ (a. will damage b. is going to damaging c. will to
0.

damage d. is going damaging) the economy in the future. It's likely that this mall _____ (a. put
1.

b. is going to put c. is putting d. will to put) many small local stores out of business. Malls are usually

ugly buildings, and fewer people _____ (a. will to want b. are going wanting c. will want d. are going
2.

to wanting) to move to the community because of it. In addition, traffic problems _____ (a. will
3.

increase b. are going to increasing c. will to increase d. are going increasing) as more people drive through

the area to get to the mall. Much of the tax money from sales _____ (a. not staying b. will not to
4.

stay c. will not staying d. is not going to stay) here. It will go to the cities where the mall companies

have their headquarters. Protect our local economy. Join us to protest against the mall. The

protest _____ (a. starts b. will to start c. starting d. is going start) this Saturday at 10:00.
5.

3 | ADVANTAGES OF THE NEW MALL

Complete these sentences about the advantages of the new mall. Use the correct forms of the words in parentheses. Put the words in order.

0. The new mall _____*will have*_____ 120 shops.
     (have / will)

1. It _____ on the east side of town.
       (be / will)

2. The food court _____ 20 restaurants.
         (to / have / going / be)

3. There _____ beautiful fountains in the center of the mall.
       (be / will)

4. The mall is _____ on April 6.
         (open / going / to)

5. It _____ the biggest mall in the state.
     (be / will)

6. People _____ to see movies at the mall.
       (be / able / will)

7. The mall _____ 7,000 new jobs.
       (create / will)

8. It _____ over $1 million to the city economy.
     (will / contribute)

9. There's even _____ an ice-skating rink in the mall.
         (to / going / be)

10. In addition, the mall _____ some conference rooms for people to
    (be / to / have / going)

    have business meetings.

11. There _____ live entertainment on the weekends.
    (will / be)

12. Developers think the mall _____ shoppers of all ages.
    (to / going / attract / be)

---

4 | EDITING: A JOB AT THE MALL

Victor's daughter, Melissa, is getting a job at the mall. Read her journal entry. There are five mistakes in the use of the future. The first mistake is already corrected. Find and correct four more.

     I just got a job at the mall, and I'm so excited! ~~I~~ *I'm* going to work in the food court. Finally, I'll

be able to make my own money and pay for my own clothes! I'm going visit all the stores and

find some great clothes for myself! Dad's going not to like it. He's against the mall. But he should

be happy that he won't have to give me money all the time. I'll to tell him tonight. I looked for a

job for a long time, so hopefully he'll understand. I starts on Monday!

Unit 7 Achievement Test

30 Items
Score: _____

A. 🎧 *Listen to this television commercial for an employment agency. Complete the commercial by writing the words that you hear. You will hear the recording two times.*

Looking for a job? Unhappy at work? Still in school? Where _____*will you go*_____ when you
                                                                    0.

decide to change jobs? What _____ when you graduate? Here at Jobs Are Us
                                          1.

Employment Agency, we can help you find a great job. As soon as you give us some basic

information, _____ hard for the right job for you. Before you know it, an exciting
                        2.

new job _____ yours. After you sign up with us, _____ that Jobs
                  3.   **4.**

Are Us Employment Agency is the best way to find the work you love. Call or stop by today!

B. *Reread the commercial. Find four future time clauses. Write them below. (Note: Only use words that are given in the conversation. Do not use any words that you wrote.) An example is given.*

0.   *when you decide to change jobs* _____

1.   _____

2.   _____

3.   _____

4.   _____

2 | AFTER GRADUATION

Read each numbered sentence about Nora's plans after she graduates. Then circle the letter of the answer which is closest in meaning to each numbered sentence.

0. Nora will move as soon as she graduates.
   a. Nora will move. Then she'll graduate.
   b. Nora will graduate. Then she'll move.
   c. Nora is going to graduate soon.

1. Nora will need some new furniture when she moves into her new apartment.
   a. Nora will need some new furniture. Then she'll move into her new apartment.
   b. Before Nora will need some new furniture, she moves into her new apartment.
   c. Nora will move into her new apartment. Then she'll need some new furniture.

2. Before she moves, Nora will look for a job.
   a. Nora will move and look for a job at the same time.
   b. Nora will move. Then she'll look for a job.
   c. Nora will look for a job. Then she'll move.

3. Nora wants to start working as soon as she moves.
   a. Nora will move. Then she'll start working.
   b. Nora will start working. Then she'll move.
   c. Nora will start working before she moves.

4. As soon as Nora saves enough money, she'll buy a computer.
   a. Nora will buy a computer before she saves enough money.
   b. Nora will save enough money. Then she'll buy a computer.
   c. Nora will buy a computer. Then she'll save enough money.

3 | PREDICTIONS ABOUT THE FUTURE

*Nora is visiting a psychic who is telling her about her future. Reword each of the psychic's predictions to form one sentence. Use the correct form of the verbs or the words **while**, **after**, **until**, and **as soon as**. Some items may have more than one right answer.*

You will move. Then you will begin working immediately.

You will begin working _____*as soon as*_____ you move.
0.

You will start working. Then you will meet a man named Calvin.

_____*You will meet*_____ a man named Calvin after _____*you start working*_____ .
0.　　　　　　　　　　　　　　　　　　　　　　　　0.

You are going to fall in love. Then you will get married.

You will get married _____ you fall in love.
1.

Calvin is going to get a raise. Then you are going to move to a larger apartment.

_____ as soon as _____ .
2.　　　　　　　　　　　　　　　　　　　　　3.

You're going to get settled in your new place. Then you're going to start a family right away.

_____ you get settled in your new place, you're going to start a family.
4.

You'll have your first child. Then Calvin will begin medical school a month later.

You'll have your first child _____ Calvin begins medical school.
5.

You'll work full time, and Calvin will go to school.

You'll work full time _____ Calvin goes to school.
6.

Your child will be five. Then Calvin will graduate from medical school.

By the time _____ , Calvin _____ .
7.　　　　　　　　　　　　　　　　　　　8.

Calvin will graduate. Then he'll begin his medical practice.

_____ after _____ .
9.　　　　　　　　　　　　　　　　　　　10.

Calvin will start working. Then you will quit work.

You won't quit work _____ Calvin starts working.
11.

Calvin will work for two years. Then you will move out of your apartment and into a house.

After _____ , you'll move out of your apartment and into a house.
12.

Your child will go to school, and you will work part time from home.

Your child will go to school _____ you work part time from home.
13.

4 | EDITING: PLANS FOR WORKING AT HOME

Read Nora's journal entry several years later. There are six mistakes in the use of future time clauses. The first mistake is already corrected. Find and correct five more. Remember to look at punctuation!

After summer ~~will be~~ *is* over, Clint will start school again. I can't believe that he'll be in second grade already! I want to start working from home when Clint will start school this year. As soon he does, I'll to have more time than I have now. Right now he's home all the time, and he needs attention. I think I'll work only part-time so that I'll finish working, before Clint comes home from school. I'll need a faster computer, but I won't buy one after I find one on sale.

Unit 8 Achievement Test

30 Items
Score: _____

---

1 | LISTENING: THE ACTING INTERVIEW

A. 🎧 *Kathy is interviewing at an acting agency. Listen to the conversation. Complete the conversation by writing the words that you hear. You will hear the recording two times.*

INTERVIEWER: Well, Kathy, tell me: _____*Why do you want*_____ to become an
                                                            0.

actress?

KATHY: Well, I was in a few theater performances here in town, and I loved them.

INTERVIEWER: Where _____?
                                          1.

KATHY: At the Little Black Theater downtown. I had the lead role in our last production.

INTERVIEWER: Really? _____?
                                          2.

KATHY: I played Hannah in *Denial Is a River*.

INTERVIEWER: That sounds familiar. Who wrote that play?

KATHY: Emil Sher. There was a good review of my performance in the local newspaper.

There's a copy of it in my portfolio.

INTERVIEWER: Oh? Who wrote the review?

KATHY: A reporter named Jim Carlotta. He saw the play on closing night.

INTERVIEWER: How many performances did you have?

KATHY: Twelve. And then in May came my biggest break yet.

INTERVIEWER: What happened in May?

KATHY: I had a small part in an independent film. That was fun.

INTERVIEWER: Which kinds of characters do you prefer to play?

KATHY: I like to play smart, confident women. I played a lawyer in the film.

INTERVIEWER: I see. And _____ do you relate to the most?
                                                3.

KATHY: Well, I really like scripts by Scott Hathaway.

INTERVIEWER: Oh? I haven't heard of him. _____?
                                                                    4.

KATHY: His most famous play is called *Elsewhere*. Do you know it?

INTERVIEWER: I'm afraid I don't. Well, Kathy, now I'd like you to read a script for me. . . .

B. Reread the conversation. Find two questions about subjects and two questions about objects. Write them in the table below. (Note: Only use words that are given in the conversation. Do not use any words that you wrote.) An example is given.

QUESTIONS ABOUT SUBJECTS	QUESTIONS ABOUT OBJECTS
0. *Who wrote that play?* _____	1. _____
1. _____	2. _____
2. _____	

2 | WHO GETS THE PART?

Match the questions with the answers.

Questions

_d_ 0. How many films has Kathy been in?

_____ 1. Whose acting did the director like the best?

_____ 2. Which actor is closest in age to the character?

_____ 3. How many people tried out for the part?

_____ 4. Whom did the director choose for the part?

Answers

a. He liked Kathy's.

b. Twelve people.

c. Kathy was.

d. Only one so far.

e. Kathy. She's 24.

f. Kathy has.

g. He chose Kathy.

3 | QUESTIONS FOR AN ACTRESS

Kathy is talking to the actress Sherry Reid. Read Sherry's answers and write Kathy's questions.

0. KATHY: _____ *Where did you grow* _____ up?

   SHERRY: I grew up in Philadelphia.

1. KATHY: _____ the best when you were growing up?

   SHERRY: The movies that I liked the best when I was growing up were adventure movies.

2. KATHY: _____ acting?

   SHERRY: I started acting in 1985.

3. KATHY: _____ how to act?

   SHERRY: Mrs. Weiss taught me how to act. She was a terrific acting teacher.

4. KATHY: _____ to teach you?

   SHERRY: She used a variety of methods to teach me to act.

5. KATHY: _____ acting?

   SHERRY: I started acting because my parents enrolled me in some acting classes, and I loved them. So they took me to a local talent agency, and I received lots of offers right away.

6. KATHY: _____ you in the first month?

   SHERRY: Ten people contacted me in the first month. I took a role in the movie, *The Bright Side.*

7. KATHY: _____ *The Bright Side?*

   SHERRY: Neil Martinez directed it.

8. KATHY: _____ in *The Bright Side?*

   SHERRY: They used Will Davidson's music.

9. KATHY: _____ *The Bright Side?*

   SHERRY: Twenty million people saw *The Bright Side.*

10. KATHY: _____ you to do the movie?

    SHERRY: They paid me $2 million.

11. KATHY: _____ *The Bright Side* in theaters?

    SHERRY: *The Bright Side* was in theaters for two months, then it went to video and DVD.

4 | EDITING: AFTER THE INTERVIEW

*Read Kathy's conversation about the interview with her husband Scott. There are eight mistakes in the use of **wh-** questions. The first mistake is already corrected. Find and correct seven more. (Note: There can be more than one way to correct a mistake.)*

SCOTT: How ^{did} your interview ~~went~~ ^{go}?

KATHY: It was great! I got a part in a commercial!

SCOTT: You did? Congratulations! How much they are going to pay you?

KATHY: A lot. More than I hoped for.

SCOTT: Awesome! Whom interviewed you?

KATHY: The owner of the agency.

SCOTT: Which company the commercial's for?

KATHY: Boston Global.

SCOTT: Oh yeah? Which product you going to advertise?

KATHY: Their imported furniture.

SCOTT: Which part will you to have?

KATHY: I'm going to play a wife who wants to decorate her home.

SCOTT: Who the director is of the commercial?

KATHY: His name is Hal Malloy.

SCOTT: When you start filming?

KATHY: In two weeks.

PART 1 Achievement Test

1 | LISTENING: GOING OUT

A. 🎧 *Sharon is talking to her roommate Carrie. Listen to their conversation. Complete the conversation by writing the words that you hear. You will hear the recording two times.*

CARRIE: What ___*are you doing*___ ?
                                0.

SHARON: I'm getting ready to go out for dinner.

CARRIE: Really? Where _____?
                                1.

SHARON: I'm going to the new Mexican restaurant downtown. And afterwards I'm going to a

magic show. Give me my wallet, please. It's on the bedside table.

CARRIE: Sure. Here you go. So _____ with?
                                2.

SHARON: A guy named Reggie. I met him at Veronica's party last night.

CARRIE: Oh yeah? _____ he like?
                                3.

SHARON: He's really nice. I found out that he used to live in the Philippines, just like I did. And

he speaks Tagalog.

CARRIE: Wow! Well, tell me all about what happens.

SHARON: OK. I'll tell you _____ I get home.
                                4.

B. *These sentences are based on the conversation. Circle the correct words or phrases to complete the sentences.*

0. Sharon (is getting) / gets / will get ready to go out for dinner.

1. Sharon eats / is going to eat / ate at the Mexican restaurant downtown.

2. Sharon used to meet / was meeting / met Reggie at Veronica's party the night before.

3. Sharon said, "Please to give / give / be giving me my wallet."

4. Reggie used to live / is used to live / was used to live in the Philippines.

5. Carrie said, "Let / To let / Be letting me know how it goes."

2 | AFTER THE MAGIC SHOW

Reggie and Sharon watched a magician. Now they are talking. Complete the conversation.
Use the words in the box.

are	don't speak	going to be	take
before	dressed	going to go	teach
'll call	'll drive	invite	used to be
're coming	enjoy	reappeared	~~was~~
disappeared	's getting	speak	won't be

SHARON: He _____was_____ a good magician! I _____ watching magic tricks.
   0.   **1.**

   How do you think he did that disappearing trick?

REGGIE: I'm not sure. I only saw that he _____ on one side of the stage, then
                                      2.

   he _____ on the other side. Maybe he has a twin brother who
       3.

   _____ up like him.
       4.

SHARON: Maybe. Anyway, it was cool to watch. You know, it's nice that you speak Tagalog. I

   usually _____ to anyone in Tagalog, except when I invite my Filipino
              5.

   friends over. Actually, they _____ over on Tuesday evening at 6:00. Do
                                   6.

   you want to come?

REGGIE: Sorry, I _____ a class on Tuesday evenings, so I _____ able
                 7.   **8.**

   to go. I'm _____ at school when they _____ at your house.
               9.   **10.**

   But tomorrow I'm _____ river rafting. Do you want to come with me, at
                       11.

   around ten o'clock in the morning?

SHARON: Sure! That'll be fun! I'll just have to buy some sunscreen _____ I go.
                                                                    12.

REGGIE: OK. I _____ you tomorrow when I'm ready. Well, it _____
              13.   **14.**

   late now. I _____ you home.
                15.

Name _____ Date _____

Reggie is talking to his roommate Lionel about his date with Sharon. Complete the conversation. Use the correct forms of the words in parentheses.

LIONEL: So, _____how was_____ your date with Sharon? _____?
0. (how / be)   1. (what / happen)

REGGIE: It was good. We saw Bart Groberg.

LIONEL: _____ Bart Groberg?
2. (who / be)

REGGIE: He's a magician. _____ some great tricks.
3. (he / perform)

LIONEL: So _____ about Sharon. Is she nice?
4. (tell / me)

REGGIE: Yeah, she's really nice. We have a lot in common. She _____ in the
5. (use to / live)

Philippines too, and _____ Tagalog. _____ river
6. (she / know)   7. (we / be going to / go)

rafting tomorrow.

LIONEL: That's cool. _____ Fridays off from work.
8. (you / never / use to / have)

REGGIE: I know. My boss was nice this time.

LIONEL: _____?
9. (what time / you / be / leave)

REGGIE: The boat rental place _____ at 10:30. So _____ here
10. (open)   11. (we / will / leave)

around 10:00.

LIONEL: Well, _____ how everything goes.
12. (let / me / know)

REGGIE: OK, I will.

4 | BEFORE RAFTING

Complete Sharon's conversation with her roommate before she goes rafting with Reggie.
Use the correct forms of the verbs in the box. Some items may have more than one right
answer.

be	enjoy	give	go	know	open	think
drive	get	~~go~~	hope	leave	tell	walk

CARRIE: Veronica and I _____*are going*_____ to a concert tonight. Do you want to go?
            0.

SHARON: Maybe, but I'm not sure when I _____ home. I _____
                                             1.   **2.**

ready to leave right now. Reggie and I _____ at 10:00 to go river rafting.
                                                              3.

I don't know how long I _____ out. I can call you from my cell phone
                                               4.

when I _____ what time I'll be back.
                     5.

CARRIE: OK. So, how did your date with Reggie _____ last night?
                                                       6.

SHARON: It was nice, and he was very polite. At the end of the night, he _____
                                                             7.

me home, and he even _____ the car door for me. I _____
                                     8.   **9.**

that was really nice of him. And it's great to have someone to talk to about the

Philippines. While we were driving home, he _____ me about his time
                                               10.

there. He _____ living there, and he _____ to go back
                     11.   **12.**

again.

CARRIE: It sounds like you have a lot in common.

SHARON: We do.

5 | EDITING: ON THE RIVER

Read the conversation between Reggie and Sharon on the raft. There are thirteen mistakes. The first mistake is already corrected. Find and correct twelve more. Remember to look at punctuation!

SHARON: The river is ~~being~~ really pretty.

REGGIE: I know. I love the water. I was being glad that we went to the magician last night. I thinked he was really good.

SHARON: Me too. It was a wonderful evening, and I was having a great time! I told my roommate all about the magician when I getted home.

REGGIE: Oh, good. Hey, I brought some crackers. Would you like some?

SHARON: Sure, I'm getting hungry. Before you picked me up I ate breakfast. But that was hours ago. Oh, I like these crackers. They're reminding me of when I was a kid.

REGGIE: This river is looking a lot like the Cagayan River in the Philippines. Did you ever go there?

SHARON: No, I never was there. I spended most of my time in Manila. I think it would be fun to go back. Maybe I could go this summer.

REGGIE: I think there are some good deals on tickets on the Internet right now.

SHARON: Really? I'll to look online when I will get home. I'll sending you a postcard if I go.

REGGIE: That sounds good!

PART II Diagnostic Test

1 | LISTENING: SHARING AN APARTMENT

A. 🎧 *Juan is looking for an apartment, but he can't decide if he wants to have a roommate. Listen to his conversation with Luisa. Complete the conversation by writing the words that you hear. You will hear the recording two times.*

LUISA: How's your apartment search going?

JUAN: Not too well. It's got me talking to _____*myself*_____ . I'm having trouble
0.

_____ if I should get a roommate or not. My parents want me to,
1.

but I'm not sure.

LUISA: That's really a decision you need to make for _____ .
2.

JUAN: I know. I want to live by _____ , but I can't afford to do that right
3.

now. I'm _____ that apartments are more expensive than I
4.

thought.

LUISA: Then maybe you should find _____ a roommate.
5.

JUAN: You're probably right. I did meet a guy in chemistry class the other day who's looking for

a roommate. His name is Bob. He's living by _____ right now,
6.

but he can't afford to pay the rent. He suggested that I move into the extra room in his

apartment.

LUISA: So what did you tell him?

JUAN: I told him I needed to think about it. We gave _____ our phone
7.

numbers and said we'd talk on Friday.

LUISA: That's tomorrow.

JUAN: Yes, I know, but I have some other things on my mind, too. I have a job interview today. I

hope I get the job. I'm nervous about the interview.

LUISA: Just be _____ . I'm sure you'll get the job. Then you can afford
8.

your own apartment.

B. *Reread the conversation. Then read each statement and write* **T** *(true) or* **F** *(false).*

___T___ 0. Juan and Luisa know each another.

_____ 1. Juan doesn't have enough money to live by himself.

_____ 2. His parents want him to live by himself.

_____ 3. Luisa thinks she has to decide for herself.

_____ 4. Juan told Bob to decide for himself.

_____ 5. Bob and Juan will talk to each other on Friday.

_____ 6. Luisa thinks Juan can live by himself if he gets the job.

2 | NEW ROOMMATES

Juan just moved in with his new roommate, Bob. Complete the conversation. Circle the correct words or phrases.

BOB: I'm glad you decided to move in.

JUAN: Me too. I figured (out)/ in / at my expenses and quickly realized it was better to have a
   0.
  roommate. And it seems like our schedules will work off / at / out well. We won't get in
                  1.
  ourselves' / one another / each other's way.
       2.

BOB: I agree. Between school and work, neither one of us will be here much.

JUAN: Yeah, last night I wanted to drop off / down / in some boxes, but you weren't here.
              3.

BOB: Oh, I worked until midnight. I had to set up / in / down some new computers. And in a
              4.
  few minutes I have to call off / up / on my boss and discuss the work I did.
           5.

JUAN: Hey, would you mind helping me out / up / at before you call? I have some boxes in my
             6.
  car that are kind of heavy.

BOB: Sure, no problem.

JUAN: Thanks. I appreciate it. My friend Luisa said she would help me, but this morning she
  called up / looked up / dropped up to say she had to study for a test.
      7.

BOB: I think I took an art history class with Luisa last semester. I remember we had a
  conversation about where we grew in / up / out.
           8.

JUAN: Luisa is a great friend. It didn't take us long to figure up / out / over that we have a lot
               9.
  in common.

BOB: I hate to point at / out / up the time, but we should hurry. Let's bring up those boxes.
      10.

3 | EXERCISING

Complete the conversation. Use the correct pronouns in the box.

each other	himself	himself	~~myself~~	oneself	themselves	yourself
herself	himself	itself	myself	ourselves	yourself	yourselves

LUISA: Thanks for giving me a ride to the store. I wanted to walk to give _____*myself*_____
0.

some exercise, but I knew I'd have too many bags to carry.

JUAN: It's no problem. You keep _____ really fit, don't you? I mean, you exercise
1.

a lot.

LUISA: Well, I like to be active, but I can't believe how much time I spend sitting in front of the

computer. What do you do to keep _____ in shape?
2.

JUAN: I lift weights, and I run. You know, my new roommate Bob runs marathons, so he has to

work hard to keep _____ in really good condition. He wakes up early six
3.

days a week to go running.

LUISA: I remember Bob. We met _____ last year in art history. I think at that time
4.

he was in a running club.

JUAN: I wouldn't be surprised.

LUISA: Does Bob run by _____ or with other people?
5.

JUAN: Both. Three days a week he runs by _____, and the other three he runs
6.

with his running club.

LUISA: That seems like a good balance. There are some activities like swimming that I do

by _____, but mostly I exercise with a couple friends. We push
7.

_____ to exercise together at least four times a week.
8.

JUAN: That's really great.

4 | STAYING FIT

Complete the paragraph about staying fit. Use reflexive and reciprocal pronouns. Some items may have more than one right answer.

Exercise is an important part of staying fit. People who adopt an active lifestyle for

____themselves____ will find that they have more energy for their jobs, relationships, and other
　　0.

daily activities. To start and maintain an active lifestyle, you must first remember it's important

to enjoy _____. If you don't like to run, don't run; try walking instead. Be sure to
　　　　　　1.

ask _____ how much you're enjoying the activity. Second, you must remind
　　2.

_____ to try different activities. Swim one day. Walk the next. Sometimes I
　　3.

make _____ try new activities, even if I don't think I'll like them. Varying
　　4.

activities is an effective way to lead an active life and stay fit. Third, find a partner. Studies

show that partners who exercise with _____ will continue to exercise and stay fit.
　　　　　　　　　　5.

People who exercise by _____ often lose interest and stop exercising before they
　　　　　　6.

see any results.

5 | A TRIP TO THE LIBRARY

Complete Juan and Luisa's conversation. Use **out, by, on, off, up,** *and* **into.**

LUISA: Thanks for coming with me to the library. I really had to drop ___*off*___ these books.
    0.

JUAN: No problem. I needed to pick _____ a book for a paper I'm writing.
    1.

LUISA: You know, we really didn't need to drive here. I'm afraid I'm turning _____ a lazy
    2.

person.

JUAN: I was thinking that we should have walked too, but I didn't want to point it _____.
    3.

Plus, I didn't want to carry all those books.

LUISA: Why are people becoming so lazy? Everyone takes the elevator instead of walking up the

stairs. Everyone drives instead of walking.

JUAN: I know. I do it too. It's funny. I grew _____ walking everywhere I went. Now I don't
    4.

want to walk anywhere.

LUISA: I know. I set _____ this morning planning to walk to class and instead I got in the
    5.

car and drove.

JUAN: I think it's too easy these days to be lazy. Everyone has their own car. When I was

growing up, my family got _____ with only one car.
    6.

LUISA: My family had one car too. My parents brought me _____ to ride my bike to school.
    7.

JUAN: I'm glad you mentioned this. I need to walk to school more.

LUISA: We could pick _____ a meeting place and walk together.
    8.

JUAN: That's a great idea. Where's the closest place for us to meet?

LUISA: How about the coffee shop on Fifth Street? That should work _____ for both of us.
    9.

JUAN: I'll need to set my alarm so that I wake _____ on time. I know that you don't like to
    10.

be late.

LUISA: I'm glad you finally figured that _____.
    11.

6 | EDITING: TALK BETWEEN ROOMMATES

Read Bob and Juan's conversation. There are twelve mistakes in the use of reciprocal pronouns, reflexive pronouns, and phrasal verbs. The first mistake is already corrected. Find and correct eleven more.

BOB: What time do you wake in the morning? *(up inserted)*

JUAN: Well, I figured up I need about nine hours of sleep. So I get up around 9:00 or sometimes 10:00. Why do you ask?

BOB: I get me out of bed by 6:00 every day so that I can go running before class. And I like to play music in the morning. But I can turn it if it's too loud for you.

JUAN: 6:00?! I know some people who can't get them out of bed until noon. But don't worry about the music. I can sleep through anything.

BOB: That's great. A friend of mine who went out to win lots of races told me that he listened to music before running. I thought it might help me.

JUAN: Whatever you need to do to keep your energetic is fine with myself. I like to play music at night while I study. Will that bother you?

BOB: Usually I can study with music. But if I'm working on math, I need to be by me in a room with no distractions.

JUAN: I understand. I had a friend who lived himself and still needed to go to the library because his neighbors were noisy. Don't worry. This kind of problem is easy to work in. I'll be sure to tell you before I play music.

BOB: Sounds good. It's great that we can discuss things with you and me.

Unit 9 Achievement Test

1 | LISTENING: AN OPTIMISTIC PERSON

🎧 *Tom and Sara are discussing what it means to be an optimistic person. Listen to their conversation. Complete the conversation by writing the words that you hear. You will hear the recording two times.*

TOM: What do you think it means to be an optimistic person? To me, optimistic people see

_____*themselves*_____ and the world around them in a positive way.
      0.

SARA: I think being an optimistic person means looking for the positive in the situation

_____, whether it's good or bad.
    1.

TOM: I think so too. My sister describes _____ as an optimistic person, but I don't
                 2.

think she is.

SARA: Why not?

TOM: Well, for example, she's always complaining that her boss doesn't like her. She says that's

the reason she didn't get a promotion last year.

SARA: Hmmm. I see what you mean. How about you? Would you describe _____
                                       3.

as an optimistic person?

TOM: Yes, I do describe _____ as optimistic. When my car broke down last week,
               4.

I had to take the bus. It took longer than driving, but I decided to enjoy the trip and read

the newspaper.

SARA: Well, people can learn from _____. Maybe you should talk to your sister
                   5.

about what it means to be an optimistic person.

TOM: Good idea. We could help _____ deal with life's problems.
               6.

2 | HELP YOUR CHILD BE OPTIMISTIC

Complete this excerpt from a parenting magazine about how to raise an optimistic child.
Circle the correct words.

Optimism is an important skill that parents can teach their children and (themselves)/

yourselves / theirselves. Some parents think this is a difficult task, but it's not that hard if you
0.

know what to do.

The first step parents must take is to teach their children to think optimistically about

himself / themselves / herself. Parents can do this by modeling what it means to be a positive
1.

thinker. Parents should think about the way they react to problems individually and with

each other / oneself / theirselves. How does Mom react when she has had a bad day? Does she
2.

blame the problem itself / himself / themselves? Or does she push herself / himself / itself to try
3. **4.**

to find a solution? How does Dad act when he receives bad news? Does he ignore the problem?

Does he blame himself / herself / itself? Or does he tackle the problem? Do Mom and Dad help
5.

itself / each other / yourselves find solutions?
6.

Secondly, pay attention to how your child reacts to situations. For example, if your son fails

a test in school, does he blame the teacher? Does he give up? If so, teach your son that he can

promise himself / herself / itself to study harder the next time. Does your daughter have
7.

problems interacting with other children? You can teach her that people talk to

one another / myself / theirselves in order to resolve daily conflicts. Once children are
8.

exposed to optimistic behavior, they can then teach himself / themselves / herself to be positive
9.

in any given situation.

Parents can't always fix their children's problems, but they can offer extra support during

times of stress. Teaching your children to be positive thinkers will help them learn for

himself / herself / themselves what it means to be positive and successful people.
10.

3 | WHO IS OPTIMISTIC?

Complete the conversation. Write the correct reflexive or reciprocal pronouns.

BOB: Do you think of _____yourself_____ as an optimistic person?
                        0.

RACHEL: Yes, I try to be as optimistic as I can.

BOB: Do you remember meeting my friend Mike last summer? Would you say that he's an

optimistic person?

RACHEL: Yes, I do remember meeting him. He had just lost his job, but he seemed positive that

he would find an even better job. Did he?

BOB: Yeah, he did. He found a job where he has lots of time for _____, and it
                                                                    1.

pays well too. I would say that Mike is an optimistic person.

RACHEL: I would too, but do you think he sees _____ that way?
                                                2.

BOB: I think he does.

RACHEL: Good, because I think how we see _____ is even more important than
                                           3.

how other people see us.

BOB: I think you're right.

4 | OPTIMISM AND YOUR HEALTH

*Complete the conversation. Use the correct pronouns in the box. Some items may have
more than one right answer. Some words can be used more than once.*

each other	himself	myself	themselves	yourselves
herself	itself	one another	yourself	

RACHEL: Sometimes I have to remind _____myself_____ to stay positive when I'm
                                              0.

having a bad day.

BOB: You know, I just read an article about people having healthier, happier lives by talking

to themselves.

RACHEL: That sounds a bit strange. Instead of talking about their problems to

_____, people just talk to _____?
        1.   **2.**

BOB: Not exactly. It's not that people aren't supposed to talk to _____.
      3.

But the article suggests that talking to _____ can change a
      4.

negative situation to a positive one.

RACHEL: But people will think I'm crazy!

BOB: Well, don't talk to _____ in public. Instead, stand in front of
      5.

your mirror each morning and tell yourself that you will have a great day.

RACHEL: Have you tried to talk to _____?
      6.

BOB: I have. I just say to _____, "Bob, you will have a great day
      7.

today." I think it works.

RACHEL: OK, well, I'll try it and let you know.

| 5 | **EDITING: BE AN OPTIMISTIC PERSON ALL THE TIME!** |

Read the paragraph. There are five mistakes in the use of reflexive and reciprocal pronouns.
The first mistake is already corrected. Find and correct four more.

    The true measure of being healthy is how optimistic you are about ~~myself~~ *yourself* and your life. You

can learn how to control your thinking so that you feel good about almost any situation. First,

instead of looking at a problem as permanent, yourself, as an optimistic person, can see it as a

temporary problem that has a solution. You may see the problem as a challenging situation that

you can resolve alone or with another person. Optimistic people rely on each to discover

solutions together. Secondly, when something goes wrong, don't take it personally. Once you

learn that you can't control everything by himself, you are on the road to becoming an optimistic

person. You can believe in you and the world around you.

Unit 10 Achievement Test

1 | LISTENING: MOVIE PLANS

A. 🎧 *Pablo is going to his friend Carmen's apartment to watch a movie with her. Listen to their conversation. Complete the conversation by writing the words that you hear. You will hear the recording two times.*

PABLO: I'll _____*pick up*_____ the movie on my way to your place. What time do you want
0.

me to get there?

CARMEN: Oh, I don't know. I still have some work to do. I need to write up my lab report and

hand it in. Then I have to _____ how much time I need to study for my
1.

chemistry test tomorrow.

PABLO: Do you think you'll be finished by 8:00?

CARMEN: Probably. I just need to _____ my notes. That's enough studying for me
2.

to get by.

PABLO: OK. Do you care what kind of movie I _____?
3.

CARMEN: Get something funny or something romantic.

PABLO: How about an old classic movie like *Casablanca*? I can't pass that movie up!

CARMEN: Sounds good. Listen, can you _____ the movie tomorrow while I'm
4.

taking my test?

PABLO: Sure. I'm going to the library now to _____ some information for a
5.

paper I have to write. I'll call you when I _____ from there to find out if
6.

you're done studying.

CARMEN: Great. I'll talk to you then.

B. *Reread the conversation. Find four phrasal verbs. Write them below. (Note: Only use words that are given in the conversation. Do not use any words that you wrote.) An example is given.*

0. *write up* _____

1. _____

2. _____

3. _____

4. _____

| 2 | HOMEMADE TORTILLAS |

Pablo and Carmen are talking about where to buy their favorite food, homemade tortillas. Complete the conversation. Use the correct phrasal verbs in the box.

drop off	go on	pass up	turn into	~~was growing up~~
figured out	look over	set up	wake up	

PABLO: Do you know what I miss most about Mexico? Homemade tortillas. When I

_____*was growing up*_____ in Mexico, my mom made them every morning.
　　　　　　　　　0.

CARMEN: I miss homemade tortillas too, but I found a store that sells them. The only problem is

that you have to _____ early to buy them. I _____ that
　　　　　　　　　　　1.　　　　　　　　　　　　　　　　　**2.**

the freshest tortillas are available when the store opens at 6:00 A.M.

PABLO: How about taking me there tomorrow? We should _____ a time to meet.
　　　　　　　　　　　　　　　　　　　　　　　　　　　　　　　　3.

CARMEN: OK, meet me at the coffee shop at 5:45. If you're not there by 6:00, I'll

_____ without you.
　　　4.

PABLO: OK, OK. I don't want to _____ the opportunity to get fresh tortillas,
　　　　　　　　　　　　　　　　　　　5.

but in case I'm not there, you can _____ some tortillas at my house.
　　　　　　　　　　　　　　　　　　　　　　6.

CARMEN: Very funny. You'd better be on time.

PABLO: OK, I promise, I'll be there!

3 | LIFE IN MEXICO

Pablo and Carmen are talking about living in Mexico. Complete the conversation. Circle the correct words.

CARMEN: So, Pablo, where are you from? I mean, what city?

PABLO: I was brought (up) / back / out on a small farm in southern Mexico. I helped my father
           0.
over / at / out in the fields. But then we moved to the city. Now my family lives in
1.
Mexico City. It's a big change for them. Instead of working in the fields, my father
puts into / on / off a suit and goes to work. What about you?
     2.

CARMEN: I grew up near the border between the United States and Mexico. I learned how to
speak English when I was six years old. I picked up / out / on English easily. That has
               3.
been really helpful for me.

PABLO: I bet!

CARMEN: I visited Mexico City once. Does your family like it there?

PABLO: Well, my dad misses our small town, but my mom always points out / by / into that
                       4.
there are more opportunities in a bigger city and that life is better for our family there.
I came to the United States for that reason too. When did you come here?

CARMEN: My family moved to California when I was ten. I attended elementary school, and my
sister went out / on / up to college. She's ten years older than me.
      5.

PABLO: You know, Carmen, it's nice talking to you. I'm glad we signed into / up / out for the
                             6.
same class.

CARMEN: Me too.

PART II

4 | EDITING: DINNER PLANS

Pablo and Carmen are going out to dinner. Read their conversation. There are nine mistakes in the use of phrasal verbs. The first mistake is already corrected. Find and correct eight more. (Note: There can be more than one way to correct a mistake.)

PABLO: I only have $10 for dinner.

CARMEN: I have $20. Do you think we can ~~get out~~ *get by* with only $30?

PABLO: Well, I can use my credit card. I can help out you if you order something expensive. Let's go to the restaurant, look on a menu, and then decide.

CARMEN: OK, but first I need to take down these shoes and put out my sneakers. They're more comfortable.

PABLO: Where I was brought on, women never wore sneakers out to dinner.

CARMEN: Oh, really? Where I grew in California, everyone wore sneakers everywhere.

PABLO: My dad always points how different things are here in the United States.

CARMEN: Hmmm. Do you want to think over this?

PABLO: What do you mean?

CARMEN: I thought you might be embarrassed to eat dinner with a woman wearing sneakers.

PABLO: Ha-ha. Very funny. Let's go.

PART II Achievement Test

| 1 | LISTENING: JOB OPPORTUNITY |

A. 🎧 *Three friends are talking about an opportunity for a new job. Listen to their conversation. Complete the conversation by writing the words that you hear. You will hear the recording two times.*

JOHN: I have to write _____*myself*_____ a note.
0.

LISA: Why?

JOHN: I _____ to meet with my anthropology professor tomorrow, and I'm afraid
1.

I might forget about it.

BILL: Then yes, you'd better write _____ a note. What's your meeting about?
2.

JOHN: My professor _____ to make a documentary, and he's looking for two
3.

students to help him _____ the project.
4.

LISA: What's the documentary about?

JOHN: The culture of a small village in South America. He spent last summer studying it.

LISA: Did he live with the villagers?

JOHN: No, he lived _____ just outside the village.
5.

LISA: Hmmm. What kind of qualifications do the students need to have?

JOHN: Well, the students must see _____ as optimistic and flexible people. And
6.

they have to be prepared to work long hours.

LISA: Is your professor only looking for anthropology students?

JOHN: Oh, no. The positions are open to any students.

LISA: The project sounds interesting. I can see myself working on it. Since we know

_____, you could recommend me for the job, couldn't you?
7.

BILL: That's a great idea, Lisa. You promised _____ a fun and challenging job this
8.

summer. It sounds like this could be it.

JOHN: Lisa, I don't know why I didn't think of that myself. Of course I'll recommend you, and

I'll bring you an application to fill out.

B. Reread the conversation. Then read each statement and circle **T** *(true) or* **F** *(false).*

(T) **F** 0. John, Lisa, and Bill know one another.

T **F** 1. John and the professor will talk with each other about the project tomorrow.

T **F** 2. The professor wants to make a documentary by himself.

T **F** 3. The professor himself lived in the village last summer.

T **F** 4. Lisa, John, and Bill studied a small village themselves.

T **F** 5. Lisa lived with the villagers herself.

T **F** 6. In order to get the job, the students must see themselves as anthropologists.

T **F** 7. Lisa wants to get a fun job for herself this summer.

T **F** 8. John thought of recommending Lisa himself.

2 | AT BILL AND JOHN'S APARTMENT

Lisa is visiting Bill and John's apartment. Complete the conversation. Circle the correct words or phrases.

BILL: Lisa, thanks for working out /(bringing over)/ getting by your new CD for us to listen to.
　　　　　　　　　　　　　　　　　　　0.

LISA: Sure, any time. Why don't you pick out / take off / go on some of your CDs to play too?
　　　　　　　　　　　　　　　　　　　　　　　　1.

JOHN: I'll do it. Bill just got back / took off / pointed out from work.
　　　　　　　　　　　　　　　　　2.

BILL: Thanks, John. I want to change my clothes and figure out / bring up / look up what we're
　　　　　　　　　　　　　　　　　　　　　　　　　　3.

　　　going to eat for dinner. I said I would cook.

JOHN: I'll clean up / clean out / clean off the kitchen. It's pretty messy.
　　　　　　　4.

LISA: I'll help.

JOHN: Thanks. Wow, I'm really hungry. I only ate an apple for lunch today. I don't know why I

　　　thought I could get over / get by / get away on just that.
　　　　　　　　　　　　5.

LISA: I'm hungry too. I just got down / got back / got out from the gym, and I could eat
　　　　　　　　　　　　　　　6.

　　　something while we make dinner. I'll go to the store and get some chips.

BILL: This dinner is turning off / turning out / turning into a lot of work!
　　　　　　　　　　　　　　　7.

JOHN: I have a better idea. Let's look at / look over / look up the number for that new pizza
　　　　　　　　　　　　　　　　　　8.

　　　place in the phone book. I think they deliver.

BILL: I'll get the phone book. Here's the number. Turn up / Turn down / Turn over the music
　　　　　　　　　　　　　　　　　　　　　　　　9.

　　　while I call.

3 | TIME TO REGISTER FOR CLASSES

John and Lisa are discussing which classes to take next semester. Complete the conversation. Use correct phrasal verbs in the box. Some items may have more than one right answer.

fill out	keep on	pick out	set up	talk over
found out	pass up	pick up	~~sign up~~	work out

LISA: Have you registered for next semester's classes yet?

JOHN: No. I can't believe it's time to _____*sign up*_____ for classes already! I still need to
0.

_____ my schedule with my advisor. I want to discuss the classes I'm
1.

considering.

LISA: I thought you went to see her last week.

JOHN: No, I _____ that I need to make an appointment. There were a lot of
2.

students waiting to see her.

LISA: When will you _____ the appointment? If you wait too long, you won't be
3.

able to get the classes you want.

JOHN: I know, but I don't have the course catalog yet. I still need to _____ a copy.
4.

Then I can decide which classes I can take.

LISA: Here, I have a copy with me. Now you can _____ your classes and make
5.

the appointment.

JOHN: Thanks, Lisa. What would I do without you?

4 | WAITING IN LINE

John made an appointment with his advisor, but he still needs to wait in line to see her. Read the conversations he hears while he waits. Complete each conversation with the correct pronoun. Write the letter of the best answer on each line.

0. **A:** Which class should I take, the one with Professor Jones or the one with Professor Martin?

    B: Gee, I don't know. I think you need to decide for ____*a*____ (a. yourself b. himself c. themselves d. herself).

1. **A:** Do you know what Mark did yesterday? He bought _____ (a. herself b. themselves c. himself d. myself) a motorcycle.

    B: Oh, wow!

2. **A:** Maria lost her wallet last night.

    B: Oh, too bad. Was there a lot of money in it?

    A: No, but the wallet _____ (a. herself b. itself c. himself d. themselves) was a good one.

3. **A:** What's the matter?

    B: My sister and I had an argument this morning, and now we're not speaking to _____ (a. ourselves b. herself c. both d. each other).

4. **A:** My brother has a job interview today, and he's nervous about it.

    B: Tell him just to be _____ (a. himself b. yourself c. themselves d. one another) and he'll do fine.

5. **A:** So, you and your sisters are all on different swim teams. Do you ever compete against _____ (a. yourselves b. one another c. ourselves d. themselves)?

    B: Sometimes. It can be pretty interesting.

6. **A:** I just decided to go to New York next month.

    B: That's great. Are you going with friends or by _____ (a. ourselves b. themselves c. yourselves d. yourself)?

7. **A:** I just can't get up early in the morning. How do you guys do it?

    B: We tell _____ (a. ourselves b. ourself c. yourself d. yourselves) we have no choice—and we just do it!

8. **A:** Ji-Eun's quitting school and getting a job.

    B: Really? How do you know?

    A: She told me _____ (a. himself b. herself c. myself d. ourselves).

9. **A:** This line is too long! I'm coming back later.

    B: Oh, relax. Tell _____ (a. myself b. yourselves c. ourselves d. yourself) that waiting in line teaches patience.

5 | NEED A JOB?

John, Lisa, and Bill are shopping for school supplies. Read their conversation. Find two reflexive pronouns and two reciprocal pronouns. Write them in the table below. An example is given.

LISA: Look at how expensive everything is! This is why I need a job. I'm tired of taking out student loans to pay for everything. The loans themselves are going to cost a lot of money in the future!

BILL: I know what you mean. Loans are not always the answer. By borrowing money now, we're only creating problems for ourselves later.

JOHN: Yeah, it's much better if you have a job and can take care of yourself by paying your own way.

LISA: Yes, but in the meantime, how can I afford these supplies? Should I put them on a credit card?

BILL: No, don't do that. Here, I'll lend you some money.

LISA: I don't know. I hate to borrow money from people.

BILL: It's fine. We've known each other a long time. I know you'll pay me back when you have a job.

LISA: Of course I will. Thanks so much. It's so nice that we can all depend on one another.

REFLEXIVE PRONOUNS	RECIPROCAL PRONOUNS
0. _themselves_	1. _____
1. _____	2. _____
2. _____	

6 | THE JOB SEARCH

Lisa is still looking for a job. Complete her conversation with John. Use reflexive pronouns, reciprocal pronouns, and particles for phrasal verbs. Some items may have more than one right answer.

LISA: I spent all week trying to find a job, but I still couldn't find anything.

JOHN: You have to keep telling _____*yourself*_____ you'll find something soon. Maybe you
           0.
        should relax for a couple of days—watch TV, call _____ some friends.
                                                                       1.

LISA: No, I think I should keep pushing myself to find a job. I have bills to pay and no money. I
        don't want to pass _____ any opportunity.
                                2.

JOHN: Did you check the job board at school? That's how Bill found a job.

LISA: I checked the board yesterday, but there was nothing I was interested in.

JOHN: I know. It's hard. Job hunting _____ can be a full-time job.
                                            3.

LISA: It sure can be!

JOHN: I know that you'll find something soon.

LISA: You know, my family used to own a restaurant and sometimes I worked in the kitchen.
        Maybe I'll go to the restaurant near my apartment and introduce _____ to
                                                4.
        the manager.

JOHN: Sounds like a good idea.

LISA: Thanks for talking this _____ with me.
                                5.

JOHN: You don't need to thank me. Good friends help _____.
                                                      6.

7 | EDITING: LISA'S FIRST DAY OF WORK

Read the conversation between Bill and John about Lisa's first day of work. There are twelve mistakes in the use of reciprocal pronouns, reflexive pronouns, and phrasal verbs. The first mistake is already corrected. Find and correct eleven more.

BILL: So, Lisa found ~~her~~ *herself* a job.

JOHN: Yes, but she called up me last night and told me her first day of work as a waitress was miserable. She says she thought it up and she has no confidence in her.

BILL: Sounds like her first day turned into a disaster. What happened?

JOHN: Well, she figured up that she can't carry a tray.

BILL: Don't tell me. Did she spill food on her?

JOHN: Worse! She spilled on some customers! She picked the tray, and it was too heavy. A few plates of food fell on them.

BILL: Then what happened?

JOHN: Well, the customers were angry. They left the table. Lisa just sat out and started crying.

BILL: That sounds horrible. Did they leave the restaurant?

JOHN: No, they cleaned them up in the bathroom. But they didn't want Lisa to be their waitress after that. They weren't very happy with herself.

BILL: I don't understand. Lisa told me she grew working in her family's restaurant.

JOHN: Yes, that's true. But she worked in the kitchen with the cooks. She helped out them by preparing the vegetables. So she has no experience serving customers.

BILL: Well, she'll have to find a way to keep herself optimistic.

JOHN: I agree, but sometimes it's hard to keep yourself optimistic when you're dropping food on your customers.

PART III Diagnostic Test

1 | LISTENING: THE BIG IDEA

A. 🎧 *Andy and Taylor are brothers. They want to build a treehouse. A treehouse is a wooden structure built in the branches of a tree for children to play in. Listen to Andy and Taylor's conversation. Complete the conversation by writing the words that you hear. You will hear the recording two times.*

ANDY: Look at all that wood left over from building the house. They

_____*shouldn't*_____ throw it out like that. Hey, *we* should use it for
0.

something.

TAYLOR: I know! _____ a treehouse out of that kind of wood?
1.

ANDY: I think so. Actually, that's a great idea! _____ it in the tree by
2.

the fence?

TAYLOR: I don't know if Mom and Dad will let us. Let's go ask Dad. We can convince him.

ANDY: OK. . . . Dad!

MOM: Could you please shut the door?

ANDY: Sorry, Mom. Dad! _____ a treehouse in the tree by the fence,
3.

please?

DAD: Well, a treehouse sounds like a good idea. But there's one problem. The tree by the

fence _____ hold the weight of a treehouse.
4.

TAYLOR: _____ it in a different tree then?
5.

DAD: Sure. You should build it in the tree on the side of the house. That one

_____ the weight.
6.

ANDY: Thanks, Dad! This is going to be great.

DAD: I think so, too. I always wanted a treehouse when I was a kid, but I

_____ have one.
7.

B. *Reread the conversation. Find one statement of advice, one statement of ability, one request, and one suggestion. Write them in the table below. (Note: Only use words that are given in the conversation. Do not use any words that you wrote.) An example is given.*

ADVICE	ABILITY	REQUEST	SUGGESTION
0. *Hey, we should use it for something.* 1. _____ _____	1. _____ _____	1. _____ _____	1. _____ _____

2 | GATHERING THE MATERIALS

Andy and Taylor are getting ready to build their treehouse. Complete the conversations. Circle the correct words or phrases.

TAYLOR: This is a lot of wood! (Can)/ Let's / Would you mind you help me move it closer to
0.
the tree?

ANDY: Sure, but we could / couldn't / can't carry it all ourselves. It's too heavy.
1.

TAYLOR: Why don't / Why not / Let's not we get Dad to help us?
2.

ANDY: Good idea. Would you go / going / to go ask him?
3.

TAYLOR: Sure.

TAYLOR: Dad, could you to help / helping / help us move the wood for the treehouse?
4.

DAD: Sure. But we ought wearing / wear / to wear gloves so that we don't hurt our hands.
5.

MOM: You 'd better / shouldn't / couldn't not forget to close the door!
6.

DAD: Would you mind to close / close / closing the gate, too? I don't want the dog to get out.
7.

ANDY: Sure. But why not / how about / let's put him inside? We're going to be coming in and
8.
out of the gate a lot with the wood.

DAD: That's fine. Should / Would / Had better you bring him inside, please?
9.

ANDY: No problem.

3 | BUILDING THE TREEHOUSE

Andy and Taylor are building their treehouse. Read the conversations. Complete the conversations with the correct phrases. Write the letter of the best answer on each line.

ANDY: We have all the wood. Now ___*a*___ (a. can we start b. ought we start c. would we start) the
0.

treehouse?

TAYLOR: Not quite yet. How about _____ (a. finding b. to find c. we finding) the rest of our
1.

supplies first? _____ (a. Could you to get b. Could you get c. Could you getting) some nails,
2.

please?

ANDY: I looked earlier, but I _____ (a. can't b. wasn't able to c. could) find them. I'll go ask
3.

Dad.

ANDY: Hey, Dad, _____ (a. may we use b. may we using c. we may use) some nails?
4.

DAD: Yes, _____ (a. you can't b. you will c. you may). They're in a can on the table in the
5.

garage. _____ (a. Do you minding if b. Do you mind if c. Do you mind) I watch you work?
6.

ANDY: No. _____ (a. Maybe we couldn't b. Maybe we would c. Maybe we could) all work on it
7.

together.

DAD: Now that's a great idea.

TAYLOR: _____ (a. Were you able to find b. Were you able to finding c. Were you able find) the nails?
8.

ANDY: Yeah. Here they are. _____ (a. Had we better build b. Ought we to build c. Should we build) a
9.

ladder first?

DAD: No, I think the ladder should come last.

4 | SHOWING THE TREEHOUSE

Andy and Taylor finished their treehouse. Complete the conversations. Use the correct forms of **can (not), could (not), (not) be able to, may (not) , will (not),** *or* **would (not).** *Some items may have more than one right answer.*

TAYLOR: We should show Mom our treehouse. _____*Can*_____ you go in and get her? I
0.

shouted to her, but I guess she _____ hear me.
1.

ANDY: Sure.

MOM: Wow. That's really high. _____ you _____ get down from
2.

there later? And _____ you get down by yourselves?
3.

ANDY: Of course! We have a ladder, see? And it's really not that high. You _____
4.

climb up too.

MOM: You think I can do it? OK, here I come . . . .

ANDY: But you _____ come up here tonight only because it's new. Normally it's
5.

just for kids—no parents allowed!

TAYLOR: Yeah. After this, you _____ come up here without our permission.
6.

MOM: OK. Wow! This is really nice up here.

TAYLOR: I know. _____ you take our picture?
7.

MOM: I _____ carry the camera with me when I climbed up the ladder. It's still
8.

on the ground.

ANDY: That's too bad. Would you please take one later?

MOM: Sure I _____. Now let's climb down. It's time for dinner.
9.

TAYLOR: May Andy and I eat up here?

MOM: No, you _____. We're going to eat together in the kitchen. But you can
10.

come right back out after dinner.

5 | TALKING ABOUT THE BOYS

The parents are talking about their sons. Complete the conversation. Use the correct forms of the words in parentheses to give advice or make suggestions. Put the words in the correct order.

MOM: The boys really enjoyed building their treehouse. _____*We should encourage*_____
    0. (encourage / should / we)

    them to do more activities like that.

DAD: _____*Why don't we suggest*_____ that they make some improvements to the
    0. (not / we / why / suggest)

    treehouse?

MOM: That sounds like a good plan. _____ some material for
    1. (could / we / maybe / get)

    a roof.

DAD: Certainly. And I think _____ it themselves, unless they
    2. (the boys / build / should)

    ask for help. _____ them what other improvements
    3. (ask / to / I / ought)

    they want to make. _____ with me to the hardware
    4. (had / go / they / better)

    store to pick out what they want.

MOM: _____ them tomorrow?
    5. (about / take / how)

DAD: Sure. Also, _____ them pay for it. It won't be that
    6. (not / we / make / should)

    expensive, and we can set a price limit.

MOM: I agree. _____ to them about it at dinner tonight.
    7. (talk / let's)

6 | EDITING: SHOPPING FOR MORE MATERIALS

Read the conversation between the boys and their dad at the hardware store. There are fifteen mistakes. The first mistake is already corrected. Find and correct fourteen more. (Note: There can be more than one way to correct a mistake.)

ANDY: Can we ~~looking~~ *look* at the wood for the roof now?

DAD: Let's to get the wood last so we don't have to carry it around the store. We should buying more nails. Taylor, can you get please some? They're over there.

TAYLOR: Sure, no problem.

ANDY: Why don't we put a refrigerator in the treehouse? Could we buying one, Dad?

DAD: No, I don't think so.

TAYLOR: Why not getting just a small one?

DAD: You can't use a refrigerator without electricity.

TAYLOR: Oh, right. Too bad. A refrigerator would be pretty cool.

ANDY: Well, we'd better to think of something else to get.

DAD: Andy, my hands are getting full. Would you mind holding these tools?

ANDY: Sure. Give them to me. Hey, how about having a pole to slide down like a firefighter?

DAD: That sounds like fun.

TAYLOR: When had we better buy the pole? Right now?

DAD: Well, I think you ought wait until you have more practice with building things. That might be a little complicated.

TAYLOR: I couldn't wait for you to teach us more about building stuff. By the time you teach us everything you know, we can make lots of improvements on the treehouse.

ANDY: Dad, do you mind we look around a little? We might get some good ideas for improvements.

DAD: That's fine. But we ought not take too long. Mom needs to use the car today too, and she can't going anywhere until we get home.

Unit 11 Achievement Test

30 Items
Score: _____

A. 🎧 *Estella Flores is an actor. Listen to her conversation with Greg, who works at an acting agency. Complete the conversation by writing the words that you hear. You will hear the recording two times.*

ESTELLA: Thanks for seeing me today, Greg. I'm sorry I had to cancel my appointment last week.

GREG: No problem. A lot of people are looking for an actor like you. I just need to ask you a

few questions. I have a client who is looking for someone to play a small part in a

television series. _____*Are you able to work*_____ next month?
                                            0.

ESTELLA: Absolutely. I _____ anytime.
                                            1.

GREG: OK, great. Now, I have another client who needs some singers for a musical comedy.

Can you sing?

ESTELLA: Well, actually, no, I can't sing very well.

GREG: That's OK. _____?
                                            2.

ESTELLA: I've taken a lot of lessons, and yes, I can dance pretty well.

GREG: Great. _____ the role of an old woman?
                                            3.

ESTELLA: Well, I've never done it before. But I'm sure I can do it.

GREG: OK. _____ comedy?
                                            4.

ESTELLA: Yes. In fact, most of my work has been in comedy.

GREG: Great. I'll make sure that people look at your résumé, OK?

ESTELLA: Thanks! Again, I'm sorry I couldn't come in last week.

GREG: Oh, that's OK. We should have some work for you soon.

B. Reread the conversation. Find four phrases that express ability. Write them below. (Note: Only use words that are given in the conversation. Do not use any words that you wrote.) An example is given.

0. _____ *Can you sing* _____

1. _____

2. _____

3. _____

4. _____

2 | GREG'S E-MAIL

Read Greg's e-mail to the producer of a television show. Complete the e-mail with the correct verb forms. Write the letter of the best answer on each line.

Hello Collin,

Estella Flores _____*b*_____ (a. cans start b. is able to start c. could start d. was able to start) work next
               0.

month, so she should be available for the television series. She _____ (a. couldn't meet b. didn't
                                                                       1.

able to meet c. couldn't to meet d. couldn't met) me last week because she was out of town, but I finally

met her today. After talking with her, I _____ (a. can recommends b. 'm able recommend c. could
                                              2.

recommends d. 'm able to recommend) her very highly. She _____ (a. can does b. cans do c. does able
                                                               3.

to do d. can do) a variety of roles.

I have a meeting in a few minutes. But I _____ (a. am able call b. can call c. can to call
                                              4.

d. couldn't call) you later today to give you more details about the interview.

Greg

---

3 | ENRIQUE CRUZ

Complete these sentences about actor Enrique Cruz. Use **can, could,** *or the correct form of* **be able to** *and the verbs in parentheses. Some items may have more than one correct answer.*

When he was younger, Enrique Cruz _____*could memorize*_____ his lines very quickly.
                                        0. (memorize)

When he made his first movie in 1985, Cruz _____ his lines in just a
                                                1. (learn)

few days.

Audiences admire Enrique's ability to portray a wide variety of characters. He

_____ in many kinds of roles. He _____
        2. (act)   **3. (play)**

characters of different ages and nationalities. He _____ in 12 different
                                                        4. (speak)

accents. When his movie *The Frenchman* came out last year, people _____
                                                                        5. (not / tell)

that he wasn't really French because his accent was so good.

Here's something a lot of people don't know about Enrique: He's very interested in music.

He _____ very well, and he's learning to play the piano. His next
        6. (sing)

movie is going to be about a musician. By the time they film it next year, Enrique

_____ some of the music himself. Now he is working hard and
        7. (perform)

practicing a lot. He says he wants _____ all the music for the movie.
                                        8. (play)

For a long time, Enrique was also known for his dancing. He _____
                                                                9. (dance)

very well until he hurt his knee last year. But now he _____ at all.
                                                            10. (not / dance)

In one action scene in his first movie, Enrique _____ his own stunts.
                                                    11. (perform)

But he _____ his own stunts anymore because of his bad knee.
            12. (not / do)

Enrique was recently in the hospital for knee surgery. But he's doing better now, and he

_____ to the lifetime achievement awards ceremony next week.
        13. (go)

| 4 | EDITING: ESTELLA'S JOURNAL |

An audition *is a short performance in which an actor shows his or her abilities to play a certain role. Estella has an audition tomorrow. Read her journal entry. There are six mistakes in the use of* **can, could,** *and* **be able to.** *The first mistake is already corrected. Find and correct five more.*

July 14

        was
    I ~~am~~ finally able to have my interview with Greg Rollins yesterday. I was able to tell him all about my talents as an actor. Then today he called and asked me to audition for a role on a new TV show. The audition is tomorrow. I can't waiting! It's so exciting! And here's the best part: I'll be able meet Enrique Cruz, who's going to be on the show! He's my favorite actor! I could never wait for his movies to come out when I was young. One day last summer, I could catch a glimpse of him at a studio, but I didn't actually meet him. Anyway, I can to go to the studio tomorrow for my audition. Greg sent me a script to read at the audition. I'm going to study it all night. By tomorrow I can say my lines really well. I hope I get this job!

Unit 12 Achievement Test

30 Items
Score: _____

1 | LISTENING: AT THE COMPANY PICNIC

A. 🎧 *Damian, a new employee, is at a park with his daughter Jody for his company's picnic. Listen to the conversation. Complete the conversation by writing the words that you hear. You will hear the recording two times.*

DAMIAN: Excuse me. _____*Could we sit*_____ here next to you?
0.

STAN: _____. I'm Stan, and this is Becky. We work in the art
1.

department.

BECKY: Hi.

DAMIAN: Nice to meet you both. I'm Damian, and this is my daughter, Jody. I'm in sales. I just

started on Monday.

STAN: Welcome to the company.

DAMIAN: Thanks. Hey, Stan, _____ you a favor?
2.

STAN: Certainly.

DAMIAN: Could I borrow your cell phone? I need to call my wife and give her directions to get

here, but my battery's dead.

STAN: I'm sorry, but my phone's in the car.

BECKY: Here, _____ mine.
3.

DAMIAN: Thanks so much. Oh, do you mind if my daughter plays her video game? It's a little

noisy.

STAN: No, not at all.

JODY: Hey, Dad. _____ get something to eat? I'm hungry.
4.

DAMIAN: Sure. The food is right over there. I'll call Mom, and I'll meet you there in a minute.

B. *Reread the conversation. Then read each statement and circle* **T** *(true) or* **F** *(false).*

(T) **F** 0. Damian asks permission to sit near Stan.

T **F** 1. Stan allows Damian to use his cell phone.

T **F** 2. Damian asks permission for Jody to play her game.

T **F** 3. It's not OK for Jody to play her game.

T **F** 4. Damian doesn't give Jody permission to eat something.

---

2 | LOOKING FOR THE TENNIS COURTS

Damian and Jody want to play tennis. Complete the conversation between Damian and a park worker. Circle the correct words or phrases.

WORKER: Can you help / (Can I help) / I can help you find something?
0.

DAMIAN: I don't think so, but we have another question: May please we / May we please /
1.

Please we may use those tennis courts over there?

WORKER: No, sorry / you mayn't / you can. They're being repaired. But you can use the ones
2.

behind the pool—over there.

DAMIAN: Oh, good, thanks. Do you mind if I to ask / asking / ask you another question?
3.

WORKER: Not at all.

DAMIAN: Can we take / Can we to take / We can take our sodas on the court with us?
4.

WORKER: Of course. There's a little table near the benches you can put them on.

---

3 | QUESTIONS AND ANSWERS AT SCHOOL

Read these statements. Use the words in parentheses to write questions that ask for permission. Then write appropriate short answers or informal expressions. (Note: There can be more than one way to answer the questions.)

Tom wants to bring a drink into the computer lab.

TOM: _____*Can I bring a drink into the computer lab*_____?
0. (can)

COMPUTER TEACHER: ____*Sorry, you can't*____. No drinks are allowed in the lab.
0.

Sarah wants to call Laura tonight.

SARAH: _____?
1. (do you mind if)

LAURA: _____. I'll be home all night, so anytime is fine.
2.

Bart wants to borrow $5 from Cindy.

BART: _____? I'll pay you back tomorrow.
                         3. (can / please)

CINDY: _____. Here you are.
              4.

Tom wants to check out this book from the library.

TOM: _____?
                         5. (may)

LIBRARIAN: _____. You have an overdue book. You need to return
                 6.

the overdue one before you can take out any others.

Maria wants to turn in her paper tomorrow.

MARIA: _____? I was sick yesterday.
                       7. (could)

TEACHER: OK, but no later than tomorrow.

Sam wants to give the teacher his homework after class.

SAM: I forgot my homework. It's in my locker. _____?
                                  8. (can)

TEACHER: No, you can't. I'm leaving right after class.

Lola wants to use Ben's dictionary.

LOLA: _____?
                        9. (could)

BEN: _____. I'm using it now. I'll be finished in a few
               10.

minutes, though.

Mario wants to borrow Kathy's blue pen.

MARIO: _____?
                     11. (can)

KATHY: Certainly! Here you go.

Stephan wants to go to the bathroom.

STEPHAN: _____?
                     12. (may)

TEACHER: Of course. But please hurry back.

Randy wants to get a book from his locker.

RANDY: _____?
                     13. (may)

TEACHER: Not right now. You can go during lunch.

4 | EDITING: AT THE LIBRARY

Carolyn is at the library. Read her conversation with the librarian. There are six mistakes in the use of **can, could, may,** *and* **do you mind if**. *The first mistake is already corrected. Find and correct five more. (Note: There can be more than one way to correct a mistake.)*

LIBRARIAN: Can I ~~may~~ help you?

CAROLYN: Yes, I'm returning an overdue library book. Can I pay the fine now?

LIBRARIAN: Yes, you could.

CAROLYN: And I also want to check out these books.

LIBRARIAN: OK. May I saw your library card, please?

CAROLYN: I sorry, but I left it at home. Can I get the books without it?

LIBRARIAN: Sure. I just need another form of identification, and then you can pay the fine. Can I

see please your driver's license?

CAROLYN: Uh-oh. I don't have any identification with me. Do you mind I just pay the fine later?

LIBRARIAN: That's fine, but you can't check out any books until you pay the fine.

CAROLYN: OK. Thank you for your help.

Unit 13 Achievement Test

1 | LISTENING: PHONE CONVERSATION

A. ◯ *Gabe and Jackie are married. Listen to their telephone conversation. Complete the conversation by writing the words that you hear. You will hear the recording two times.*

JACKIE: Hello?

GABE: Hi, honey. What are you up to?

JACKIE: I'm checking my e-mail. We got a message from our landlord, but I haven't read it yet.

GABE: Oh, really? ____*Can you open*____ it now?
                              0.

JACKIE: Yeah, hold on a minute . . . OK. It says, "Hi, Gabe and Jackie, I'm going out of town

next week. _____ the flowers in front of the apartment building?
                          1.

I'll take $50 off your rent for the month. _____ me know as
                                                              2.

soon as possible? Thanks!" Do you want to do it?

GABE: Sure. It won't be much work. _____ him back?
                                                  3.

JACKIE: No problem.

GABE: Great. Listen, I'm about ready to leave the office. Is there anything you need me to get

on the way home?

JACKIE: Yes, _____ some milk and cheese, please?
                        4.

GABE: Sure. Do you need anything else from the grocery store?

JACKIE: No, but _____ by the bank to get some cash?
                          5.

GABE: Not at all. Anything else?

JACKIE: Just one more thing. _____ a movie to watch tonight?
                                          6.

GABE: I'm sorry, I can't. I don't have my video rental card. They won't let me rent a movie

without it.

JACKIE: Too bad. Oh well. See you in a little bit.

B. *Read the conversation. Find four responses to requests. Write each response in the correct category below. An example is given.*

GABE: We have to do a lot this weekend. But if we each do a few things, it won't take too long.

JACKIE: OK. Could you return the movie to the video store?

GABE: Sure. Do you want to get another one?

JACKIE: I don't think so. We might not have time to watch it. Can you pay the phone bill too?

GABE: No problem. Now, we need to find someone to repair the roof. Would you mind calling some people?

JACKIE: Not at all. But will you please fix the wall in the bathroom? It's really bothering me.

GABE: Of course. I can do that today.

JACKIE: Great! Can I help you?

GABE: Yes, you can. Oh, could you pick up our clothes from the dry cleaners?

JACKIE: I'm sorry, I can't today. They're closed on the weekends.

RESPONSES: WILL DO WHAT THE PERSON REQUESTS	RESPONSE: WILL NOT DO WHAT THE PERSON REQUESTS
0. *Sure.*	1. _____
1. _____	
2. _____	
3. _____	

---

2 | CLEANING THE HOUSE

Gabe and Jackie are cleaning the house. Read their short conversations. Complete the conversations. Write the letter of the best answer on each line.

JACKIE: Could you ___a___ **(a. vacuum b. to vacuum c. vacuum please)** the living room, please?
　　　　　　　　　0.

GABE: I'm sorry, but I _____ **(a. couldn't b. wouldn't c. can't)**. Jill has our vacuum cleaner.
　　　　　　　　　　　　1.

JACKIE: Would you mind _____ **(a. put b. putting c. putting please)** away the DVDs?
　　　　　　　　　　　　　　2.

GABE: _____ **(a. Certainly b. Sure I will. c. Not at all)**. I'll do it right after lunch.
　　　3.

GABE: Will _____ (a. please you organize b. you please organize c. you organize please) the mail?
                4.

JACKIE: OK.

GABE: _____ (a. Would please you fold the laundry b. Would you fold please the laundry c. Would you fold
           5.

the laundry, please)? It's in the dryer.

JACKIE: Sorry, I _____ (a. can't b. couldn't c. wouldn't) right now. I have to make a phone call.
                    6.

GABE: I'll take this garbage out. _____ (a. Can you open please b. Can please you open c. Can you
                                         7.

please open) the door?

JACKIE: Sure. Would you mind picking up those newspapers on the floor?

GABE: _____ (a. Certainly b. Not at all c. Sure I will). Let me go get another trash bag.
           8.

JACKIE: _____ (a. Cans you wash b. Can you wash c. Can you washes) the windows?
           9.

GABE: Sure. _____ (a. Would you give b. Would you giving c. Would you to give) me the paper towels?
                10.

JACKIE: _____ (a. Please could you make b. Could you make please c. Could you please make) the bed?
           11.

GABE: Certainly. _____ (a. Will you clean b. Will you cleaning c. Will you to clean) the bathroom?
                    12.

JACKIE: I hate cleaning the bathroom! _____ (a. Please would you do b. Would you please do c. Would
                                          13.

you do please) it?

GABE: That depends! _____ (a. Will you do b. Will you doing c. Will you to do) something for me?
                       14.

JACKIE: I suppose so. But _____ (a. could you choose please something easy b. could please you choose
                             15.

something easy c. could you choose something easy, please)? I'm tired from all this work!

3 | EDITING: IN THE EVENING

Gabe and Jackie are relaxing in the evening. Read their conversation. There are six mistakes in making and responding to requests. The first mistake is already corrected. Find and correct five more. (Note: There can be more than one way to correct a mistake.)

GABE: Can you ~~X~~ put on some music?

JACKIE: Sure. Would you mind to turn on the lights?

GABE: Not at all. Then could you makes us some hot chocolate?

JACKIE: Sorry, I couldn't. We don't have any. Do you want tea instead?

GABE: That sounds good. But can you buy some more hot chocolate the next time you go

to the store?

JACKIE: Certainly. Is this music OK?

GABE: Yes. But will you turn up please the volume?

JACKIE: Not at all. Is this better?

GABE: Perfect. Thanks.

Unit 14 Achievement Test

1 | LISTENING: *MONEY MATTERS*

A. 🎧 *Listen to part of a television show called* Money Matters. *Complete the show by writing the words that you hear. You will hear the recording two times.*

CINDY: We're back with *Money Matters*. I'm Cindy Hall.

_____*What should you do*_____ if your wallet is lost or stolen?
                        0.

Russ Severson is here today to give us the answer. According to him,

_____ several things in that situation. Russ,
                        1.

let's say my wallet is missing. Should I call the police?

RUSS: Yes!

CINDY: _____ them?
                        2.

RUSS: You had better call as soon as you realize your wallet is missing. Thieves can act fast.

CINDY: Should I cancel my credit cards right away?

RUSS: Absolutely. You ought to do that right after you call the police. By the way,

_____ down the numbers of your cards or make
                        3.

a photocopy of them now, *before* you lose them. Then you'll have all the information

you need to give the credit card companies.

CINDY: When should I get new ID cards?

RUSS: That isn't as important as calling the police and your credit card companies, but

_____ new ID cards within a few days.
                        4.

CINDY: Russ Severson, great to have you on the show. I think we all

_____ attention to your excellent advice.
                        5.

RUSS: Thank you, Cindy.

B. *Reread the conversation. Find two statements of advice and two questions asking for advice. Write them in the table below. (Note: Only use words that are given in the conversation. Do not use any words that you wrote.) An example is given.*

STATEMENTS OF ADVICE	QUESTIONS ASKING FOR ADVICE
1. _____ _____	0. *Should I call the police?* _____
2. _____ _____	1. _____ _____
	2. _____ _____

C. *Reread the conversation. Then read each statement and circle* **T** *(true) or* **F** *(false).*

Ⓣ **F**   **0.** You ought to have a plan if your wallet is ever lost or stolen.

T **F**   **1.** If your wallet is lost or stolen, you'd better tell the police as soon as you can.

T **F**   **2.** You should wait for someone to return your wallet.

T **F**   **3.** You should cancel your credit cards.

T **F**   **4.** You shouldn't contact your credit card companies before you call the police.

2 | HOW CAN I PROTECT MYSELF?

Complete these questions and answers on Russ Severson's website. Use **should** *and the correct words in the box. Then give appropriate short answers.*

be concerned about identity theft	participate in online banking
~~create complicated PIN numbers~~	shop online only at secure websites
give it to them	write them down

Q: _____ *Should I create complicated PIN numbers* _____? I worry about people figuring my PIN
                                  0.

numbers out.

A: _____ *Yes, you should* _____. It's not a good idea to create PIN
                               0.

numbers based on birthdays or other significant dates.

Q: I always forget my PIN numbers. _____?
                                              1.

A: _____. Just remember to keep them in a safe
                             2.

place in your home. Don't carry them with your credit or debit card.

Q: People often ask me for my phone number. _____?
  3.

A: _____. It's not a good idea to share personal
  4.

information if you don't know why the person wants it. Only give out your phone number if

you are sure how the person will use it.

Q: Someone recently stole my friend's credit card number from an online store.

_____?
  5.

A: _____. Always make sure a website is secure
  6.

before you enter any personal information. Most online stores are completely safe. But check

into a store's reputation if you have any doubts.

---

3 | EDITING: HOW TO AVOID IDENTITY THEFT

*Read these tips from an Internet article by Russ Severson about how to avoid identity
theft. There are twelve mistakes. The first mistake is already corrected. Find and correct
eleven more.*

   leave
0. You should ~~leaving~~ any ID cards that you don't use often in a safe place at home.

1. You ought sign your credit cards as soon as you get them, and you should cancel any cards

   you don't use.

2. You should not carrying your birth certificate with you. Keep it in a safe place.

3. You should not wrote your PIN numbers on your cards.

4. You had better to shred any documents that have personal information on them.

5. You should checks your credit card accounts regularly to look for any unusual activity.

6. If you don't receive a credit card statement, you ought contact the company.

7. You shoulds change the passwords and PIN numbers for your bank accounts frequently.

8. You ought to not give your bank account information over the phone or online.

9. You ought to using passwords that are difficult for people to guess.

10. You should putting outgoing mail in a secure post office box, and you ought to remove your

    mail from your mailbox soon after it is delivered.

11. You are should protect your computer with anti-virus software.

Unit 15 Achievement Test

30 Items
Score: _____

---

1 | LISTENING: WEEKEND PLANS

A. 🎧 *Taylor and Gabriella are married. Listen to their conversation. Complete the conversation by writing the words that you hear. You will hear the recording two times.*

TAYLOR: Why don't we do something fun this weekend? _____*Let's have*_____ a
                                                                              0.
barbecue. We can cook some food outside and invite some people to come over.

GABRIELLA: Good idea! Why not invite the new neighbors, Matt and Anita?

TAYLOR: OK. We'll need to buy a few things. _____ meat for
                                                          1.
hamburgers?

GABRIELLA: I think there's a sale on steak. Maybe we could have steak instead.

TAYLOR: Well, only if it's not too expensive. _____ too much money.
                                                            2.

GABRIELLA: OK, I agree. We shouldn't spend a lot. _____ hot dogs?
                                                                  3.
They're cheap.

TAYLOR: I don't know. That doesn't sound very good. How about sausage instead?

GABRIELLA: Mmm! That sounds great! Let's get some chips too. Do we have anything for
dessert?

TAYLOR: I think we have soda, and we have ice cream. _____ ice
                                                                     4.
cream sodas?

GABRIELLA: Great idea!

B. Reread the conversation. Then read each statement and circle **T** *(true) or* **F** *(false).*

(T) **F** 0. Taylor suggested doing a fun activity.

T **F** 1. Gabriella didn't want to invite the neighbors.

T **F** 2. Taylor suggested having steak for dinner.

T **F** 3. Gabriella suggested getting some chips at the store.

T **F** 4. Taylor didn't want to have ice cream sodas.

2 | WHAT SHOULD WE DO TODAY?

Complete these suggestions. Circle the correct words or phrases.

0. (Let's)/ Let's not / How about visit the historical museum. I really want to see it.

1. It's hot outside. Maybe we could / How about / Why don't go somewhere with air

   conditioning.

2. Why doesn't / Why not / Why don't we go shopping? I need to buy some new clothes.

3. How about / Why not / Let's not have a party? We could invite a few friends to come over.

4. How about / Why don't we / Let's going to the car show?

5. Let's / How about / Maybe we go see a movie. We both want to see *Phone Call.*

6. Why doesn't / Why don't / Maybe we could take a road trip. I want to drive somewhere.

7. Let's not / Let's / How about stay home and read. I have a book I want to finish.

8. Why not / Let's not / Let's work. We need a break from work for awhile.

9. Maybe we could meet / meeting / not meeting Todd and Beth for dinner.

10. Why not / Why don't / How about go to the art festival downtown? I heard it's really good.

11. How about / Let's / Why don't cleaning the house right now? We won't have time tomorrow.

3 | GETTING READY FOR THE BARBECUE

Complete the suggestions for the barbecue with the phrases in the box. Use the correct forms of the verbs and punctuate correctly.

play some games	read a book	set up the chairs
~~get ready for the barbecue~~	make some iced tea	cook some eggs
put on some music	open the windows	eat something

TAYLOR: Gabriella, it's 4:00 already!

GABRIELLA: Well, let's _____ *get ready for the barbecue.* _____
                                          0.

TAYLOR: OK. First, let's _____ That way people will have
                                              1.

a place to sit when they arrive.

GABRIELLA: That sounds good. Hey, it's so quiet around here. Why don't you

_____
                2.

TAYLOR: Great idea. I'll play that new CD we got.

GABRIELLA: OK. You know, this room is really hot.

GABRIELLA: Maybe we could _____
                                              3.

TAYLOR: That works. Hey, what are we going to do all night? We don't want our guests

to be bored.

GABRIELLA: Why not _____
                                  4.

TAYLOR: I'll go get them. Do you think we have enough food?

GABRIELLA: Yeah, I think so. But we might need something else to drink.

TAYLOR: How about _____ It's quick and easy.
                                      5.

GABRIELLA: Good idea. I'll do it right now.

4 | EDITING: DURING THE BARBECUE

Taylor and Gabriella are having their barbecue. Read two of their conversations. There are seven mistakes in the use of suggestions. The first mistake is already corrected. Find and correct six more.

TAYLOR: Why ~~we don't~~ *don't we* get the food out? Or maybe people could start with drinks.

GABRIELLA: Yes, that sounds good. How about to bring out the lemonade first?

TAYLOR: You've been busy all day. Why you don't sit down and relax? I can get the lemonade.

GABRIELLA: OK. Thanks!

(A little while later)

GABRIELLA: Look, there are Matt and Anita. They're all by themselves. Let's to introduce them to

some people. Maybe they could to meet a few new friends.

TAYLOR: We could introducing them to Joshua and Kate.

GABRIELLA: Yeah. Maybe we could all play a game together. That will start a conversation.

TAYLOR: OK, but let's don't play anything too hard. I want to have fun!

PART III Achievement Test

1 | LISTENING: THE PROJECT

A. 🎧 *Amber and Tanisha are going to work together on a science project: building a bottle rocket. Listen to their conversation. Complete the conversation by writing the words that you hear. You will hear the recording two times.*

AMBER: Look at this assignment. Mr. Vargas _____ *shouldn't* _____ make us work
            0.
so hard! I don't even understand the project.

TANISHA: I don't really either. I just know that we have to build a rocket—you know, like
those things that travel into space.

AMBER: That sounds really complicated. He should at least give us more time.

_____ it in only four days?
        1.

TANISHA: Well, of course ours won't really go into space. We'll just make a really
simple version of a rocket. But I think we need to start working on it. I

_____ over tonight.
     2.

AMBER: That's a good idea. _____ Mr. Vargas now for a little
         3.
help? I think he's still in his classroom.

TANISHA: OK. Let's go.

MR. VARGAS: Yes?

AMBER: Excuse me, _____ to you for a minute?
       4.

MR. VARGAS: Sure. What's up?

AMBER: Could you please tell us more about the project? We _____
            5.
everything when you explained it in class.

MR. VARGAS: I think you should wait until tomorrow. I'll explain the project more to the whole
class then. After that, _____ complete it with no problems.
         6.

TANISHA: OK. But if we still have questions, _____ talk to you again?
          7.

MR. VARGAS: Of course. But don't worry. You can get a good grade on this project. It won't be
too hard.

B. *Reread the conversation. Find one statement of advice, one statement of ability, one request, and one suggestion. Write them in the table below. (Note: Only use words that are given in the conversation. Do not use any words that you wrote.) An example is given.*

ADVICE	ABILITY	REQUEST	SUGGESTION
0. *He should at least give us more time.* 1. _____ _____	1. _____ _____	1. _____ _____	1. _____ _____

2 | FINDING THE MATERIALS

Amber and Tanisha need to find the materials to make the rocket. Complete the conversation. Circle the correct words or phrases.

TANISHA: We would /(can)/ could start building the rocket as soon as we find some soda
      0.
bottles. Would you mind to look / looking / looks for some?
                 1.

AMBER: I just looked. I couldn't / wasn't able / shouldn't find any.
               2.

TANISHA: Let's not / Why don't / Why not we ask one of your neighbors? Someone
           3.
probably has some. Would you to go / going / go ask?
                 4.

AMBER: Sure.

AMBER: Hi, Mrs. Johnson. My friend and I are making a bottle rocket. Could we

to have / have / having a couple of empty soda bottles if you have any?
  5.

MRS. JOHNSON: Certainly. You know, you ought talk / to talk / talking to my husband
              6.
about making bottle rockets. He's really good at them. Here you go.

You 'd better / shouldn't / ought wash the bottles out before you use them.
      7.

AMBER: Great, thank you! Would / Should / Had better your husband answer a few
           8.
questions for us?

MRS. JOHNSON: How about / Why not / Let's ask him yourself? He's out in the garage.
      9.

AMBER: Thanks. I'll find him.

3 | STARTING THE BOTTLE ROCKET

Amber and Tanisha are ready to build their bottle rocket. Complete the conversations with the correct phrases. Write the letter of the best answer on each line.

AMBER: OK, we have the soda bottles. ____*a*____ (a. Can we start b. Ought we start c. Would we start)
0.
now?

TANISHA: I think so. Oh wait. How about _____ (a. to getting b. we getting c. getting) all the
1.
other materials first? I don't think we have any tape here. _____ (a. Could you find
2.
b. Could you finding c. Could you to find) some, please?

AMBER: I looked earlier, but I _____ (a. couldn't able to b. wasn't able to c. can't) find any. I'll go
3.
ask my mom.

AMBER: Mom, do we have any tape? And _____ (a. may we used b. may we use c. may use) it for
4.
our bottle rockets?

MOM: Yes, _____ (a. you will b. you can't c. you may). I think we have some in the desk
5.
drawer. _____ (a. Do you mind if b. Do you mind c. Do you minding if) I watch while you
6.
work? I'm interested in how you do this.

AMBER: Not at all. Hey, _____ (a. maybe you would help b. maybe you couldn't help c. maybe you
7.
could help) us.

MOM: Sure. I'll help if I can.

TANISHA: _____ (a. Were you able find b. Were you able to find c. Were you able to finding) some tape?
8.

AMBER: Yeah. Here it is. _____ (a. Ought we to start b. Had we better start c. Should we start) now?
9.

TANISHA: Absolutely.

4 | THE PRACTICE LAUNCH

Amber and Tanisha finished their bottle rocket. Now they're ready to launch it, or send it into the sky. Complete the conversations. Use the correct forms of **can (not), could (not), (not) be able to, may (not), will (not),** *or* **would (not).** *Some items may have more than one right answer.*

TANISHA: We should show your mom our rocket. _____ *Can* _____ you ask her to

        0.

come out?

AMBER: Sure.

MOM: Oh, wow! It looks good! _____ you _____

        1.

launch it tomorrow?

AMBER: Yeah. It's going to be awesome!

MOM: _____ you launch it tonight too so I get to see it?

       2.

AMBER: Yeah! Then you _____ see how high it goes.

       3.

MOM: OK! You _____ invite a couple friends over and show it to

       4.

them too. But you _____ invite more than a few people.

       5.

AMBER: Mom, _____ you record the launch with the video camera?

       6.

AMBER: Sorry, I _____ find it when I looked yesterday.

       7.

TANISHA: Would you try to record us with your camera phone?

AMBER: Sure I _____. Oh wait, my new phone doesn't have a video

       8.

recorder. When I had the old phone I _____ remember to use

       9.

the video feature. That's why I didn't get it on my new phone.

AMBER: May I run over to Sarah's house and borrow her video camera?

MOM: No, _____. Sorry, but it's almost supper time. Maybe after

       10.

we eat.

5 | TALKING ABOUT AMBER

Amber's parents are talking about her. Complete the conversation. Use the correct forms of the words in parentheses to give advice or make suggestions. Put the words in the correct order.

MOM: Amber has really enjoyed this project. She said she wants to build other rockets.

_____*Why don't we help*_____ her do that?
    0. (not / we / why / help)

DAD: That's a good idea. _____ her to get a rocket kit?
                1. (about / encourage / how)

MOM: OK. _____ a little research on the Internet to see which
        2. (should / do / she)

kind she wants to build next. Then _____ a kit.
                    3. (could / she / pick out / maybe)

DAD: Yeah, _____ what kind she wants to make.
        4. (ask / had / we / better)

MOM: I think _____ her pay for part of it.
            5. (should / we / make)

DAD: Yes, I agree. But _____ her find one that isn't too
                6. (help / we / ought / to)

expensive. _____ to her about it tonight.
        7. (talk / let's)

6 | EDITING: A MORNING OF ERRANDS

Amber and her dad are shopping. Read their conversation. There are fifteen mistakes in the use of modals. The first mistake is already corrected. Find and correct fourteen more. (Note: There can be more than one way to correct a mistake.)

AMBER: Hey, Dad, can I ~~to~~ show you the rocket kits that I want?

DAD: Sure. Let's to compare them.

AMBER: Well, I like both of these. Can please I get two?

DAD: Certainly. But you should remembering that you're paying for part of them.

AMBER: I know. I want them. They're really cool. Hmmm . . . I couldn't imagine how to make a rocket with these.

DAD: Why not asking someone? Excuse me, sir. Could you helps us with these rocket kits?

CLERK: Of course. Would you mind waiting for just a few minutes?

DAD: Sure. We're not in a hurry.

AMBER: We'd better to get Mom a new battery for her cell phone while we're shopping today. She can't even having it on a whole day without the battery going dead. Should we get that here?

DAD: No, we ought not. It's too expensive. Do you mind we stop by the electronics store on the way home?

AMBER: No, I don't.

DAD: They have a new battery for her phone. After we buy her that, she will can use her phone several days without charging the battery.

AMBER: Great! When had we better give it to her? How about her birthday?

DAD: Well, I think we ought give it to her right away. She needs it now.

PART IV Diagnostic Test

1 | LISTENING: OLD FRIENDS

🎧 *Listen to this conversation between Connie and Donna, who were friends in high school. Complete the conversation by writing the words that you hear. You will hear the recording two times.*

CONNIE: Donna! What a surprise to see you! I ____*haven't seen*____ you since high school!
0.

DONNA: Hi, Connie! Wow, you _____ a bit since then!
1.

CONNIE: Thanks! What are you doing in Boston? Do you live here?

DONNA: Yeah, I _____ here since I graduated. How about you?
2.

CONNIE: I _____ in Wisconsin for a few years, but I _____ here. I
3. **4.**

remember that you _____ to open your own hair salon. Did you?
5.

DONNA: Yes, I _____ in the beauty business for a while now, and I
6.

_____ my first salon a few years ago. Actually, I _____ a
7. **8.**

second one.

CONNIE: Wow! That's exciting! I _____ something else about you. Someone told
9.

me that you _____ a book. Is that right?
10.

DONNA: Yes. Actually, I _____ it. It's called *Becoming Beautiful: Beauty Tips for*
11.

Women.

CONNIE: I'd love to read it! Hey, are you busy right now?

DONNA: No. Do you want to get some coffee?

CONNIE: Sure. I _____ a chance to relax for days.
12.

DONNA: I know the perfect coffee shop.

2 | BEAUTY SALON OF BOSTON

Read this information on the Beauty Salon of Boston website. Complete the information with the correct verb forms. Write the letter of the best answer on each line.

If you want personalized service and exceptional quality, then you ___*b*___ (a. came b. 've

0.

come c. 've been coming) to the right place. Women all over Boston _____ (a. have been talking

1.

b. have talked c. talked) about Beauty Salon of Boston for the past three years. Beauty Salon of

Boston _____ (a. has been open for b. has opened for c. has been open since) 2002. Since then, we

2.

_____ (a. opened b. 've been opening c. 've opened) a second store. We _____ (a. already have

3.   **4.**

become b. 've already become c. 've become already) Boston's favorite salon, according to *The Globe's*

"Readers' Favorites." We _____ (a. 've been b. 've been being c. was) their favorite for the past

5.

two years. You _____ (a. haven't never seen b. 've ever seen c. 've never seen) a beauty salon like

6.

ours. What's the secret to our success? We _____ (a. 've provided b. provided c. 've been provided)

7.

quality service at affordable prices since the very beginning. We've also helped the community.

Last year, we _____ (a. 've donated b. donated c. 've been donated) $25,000 to local charities. And

8.

we offer discounts to students and senior citizens.

If you _____ (a. wanted b. 've ever wanted c. 've been wanted) to work in a truly first-rate

9.

salon, click here for employment opportunities. We always have entry-level openings. We

_____ (a. 've also been looking b. been looking c. been also looking) for an accountant. If you would

10.

like to apply for the position, click here.

3 | CONVERSATION OVER COFFEE

Complete the conversation between Connie and Donna. Use the present perfect form of each verb. Use contractions when possible.

CONNIE: You know, I _____'ve_____ always _____wanted_____ to live in Boston. Sometimes I can't
                                0. (want)

        believe I'm really here.

DONNA: _____ the city so far?
            1. (you / enjoy)

CONNIE: _____. It's a great place.
          2. (yes / have)

DONNA: What did you do in Carefield?

CONNIE: I was an accountant. I _____ as an accountant for seven years.
                                  3. (work)

        Among other things, I _____ the finances for a construction
                           4. (manage)

        company, and I _____ tax returns for T & S Block.
                      5. (process)

DONNA: _____ a job here yet?
         6. (you / find)

CONNIE: Well, I _____ at several places, but I haven't had any offers.
              7. (apply)

DONNA: _____ ever _____ working for someone you know?
                     8. (you / consider)

CONNIE: Well, no, I _____ about it. Why?
          9. (never / think)

DONNA: I need an accountant. If you like, I can show you the salons and tell you what I need.

CONNIE: Wow! OK.

4 | CONNIE'S BLOG

*Complete this posting on Connie's blog, or online journal, about her meeting with Donna.
Circle the correct words or phrases.*

    I (ran)/ have run into an old friend from high school, Donna Washington, yesterday.
       0.
She lived / 's lived here in Boston since she finished high school. She owned / 's owned her
     1.   **2.**
own beauty business since 2002. I 've already seen / have seen already her salons, and it
                            3.
seems like business never was / has never been better. Her previous accountant
                    4.
has recently quit / recently has quit, and she has looked / 's been looking for a new one.
     5.   **6.**
She has been calling / 's called me twice to talk about working for her. I'm not sure yet if I'll
       7.
take the job because I didn't finished / haven't finished exploring other opportunities.
             8.

5 | CONNIE'S MOVE TO BOSTON

Complete these sentences about Connie's move to Boston. Use the words in parentheses and the correct form of each verb. Use contractions when possible. Some items may have more than one right answer.

0. Connie _____'s been_____ in Boston for two weeks.
   (be)

1. She _____ in Wisconsin for four years.
   (live)

2. She _____ her other job at T & S Block.
   (recently / quit)

3. She _____ a place to live.
   (already / find)

4. She _____ a job for a few weeks.
   (look for)

5. She _____ a job yet.
   (not / accept)

6. Donna _____ her to be the new accountant for the salons.
   (ask)

7. Some of the employees of the salons _____ Connie yet.
   (not / meet)

8. Donna _____ them much about her, and they're very curious.
   (not / tell)

9. Connie _____ to interview for other jobs.
   (continue)

10. In fact, she _____ two other job offers since Donna's offer.
    (receive)

11. She _____ with Donna twice this week.
    (meet)

12. She _____ up her mind about Donna's job offer yet.
    (not / make)

6 | EDITING: CONNIE'S BLOG, PART 2

Read Connie's most recent blog posting. There are ten mistakes. The first mistake is already corrected. Find and correct nine more. (Note: There can be more than one way to correct a mistake.)

                                    decided

      Well, last month I've decided to accept Donna's offer to be the new accountant for her salons.

I've been there since three weeks now, and I've enjoy every minute of it. Donna was really nice to

work with so far. Last week I've need to catch up on some work that the old accountant didn't

do. There was a lot of work, but I already finish it all. I've never enjoyed a job as much as I'm

enjoying this one. I've already been having my hair cut, and I'm met a lot of the people who

work in the salons. They're all very nice. I've had recently a couple of the girls over for dinner.

Donna and her husband have already came over twice. I've been hoping to have a large dinner

party for everyone sometime soon.

Unit 16 Achievement Test

1 | LISTENING: COMPUTER TALK

🎧 *Listen to this conversation between classmates Tricia and Scott. Complete the conversation by writing the words that you hear. You will hear the recording two times.*

TRICIA: I heard that you ____'ve designed____ some websites.
0.

SCOTT: Yes, I _____ a few for friends, but nothing professionally.
1.

I _____ five or six websites _____ I started studying
2.   3.

computer science. I'm interested in becoming a website designer.

TRICIA: Oh, really? How long _____ computer science?
4.

SCOTT: _____ two years.
5.

TRICIA: Do you know Gerald West?

SCOTT: The guy who used to go to school here? He graduated, right?

TRICIA: Yeah, with a degree in Web design. He _____ hundreds of websites
6.

for businesses. That's all he's done _____ he graduated. I think
7.

he _____ a lot of money. You ought to e-mail him and talk to him
8.

about his experiences.

SCOTT: That's a good idea.

Name _____   **Date** _____

*Scott and Chris are discussing what they've done since high school. Complete the conversation. Use **since** or **for**.*

SCOTT: Chris? How are you!

CHRIS: Oh, hi, Scott! I'm fine. I haven't seen you ____*for*____ a long time. It's good to see you!
  0.

SCOTT: It's good to see you, too! Do you work here?

CHRIS: Yeah! I've worked at the post office _____ we graduated. What about you? Where
  1.

have you been _____ the last few years?
  2.

SCOTT: I'm still in school. I've actually changed my major twice _____ I started. I've been
  3.

studying computer science _____ the past two years. Hey, have you seen any of our
  4.

other friends _____ you moved away from Sun Valley?
  5.

CHRIS: Well, I didn't go home much _____ the first couple of years, but _____ my
  6.   **7.**

brother started playing high school sports a couple years ago, I've gone home more

frequently.

SCOTT: How are the high school teams doing?

CHRIS: Well, the football team hasn't won the championship _____ we played!
  8.

SCOTT: We sure were good! You know, I don't think I've played football _____ then. Hey,
  9.

we should get together sometime, Chris.

CHRIS: Sounds good! Here's my number.

SCOTT: Great. I'll give you a call.

3 | QUESTIONS FOR A PRO

*Complete the conversation between Scott and Gerald about being a Web designer. Use the present perfect form of each verb and **since** or **for**.*

SCOTT: ___Have you worked___ as a website designer for a long time?
0. (work)

GERALD: Yes, I _____ it _____ several years.
1. (do)   2.

SCOTT: How many websites have you created?

GERALD: Oh, I _____ about 300 websites _____ I started.
3. (create)   4.

SCOTT: _____ any awards?
5. (receive)

GERALD: Yes. Actually, I _____ three major awards _____ 2003,
6. (win)   7.

when I started my own business.

SCOTT: _____ a lot of money _____ that time?
8. (earn)   9.

GERALD: At first I didn't earn much, but I _____ a lot of money in recent years.
10. (make)

4 | EDITING: SCOTT'S WEBSITE

Read Scott's website. There are four mistakes in the use of the present perfect. The first mistake is already corrected. Find and correct three more.

                                                        I've
About me: I'm Scott Johnson, and I̶ been a web designer and a computer science major since

two years. For I started studying computer science, I've help some friends build their websites.

I'd be happy to help you with your Web design needs. Contact me at sjohnson@uua.edu.

PART IV

Unit 17 Achievement Test

30 Items
Score: _____

---

1 | LISTENING: HARD TO PLEASE

🎧 *Listen to this conversation between Lori and her friend David, who is sick. Complete the conversation by writing the words that you hear. You will hear the recording two times.*

LORI: Would you like a glass of orange juice?

DAVID: Thanks, but I ___*'ve already had*___ three glasses.
                                                    0.

LORI: Have you looked at today's paper _____? I bought you a copy.
                                                                            1.

DAVID: Oh, thanks, but I _____ two papers and three magazines this morning
                                      2.

   already.

LORI: OK. _____ the movie *Playing by Ear* yet? I hear it's available on DVD now.
                3.

DAVID: Yep, I've _____ seen it.
                            4.

LORI: Is there anything you _____ yet?
                                           5.

DAVID: Well, I _____ a nap yet, but I think I'm ready for one.
                      6.

LORI: OK. I'll leave you alone then. Have a good nap.

---

2 | WHAT HAS DAVID DONE?

Complete these sentences. Use the present perfect forms of the verbs in parentheses with
already *and* **yet** *to write affirmative and negative statements.*

(get)

0. AFFIRMATIVE: David _____*has already gotten*_____ a lot of rest.

0. NEGATIVE: But he _____*hasn't gotten*_____ well _____*yet*_____.

(drink)

1. AFFIRMATIVE: He _____ a lot of orange juice.

2. NEGATIVE: But he _____ much water _____.

(read)

3. AFFIRMATIVE: He _____ today's papers.

4. NEGATIVE: But he _____ any books _____.

(eat)

5. AFFIRMATIVE: David _____ lunch.

6. NEGATIVE: But he _____ dinner _____ .

(take)

7. AFFIRMATIVE: He _____ his medicine.

8. NEGATIVE: But he _____ a nap _____ .

3 | BACK IN THE OFFICE

*Read this conversation between David and his assistant at work. Complete the
conversation with the correct phrases. Write the letter of the best answer on each line.*

JACK: Oh, hi, David! Welcome back. How are you feeling?

DAVID: I'm feeling much better, thanks. In fact, ___*b*___ (a. I already have exercised b. I've already
    0.
exercised c. Have I already exercised) this morning. How's it going at the office?

JACK: Pretty good. _____ (a. Have you receive my e-mail already b. Have you received my e-mail yet
    1.
c. Have yet you received my e-mail)?

DAVID: No, I haven't.

JACK: Well, _____ (a. I've already finished b. already I've already finished c. I have finished yet) most of
    2.
the work you left for me.

DAVID: That's great. Have the Porter contracts _____ (a. arrive already b. arrive yet c. arrived yet)?
    3.

JACK: Five of them have come in, but the others _____ (a. no have gotten here yet b. haven't
    4.
gotten here yet c. haven't got here yet).

DAVID: I wonder where the rest of them are. I assume you _____ (a. have called already b. have
    5.
yet called c. have already called) Mary Porter.

JACK: Yes. She said she _____ (a. hasn't mailed the rest yet b. no has mailed the rest yet c. hasn't
    6.
mailed the rest already), but she said she would send them this afternoon. Oh, and she

_____ (a. has decided already b. already has decided c. has already decided) to do all her future
    7.
business with you.

DAVID: That's great news! What about my plane reservations to Chicago?

JACK: _____ (a. I've made already b. I've already made c. I did already make) them. Oh, _____
        8.   9.

(a. has anyone told b. have anyone told c. anyone has told) you about Mr. Sutton's party yet?

DAVID: Yes, _____ (a. I've already written b. already I've written c. I had written already) it on my
        10.

calendar. I'll be there. And listen—you're doing a great job. Thanks.

---

4 | EDITING: NURSE'S NOTES

*David is at the doctor's office. Read the nurse's notes for the doctor. There are seven mistakes in the use of the present perfect, **already**, and **yet**. The first mistake is already corrected. Find and correct six more.*

David's already ~~be~~ *been* here twice this winter with cold symptoms. He's had his present cold for

four days yet, and he's now starting to feel somewhat better. He's received already his flu shot,

and he has already have a complete physical. David usually gets allergies in the spring, and he

have already bought his allergy medication, but he hasn't start to use it yet. He went to his

allergist for more testing, but the results haven't come back already.

Unit 18 Achievement Test

1 | LISTENING: MOTHER'S DAY

A. 🎧 *Listen to this conversation between two friends, Liz and Beth. Complete the conversation by writing the words that you hear. You will hear the recording two times.*

LIZ: Are you looking forward to Mother's Day?

BETH: Oh, sure. I _____*'ve always enjoyed*_____ Mother's Day. My children have done some
                                                  0.

wonderful things for me over the years to celebrate.

LIZ: Oh, really? Like what?

BETH: They _____ me lovely notes. They've taken me out
                              1.

to dinner _____. And they've sent me flowers
                    2.

_____.
        3.

LIZ: That's nice. Have they _____ Mother's Day?
                                        4.

BETH: No, never. I'm a lucky woman!

B. *Liz and Beth are still talking. Read the rest of their conversation. Complete the conversation with the correct phrases. Write the letter of the best answer on each line.*

BETH: And I don't just get things from my children on Mother's Day. My husband ___*a*___
                                                                                  0.

(**a.** has always given **b.** has given always **c.** has always give) me wonderful presents, too.

LIZ: Oh, yeah? What _____ (**a.** have he done **b.** has he done **c.** has he do) for you in past years?
                        1.

BETH: Well, _____ (**a.** he's given always **b.** he gave always **c.** he's always given) me the "day off."
            2.

He's sent me to the spa for the day _____ (**a.** always **b.** often **c.** several times). _____
                                              3.   **4.**

(**a.** He's often taken **b.** He's taken often **c.** He takes often) days off from work and spent them with

me. He _____ (**a.** 's ever missed **b.** 's never missed **c.** 's missed never) a Mother's Day!
        5.

LIZ: How wonderful!

PART IV

2 | MOTHER'S DAY PLANS

Howard and Leanne are Beth's children. They're making plans for Mother's Day. They want to do something different for their mother this year, so they're trying to remember what they did in past years. Complete their questions and answers. Use the present perfect and the words in parentheses.

(we / have)

0. _____*Have we ever had*_____ a picnic in the park?

0. No, _____*we've never had*_____ a picnic in the park.

(we / make / her)

1. _____ breakfast in bed?

2. No, _____ breakfast in bed.

(we / buy / her)

3. _____ tickets for a show?

4. No, _____ tickets for a show.

(we / forget)

5. _____ about Mother's Day?

6. No, _____ about Mother's Day.

(Mom / complain)

7. _____ about her present?

8. No, _____ about her present.

3 | CLEANING HOUSE

Howard and Leanne have decided to clean the house for their mom. Complete the
sentences. Use the present perfect and the words in parentheses.

0. They _____'ve organized_____ the cupboards.
   (organize)

0. Leanne ____has just finished washing the dishes____.
   (just / finish washing the dishes)

1. Howard _____ the carpet.
   (vacuum)

2. Leanne _____ the windows.
   (wash)

3. Leanne _____ the furniture.
   (dust)

4. Howard _____ the floor twice.
   (sweep)

5. They _____ the beds.
   (make)

6. Leanne _____ up the bookshelves.
   (straighten)

7. Leanne _____ flowers in the garden.
   (plant)

8. Howard _____ the lawn.
   (mow)

9. They _____.
   (just / water the plants)

10. Howard _____ the refrigerator.
    (clean)

4 | EDITING: THE CLEAN HOUSE

Beth is writing in her journal on Mother's Day. There are four mistakes in the use of the
present perfect and adverbs. The first mistake is already corrected. Find and correct
three more.

      had

I've ~~have~~ a nice Mother's Day. Howard and Leanne are such sweethearts. The house have

been a mess because I've been lately so busy. I haven't had time to clean when I get home from

work. I just eat and go to bed. But they've just clean everything! It's like I'm in a new house!

What a great Mother's Day gift.

Unit 19 Achievement Test

---

1 | LISTENING: BARRY'S COOKIES

🎧 *Listen to this television commercial for Barry's Cookies. Complete the commercial by writing the words that you hear. You will hear the recording two times.*

ACTRESS: _____*Have you tried*_____ the new variety of Barry's Cookies?
　　　　　　　　　　0.

ACTOR: No, I haven't! I _____ a box earlier today, but I
　　　　　　　　　　　　　　　1.

　　　　　_____ any yet. Are they good?
　　　　　　　　2.

ACTRESS: Oooo, are you kidding? They're delicious! I _____ a whole
　　　　　　　　　　　　　　　　　　　　　　　　　　　3.

　　　　　box yesterday! As for today, _____ five already . . . and
　　　　　　　　　　　　　　　　　　　　4.

　　　　　I'm going to have more after dinner!

ACTOR: Hmmm, sounds dangerous.

ACTRESS: Not at all! This new variety is low fat.

ACTOR: Low fat? And they taste good?

ACTRESS: Yes! Barry _____ it again! He always makes great-tasting
　　　　　　　　　　　　5.

　　　　　cookies.

ACTOR: Well, maybe I'll try one right now . . . Hey, what _____ to
　　　　　　　　　　　　　　　　　　　　　　　　　　　　　6.

　　　　　my box of cookies? It _____!
　　　　　　　　　　　　　　7.

ACTRESS: Oh . . . you left your cookies here? Er . . . I _____ they
　　　　　　　　　　　　　　　　　　　　　　　　　　8.

　　　　　were my cookies . . .

ANNOUNCER: Barry's Cookies: They're America's favorite!

Name _____ Date _____

Complete this transcript of a guided tour at Barry's Cookies factory. Circle the correct words or phrases.

Welcome to Barry's Cookies factory! Let me tell you a little about the company. There was a

young man named Barry Owen who has decided / (decided) to open his own cookie company. He

                                          0.

has worked / worked in a bakery for 10 years. He has saved / saved his money, and in 1979 he
     1.   **2.**

has started / started his own bakery. Since then, Barry's Cookies has grown / grew tremendously.
     3.   **4.**

Last year, the company has made / made $94 million. We 've improved / improved our
                    5.   **6.**

production capacity greatly over the years we've been in business—and we continue to do so. So

far this month we 've produced / produced 200,000 boxes of cookies!
                    7.

    Barry has worked / worked hard to create exciting new flavors, and he
                  8.

has developed / developed more than 20 cookie recipes. And even though it's only June,
          9.

this has been / was another thrilling year, as Barry introduced a brand new flavor of cookie.
          10.

Barry's Cookies are America's favorite cookies.

PART IV

3 | CHANGES

Use the words below to write sentences about how Barry's life has changed since the 1970s.

In the 1970s	Since then
0. live / in London	0. move / to Chicago
1. be / skinny	2. gain / weight
3. be / unsuccessful in school	4. become / a successful businessman
5. work / as a bakery assistant	6. learn / how to manage a company
7. be / single	8. get / married

0. *In the 1970s Barry lived in London.* _____

0. *Since then, he has moved to Chicago.* _____

1. _____

2. _____

3. _____

4. _____

5. _____

6. _____

7. _____

8. _____

4 | EDITING: BARRY'S COOKIES IN THE NEWS

Read this paragraph from an Internet article about Barry's Cookies. There are five mistakes in the use of the present perfect and simple past. The first mistake is already corrected. Find and correct four more.

                                              has become

Over the past 10 years, Barry's Cookies ~~became~~ the leading cookie company in the United States. The value of the company climbed steadily since it first opened in 1979. The company has opened markets in 12 foreign countries—last year, it has opened its first store in Mexico. Since the mid-1990s, the company sold billions of dollars' worth of cookies.

    What does Barry say about his success? "I have always wanted to make people happy. I guess I've done that. And I'm glad that people started to think of Barry's as America's favorite cookie."

Unit 20 Achievement Test

1 | LISTENING: WORLD MUSICIAN

A. 🎧 *Listen to this radio program. Complete the program by writing the words that you hear. You will hear the recording two times.*

Daniel Meyers _____*has released*_____ his twentieth album. That's right, his twentieth.
                            0.

Meyers has been one of Britain's most productive musicians for quite some time. He's been

writing music for 20 years, which means that he _____ out an average
                                                              1.

of an album per year. But more amazing than the quantity of his work is the quality. Many critics

say that every one of his albums _____ worth buying. He's studied the
                                              2.

masters of classical, blues, rock, jazz, pop, and world music, and he's picked up new musical

skills with every album. He's even _____ in different musical hotspots
                                              3.

around the world to find inspiration for each new album. This past year, he's been living on

Corfu, a Greek island in the Mediterranean Sea, where he _____ and
                                                                      4.

recording with local musicians. You can hear some of Meyers's latest music on our website at

worldradionews.net. This is Hannah Phillips, World Radio News, Washington.

B. *Reread the review. Find two verbs in the present perfect progressive and two verbs in the present perfect. Write them in the table below. (Note: Only use words that are given in the program. Do not use any words that you wrote.) An example is given.*

PRESENT PERFECT PROGRESSIVE	PRESENT PERFECT
1. _____	0. _*has been*_____
2. _____	1. _____
	2. _____

2 | DANIEL MEYERS'S WEBSITE

Complete this message that musician Daniel Meyers put on his website. Circle the correct words or phrases.

I've (released) / been releasing my newest album, which I've just finished / been finishing
     0.   **1.**

recording in Greece. On that album, I've used / been using the *zummarah,* which is a
                                        2.

woodwind instrument found in Egypt, and a Grecian *tsabouna* in many of the songs. I've

toured / been touring the United States for the past few months, and I'm loving every minute of
     3.

it. I'm working with a great group of musicians. Most of them have made / been making music
                                                                        4.

all their lives. I'm grateful to have the opportunity to work with them. The tour is a lot of fun.

We've had / been having a great time because we're really enjoying playing together. I've
              5.

planned / been planning my next album, too. It's not finished yet, but I have some great ideas.
              6.

Check back in a few weeks for more news.

3 | INTERVIEW WITH DANIEL MEYERS

Hannah Phillips is interviewing Daniel Meyers about his music career. Complete Phillips's questions and Meyers's answers. Use the present perfect or the present perfect progressive and the words below.

0. PHILLIPS: How many / albums / release?

    How many albums have you released? _____

  MEYERS: Twenty

    I've released twenty albums. _____

1. PHILLIPS: How long / you / make / music?

    _____

  MEYERS: Twenty years

    _____

2. PHILLIPS: How many / awards / receive / over the past year?

    _____

  MEYERS: Three

    _____

3. PHILLIPS: Where / tour / this month?

   _____

   MEYERS: Australia

   _____

4. PHILLIPS: How many times / tour / Asia?

   _____

   MEYERS: Six times

   _____

5. PHILLIPS: What / be / your inspiration for your recent album?

   _____

   MEYERS: My daughter

   _____

6. PHILLIPS: your daughter / listen / to the album a lot these days?

   _____

   MEYERS: Yes. She / listen / to it a lot.

   _____

4 | EDITING: WEB REVIEW

Read this review from the Internet about Meyers's new CD. There are five mistakes in the use of the present perfect and present perfect progressive. The first mistake is already corrected. Find and correct four more.

    I've been ~~listen~~ *listening* to Meyers's new CD, *The Cradle of Sound,* for the past week, and I has been struggling to find the words to describe this album. He's changed his sound many times, and in this album his sound changes with every song. Some songs are danceable and some are like lullabies, yet Meyers has been being able to create an album in which all the songs work together. In my opinion, Meyers has been creating another masterpiece in music. Dan Meyers, you've been doing great work on all of your previous albums. You have now given us pure genius.

    My rating: ★★★★★

PART IV Achievement Test

1 | LISTENING: OLD FRIENDS

🎧 *Listen to this conversation between Carlos and Doug, who were friends in high school. Complete the conversation by writing the words that you hear. You will hear the recording two times.*

CARLOS: Hey, Doug! How are you doing? I _____*haven't*_____ seen you since we

0.

played football together in high school!

DOUG: I know! It _____ a long time.

1.

CARLOS: So _____ to Los Angeles, or are you just visiting?

2.

DOUG: I've been living here _____ we graduated. What about you?

3.

CARLOS: I _____ here. So, what did you end up studying at school?

4.

DOUG: I _____ criminology, and then I _____

5.   6.

my master's degree in criminal justice.

CARLOS: Cool! If I remember correctly, you always wanted to become a detective. Did you?

DOUG: Well, I _____ a private investigator firm a few years

7.

ago, and my plan was to open up about a dozen offices around the state.

I _____ ten of them—they're in all the major cities and towns.

8.

CARLOS: Wow! I bet you _____ really hard all these years.

9.

DOUG: Yes, I have. On top of everything else, I _____ a course on

10.

professional investigation techniques.

CARLOS: I'd like to hear more about that. _____ dinner yet?

11.

DOUG: No, I haven't even _____ lunch—I'm pretty hungry.

12.

CARLOS: Why don't we get something to eat now?

DOUG: All right, let's go!

2 | CALIFORNIA PRIVATE INVESTIGATIONS

Read this information from the California Private Investigations website. Complete the information with the correct words or phrases. Write the letter of the best answer on each line.

Californians _____*a*_____ (a. have been trusting b. have trusting c. trusted) California Private
                    0.

Investigations (CPI) for years. No other private investigator firm _____ (a. has ever not been
                                                                          1.

b. has ever been c. has been ever) able to offer all that we can offer you. If you're looking for

professional service and affordable prices, you _____ (a. 've found b. 've been finding c. been found)
                                                2.

the right place. CPI _____ (a. has been in business for b. has been being in business since c. has been in
                     3.

business since) 2001. Since then, _____ (a. we've helped b. we helped c. we've help) hundreds of
                                  4.

clients. _____ (a. We've earned b. We earned c. We've earn) California's "best business award" twice.
         5.

Why are we different? _____ (a. We've proved b. We proven c. We've proven) ourselves to be
                      6.

the best at what we do for the past four years. We answer questions that other private and

government organizations _____ (a. haven't been always b. haven't always been c. have always not been)
                         7.

able to answer. Try us yourself and find out why CPI _____ (a. has become b. has been becoming
                                                     8.

c. became) California's most trusted private investigator firm.

If _____ (a. you been trying b. you tried c. you've been trying) to find someone, click here to
   9.

learn about our "People Find" service.

CPI is opening new offices near you. If _____ (a. you been considering b. you considered
                                        10.

c. you've been considering) a move to an exciting new career, click here to find out more about our

job openings.

PART IV

3 | AT DINNER

Complete the conversation between Doug and Carlos. Use the present perfect form of each verb.

DOUG: So, why did you move to Los Angeles?

CARLOS: Well, I _____'ve_____ always _____wanted_____ to live in L.A. because I have
                                                                    0. (want)

a lot of family here.

DOUG: Oh, so you _____ to L.A. before.
                                    1. (be)

CARLOS: Yeah, I _____ here many times to visit family.
                              2. (come)

DOUG: What do you do?

CARLOS: I'm an investigative reporter.

DOUG: Oh, really? Where _____ you _____?
                                                                    3. (work)

CARLOS: Well, several places. I _____ for a magazine, and I _____
                                                4. (write)   **5. (report)**

for various newspapers.

DOUG: _____ you _____ a job here yet?
                                                    6. (find)

CARLOS: Well, I _____ to a couple of newspapers since I arrived, but
                              7. (apply)

I _____ working anywhere yet.
          8. (not / start)

DOUG: You said you did investigative reporting. Have you ever thought about working as a

private investigator?

CARLOS: Yes, I _____. It sounds like interesting work.
                          9. (have)

DOUG: Well, we have more work than we can handle in our main office right here in L.A., and

I'm looking for some help. Are you interested?

CARLOS: Maybe. Tell me more about it.

4 | CARLOS'S E-MAIL

Complete this e-mail Carlos wrote to his brother about meeting Doug. Circle the correct words or phrases.

Hey Travis,

I (ran)/ have run into Doug Wells a few weeks ago. Do you remember him? The last time I
   0.

saw / have seen him was in high school. He 's been being / 's been here in L.A. ever since then
  1.   **2.**

and has opened his own private investigator firm. I 've already seen / have seen already the main
                                               3.

office. It sounds like business was / has been really good recently, but he had / 's had too much
                           4.   **5.**

work, and he 's looked / 's been looking for some help. He offered me a job last week. Since then
              6.

he has been calling / 's called me twice to try and convince me to take the job, but I haven't
            7.

decided yet / already. I'll let you know when I decide.
      8.

Talk to you later,

Carlos

5 | CARLOS'S MOVE TO LOS ANGELES

Complete these sentences about Carlos's move to Los Angeles. Use the words in parentheses and the correct form of each verb. Use contractions when possible. Some items may have more than one right answer. The first answer is already given.

0. Carlos _____*has been*_____ in L.A. for two weeks.
              (be)

1. Before that, he _____ in Seattle for three years.
                        (live)

2. He _____ a job as an investigative reporter.
          (just / quit)

3. He _____ into his new apartment.
       (already / move)

4. He _____ to find a job.
            (try)

5. He _____ a job interview for nine days.
       (not / have)

6. No one _____ to offer him work.
           (call)

7. Doug _____ him to join his private investigator firm.
       (invite)

8. Carlos _____ Doug that he'll think about the offer.
       (tell)

9. He _____ one of Doug's offices yesterday.
   (visit)

10. He _____ Doug and his team members work together a few times.
    (watch)

11. He _____ Doug give evidence in court once.
    (observe)

12. He _____ any investigative work yet, but he thinks it would be fun.
    (not / do)

---

6 | EDITING: ANOTHER E-MAIL

Read Carlos's most recent e-mail to Travis. There are ten mistakes. The first mistake is already corrected. Find and correct nine more.

Hey, Travis,

                  decided

Last month I've decided to accept Doug's job offer. I've been there since two weeks, and I've

yet learned a lot. Doug was really good to work with so far. I've need to learn a lot of things, but

I've maked progress. I've started to really like the work, and Doug already has put me in charge

of a small case. I'm met some interesting people. I've have some of them over for dinner. One guy

has came over a couple of times, and he's told me lots of useful things. I haven't gotten a big case

yet, but I think I will soon.

See you later,

Carlos

PART V Diagnostic Test

---

1 | LISTENING: SPORTS HISTORY

🎧 *Listen to this conversation between two students. Complete the conversation by writing the words that you hear. You will hear the recording two times.*

PAUL: Hey, have you decided what to write about for your history report?

MARA: No, I don't have ___*any*___ ideas, but I haven't given it _____ thought. Have you?
                      0.   **1.**

PAUL: Yeah, I think I'm going to write about the history of baseball and the World Series.

MARA: Will you be able to find _____ information?
                               2.

PAUL: Yeah, I don't think that will be a problem. I have _____ sports magazines, and I'm
                                           3.

     sure there's _____ stuff on the Internet, so I think I'll be able to find _____
                       4.   **5.**

     material. If you have a hard time thinking of a topic, I can give you _____ help.
                                                          6.

MARA: Well, if you have _____ extra ideas, I would be happy to hear them!
                         7.

---

2 | BASEBALL: REPORT ON THE WORLD SERIES

Read the beginning of Paul's report about the World Series. Complete the report with the correct words or phrases. Write the letter of the best answer on each line.

Every year in the United States, many Americans give ___*a*___ (a. a lot of attention b. a lot of
                                                      0.

attentions c. many attention d. many attentions) to the World Series. _____ (a. Many peoples b. Many
                                                                1.

people c. Much people d. A lot of peoples) consider baseball to be the nation's pastime, and the most

exciting part of baseball season is the final series of games for the championship. In fact,

_____ (a. some baseball fan b. several baseball fan c. some baseball fans d. any baseball fan) may think
     2.

of the World Series as the best part of the year.

     Since the World Series only involves teams from the United States and one team from Canada,

a lot of people wonder why _____ (a. a few winners b. the winners c. several winners d. winners) are
                                        3.

called "World Champions." In 1884, _____ (a. a little b. a few c. little d. few) newspaper reporters
                                       4.

wrote that the winning team members were "World Champions," and the name stuck.

There are two sets of teams in professional baseball in the United States, the American

League and the National League. The World Series is _____ (a. series b. some series c. many series
                                                          5.

d. a series) of seven games between the best team in the American League and the best team in the

National League. The team that wins four games wins the championship.

A few teams have won _____ (a. some time b. a great deal of time c. several times d. much time)
                       6.

at the World Series championships. The New York Yankees have won 26 times, and the

Cardinals and the Athletics have each won nine times. Eight teams haven't won _____
                                                                               7.

(a. much b. some c. a few d. any) World Series championships.

---

3 | SOCCER: THE FIFA WORLD CUP

Complete this information about the FIFA World Cup. Circle the correct words or phrases.
(Note: Ø means that you don't need a word.)

The Fédération Internationale de Football Association (FIFA) World Cup soccer event is

a /(the)/ Ø most popular international sporting event ever. A lot / A great deal / Many of people
   0.   1.

around the globe enjoy watching it, either in person or on television.

French football administrators first had the idea for the World Cup in the early part of the

20th century. They wanted to bring several / a little of / enough national championship soccer
                                          2.

teams together to compete for a world championship. The first competition was in Uruguay in

1930, followed by competitions in 1934 and 1938. (The championship games of the World Cup

occur every four years.) But then there were any / a few / a little years when there weren't
                                                      3.

any / some / the World Cup games because of World War II. The competition began again in
4.

1950. Since then, the games have taken place in many / much / a lot countries from Europe to
                                                     5.

the Americas to Asia. Several / Little / The enough teams have participated in the tournaments
                                              6.

since the first one in 1930.

In all these tournaments, there have only been seven different champions. However,

a few / much / any times there have been Ø / the / enough defeats that were surprising to
        7.   8.

many / much / a great deal of viewers, such as Cameroon's first-round defeat of the Argentinean
        9.

champions during the first game of the / a / Ø 1990 World Cup series.
                                          10.

Name _____   Date _____

---

4 | TENNIS: THE FRENCH OPEN

Complete this information about the French Open. Circle the correct words. (Note: Ø means that you don't need a word.)

The French Open, which is held in Paris every summer, is (the)/ a / Ø best international clay
           0.

court tennis competition. Men's singles at the French Open started in the / a / Ø Paris in 1891,
                                      1.

and women's singles began in 1897.

At first, only French citizens and residents could play in the competition. In 1925, the / a / Ø
                                                            2.

French Tennis Federation opened it to the / a / Ø foreign players. The / An / Ø event was played
                               3.   **4.**

at two different tennis clubs until 1928, when construction of the / a / Ø current stadium,
                                              5.

Roland-Garros, was complete.

The name of the stadium comes from the / a / Ø French hero of World War II. Before the
                                 6.

war, Roland-Garros was the / an / Ø aviation pioneer who, on September 23, 1913, was the
                            7.

first man to fly the / a / Ø plane over the / a / Ø Mediterranean Sea. He was also the / a / Ø
               8.   **9.**   **10.**

tennis player.

Although there were no competitions at Roland-Garros from 1940 to 1945 because of World

War II, the matches began again after the / a / Ø war ended. Since that time, the / a / Ø amazing
                                     11.   **12.**

players like Bjorn Borg, Mats Wilander, Chris Evert, and Martina Navratilova have competed in

the tournament. The / A / Ø level of competition is so high at the French Open that there have
                    13.

been only five French winners from the / a / Ø late 1940s until today.
                                        14.

---

5 | TENNIS: WIMBLEDON

*Complete this information about Wimbledon. Use **a, an,** or **the.** Use **Ø** if you don't need an article.*

Wimbledon, which is held in ____*a*____ a neighborhood of London, England, is probably
                                       0.

_____ most highly regarded international tennis competition. Today it is _____ only
  1.   **2.**

major tennis championship that is still played on grass courts. Twenty-two men played in

_____ first competition at _____ tennis club in 1877. Women first competed in 1884,
  3.   **4.**

and only 13 participated. Nowadays hundreds of men and women compete each year.

When _____ air travel started to become more common, more players came to
                5.

Wimbledon from all over _____ world. Since _____ event became international in 1900,
                                    6.   7.

only a few British players have won. _____ last British player to win at Wimbledon was
                                              8.

_____ woman named Virginia Wade. She won in 1977.
    9.

Wimbledon was _____ amateur event until 1968. Since then, the competition has been
                          10.

open to both _____ amateurs and professionals. Some of _____ more recent famous
                    11.   12.

players who have won Wimbledon include John McEnroe, Jimmy Connors, and Bjorn Borg,

_____ outstanding player who won Wimbledon five times in a row.
    13.

Wimbledon tournaments generally last for _____ period of two weeks. There are
                                                  14.

separate tournaments for men's singles, women's singles, men's doubles, women's doubles, and

mixed (men and women) doubles. (In a singles match, two players compete against each other. In

a doubles match, two teams of two players each compete.)

A few hundred people watched the first Wimbledon match in 1877, but now about half a

million people attend each year!

Even more action will be coming to Wimbledon. The tennis events of _____ 2012
                                                                          15.

London Summer Olympic Games will take place at the courts there.

---

6 | EDITING: DIARY

*Read Paul's diary entry about his presentation on the World Series. There are eight mistakes
in the use of quantifiers and articles. The first mistake is already corrected. Find and correct
seven more. (Note: There can be more than one way to correct a mistake.)*

October 12

                                          the
Today I gave my presentation about ~~a~~ history of the World Series. I didn't have some problems

giving my speech, and I wasn't nervous at all. My teacher is the baseball fan, and she said she

enjoyed it. She and my classmates asked a lot of question, and I was able to answer several of

them. Scott, another student who also loves the baseball, has amazing memory, and he was able

to answer many of questions I didn't know the answers to. It was actually the very enjoyable class!

Unit 21 Achievement Test

---

1 | LISTENING: 2004 NOBEL PEACE PRIZE WINNER

A. 🎧 *Listen to this conversation about Wangari Maathai, the 2004 Nobel Peace Prize winner. Complete the conversation by writing the words that you hear. You will hear the recording two times.*

CHRIS: Did you watch the TV _____*show*_____ about Wangari Maathai last night?
0.

NOEL: No. Who's that?

CHRIS: She was _____ of the 2004 Nobel Peace Prize. She's from Kenya.
1.

NOEL: Really? What did she do?

CHRIS: She started an environmental _____ there in 1976. She organized women
2.

to plant trees. Since then, thousands of women have planted more than 30 million trees

in Kenya.

NOEL: That's impressive!

CHRIS: Yeah, and she's been very active in politics too. She has been in prison for fighting against

cutting down trees and for demanding an end to corruption. She helped get rid of the

Kenyan dictator, Daniel Moi, and she helped bring peace to _____.
3.

NOEL: Wow, she did all that? It sounds like she really had a lot of _____!
4.

CHRIS: Yeah, I was impressed. And she's also really respected for her intelligence. In fact, she was

the first woman from the region to get a Ph.D.

NOEL: So what's she doing now?

CHRIS: A lot! She's _____ of the Kenyan parliament, and she's the Assistant
5.

Minister in the Ministry of Environment, Natural Resources, and Wildlife. In 2005, she

also became the first president of the African Union's Economic, Social, and Cultural

Council. So she's still doing a lot of work for the environment and for democracy.

NOEL: Too bad I missed _____. She sounds amazing.
6.

B. *Reread the conversation. Write each noun from the box below in the correct category according to its use in the conversation. An example is given.*

| democracy | environment | Kenya | peace | ~~Wangari Maathai~~ |
| dictator | intelligence | Nobel Peace Prize | region | woman |

PROPER NOUNS	NON-COUNT NOUNS	COUNT NOUNS
0. _Wangari Maathi_	1. _____	1. _____
1. _____	2. _____	2. _____
2. _____	3. _____	3. _____
	4. _____	

---

2 | ALFRED B. NOBEL

Read this information about Alfred B. Nobel and the Nobel Prizes. Complete the information with the correct words or phrases. Write the letter of the best answer on each line.

Alfred B. Nobel (1833–1896) was a Swedish chemist and engineer. He invented ___*a*___
0.
(a. many b. much c. plenty of d. a great deal of) things, including dynamite. Nobel knew that this

invention was very powerful, and he wanted _____ **(a. country b. a Country c. countries**
1.
d. the Country) to use this power to create peace. But instead, people used his invention to develop

weapons. He didn't want future generations to remember him for causing people harm. So

when he died, he left _____ **(a. many b. a lot of c. a few d. a great of)** money and instructions to
2.
establish prizes to recognize people who help _____ **(a. the man b. human c. mankind d. peoples)**.
3.

The first Nobel Prizes were given on the fifth anniversary of Alfred Nobel's death in 1901.

Each year _____ **(a. little b. a little c. few d. a few)** people who have benefited humanity win the
4.
prizes. There are prizes in six categories: peace, literature, physics, chemistry, medicine, and

economic science. There isn't _____ **(a. any b. no c. some d. many)** consideration of nationality in
5.
choosing the winners. Nobel Prize winners have helped humanity in _____ **(a. a great deal of**
6.
b. many c. a little d. much) different ways through their work, art, and inventions.

Nobel was interested in _____ (a. any b. a little c. much d. a lot of) things, not just science. He
_{7.}

loved literature and poetry, and he even wrote _____ (a. several b. enough c. few d. a great deal of)
_{8.}

poems and stories. When he died, he owned _____ (a. several b. a lot of c. a few d. a great deal of)
_{9.}

books—more than 1,500! However, most people still know Alfred B. Nobel for his _____
_{10.}

(a. creation b. creations c. Creation d. Creations) of the Nobel Prizes.

---

3 | EDITING: THE NOBEL MUSEUM

*Read this diary entry about a visit to the Nobel Museum. There are six mistakes in the use of
nouns and quantifiers. The first mistake is already corrected. Find and correct five more.
(Note: There can be more than one way to correct a mistake.)*

May 31

What a great trip! Today I arrived in Stockholm, Sweden, and so far I haven't had any
trouble
~~troubles~~.

I just got back from the nobel Museum. They have a new exhibition about Albert Einstein.

The exhibition focuses on his younger years, from 1905–1925. I didn't know many history about

Einstein, and I found the museum quite interesting. I spent a lot of times there learning about this

part of Einstein's life. He did a great many of work in his 20s and 30s, and he received the Nobel

Prize in physics when he was 42 years old.

I bought a few postcard at the museum, and I got a book about Albert Einstein too. Now

that I've been to the museum, I'm really interested to learn even more about him.

PART V

Unit 22 Achievement Test

| 1 | LISTENING: DINNER PLANS |

A. 🎧 *Ashley and Shari are talking about their dinner plans. Listen to their conversation. Complete the conversation by writing the words that you hear. You will hear the recording two times.*

ASHLEY: What do you feel like having for dinner?

SHARI: I don't know. I'd like something interesting . . . . Do you have

   __an international cookbook__ ?
   0.

ASHLEY: No, but we could go to _____ to look for one.
   1.

SHARI: Or we could look for a recipe on the Internet.

ASHLEY: That's _____. I'll go online, and we can look right now.
   2.

SHARI: Do you want to try a dish from Asia?

ASHLEY: Sure, how about an Indian dish? _____ of mine made an
   3.

   amazing curry once. I remember that it was a chicken curry, and it had potatoes,

   tomatoes, and lots of spices.

SHARI: Well, why don't we try a beef curry this time?

ASHLEY: Let's see what we can find . . . . How about this one?

SHARI: Oh, that looks like _____ recipe. It doesn't look too hard.
   4.

ASHLEY: I think we'll have to go to the supermarket to buy some things, though. Actually, there's

   a great international market not too far from here. They have spices and things from

   around _____.
   5.

SHARI: That sounds great. Why don't we write down the ingredients and go?

B. Reread the conversation. Find two phrases with definite articles and six phrases with indefinite articles. Write them in the table below. (Note: Only use words that are given in the conversation. Do not use any words that you wrote.) An example is given.

PHRASES WITH DEFINITE ARTICLES	PHRASES WITH INDEFINITE ARTICLES
0. *the Internet*	1. _____
1. _____	2. _____
2. _____	3. _____
	4. _____
	5. _____
	6. _____

2 | PLANS FOR TOMORROW NIGHT

*Complete Ashley and Shari's conversation about their plans for tomorrow night. Use **a, an,** or **the**. Use Ø if you don't need an article.*

ASHLEY: Hey, do you have plans for tomorrow night?

SHARI: No. I was going to go to ____*a*____ baseball game, but I couldn't get _____ ticket.
　　　　　　　　　　　　　　　　　0.　　　　　　　　　　　　　　　**1.**

ASHLEY: Well, I was listening to the radio, and the weatherman on station 98.9 said that a storm

　　　　may be coming through _____ area. So they may cancel _____ game.
　　　　　　　　　　　　　　　　　2.　　　　　　　　　　　　　　**3.**

SHARI: Well, I don't feel so bad then. Maybe I'll just go to the movies. Do you have _____
　　　　　　　　　　　　　　　　　　　　　　　　　　　　　　　　　　　　　　4.

　　　　plans?

ASHLEY: Well, I was planning to go to _____ art exhibition. It's downtown at _____
　　　　　　　　　　　　　　　　　　　　5.　　　　　　　　　　　　　　　　**6.**

　　　　Carlson Museum. It's supposed to be _____ awesome show. Do you want to go?
　　　　　　　　　　　　　　　　　　　　　　　7.

SHARI: Sure. What is _____ exhibition about?
　　　　　　　　　　　　8.

ASHLEY: It's a Picasso exhibition. And it will only be in town for _____ next two weeks. I
　　　　　　　　　　　　　　　　　　　　　　　　　　　　　　　　9.

　　　　want to see it because I really love _____ paintings and all kinds of art.
　　　　　　　　　　　　　　　　　　　　10.

SHARI: That sounds great! Do you want to go to _____ new Mexican restaurant on Edison
11.

Street afterwards? I haven't been there yet, and I've heard it's the best place in the city to

get _____ tacos.
12.

ASHLEY: Sure. Why don't we go around 6:00?

SHARI: Sounds good.

---

3 | EDITING: VACATION PLANS

*Read this e-mail from Ashley to Shari about their vacation plans. There are six mistakes in
the use of definite and indefinite articles. The first answer is already given. Find and correct
five more. (Note: There can be more than one way to correct a mistake.)*

Shari,

    Hi! Thanks again for inviting me to *the* lake next week! It will be nice to have vacation from

work. I'm really looking forward to a peace and quiet, and I'll bring the good book to read.

    When you have a minute, can you send me a phone number of your house there? I'd like to

give it to my parents so they can reach me.

    I can't wait. You're a awesome friend! See you next week!

Ashley

PART V Achievement Test

1 | LISTENING: CULTURAL STUDIES

🎧 *Listen to Janet and Sam's conversation about their class schedules. Complete the conversation by writing the words that you hear. You will hear the recording two times.*

JANET: Hey, what are you doing?

SAM: I'm planning my class schedule for next semester, but I still need one more class. How do you like your cultural studies class?

JANET: It's really good. I've learned _____ *a lot of* _____ new things about cultures around
         0.
the world.

SAM: Do you have _____ homework in that class?
                  1.

JANET: Well, we really don't have _____ assignments to hand in, but there
                                  2.
is _____ reading. The good part is that the professor doesn't give us
   3.
_____ boring things to read. And there's just one big project: We have
4.
to write a research paper about a custom from a culture other than our own.

SAM: That sounds interesting. Do you have _____ ideas of what you'll write
                                          5.
about?

JANET: Well, I have _____ ideas, but I haven't decided yet. I may write about
                    6.
customs related to food. I'm going to the library tomorrow to do _____
                                                                  7.
research on the topic.

2 | JAPANESE CHOPSTICKS

Read this information from Janet's research paper about Japanese chopsticks. Complete the information with the correct words or phrases. Write the letter of the best answer on each line.

Chopsticks, or pairs of thin sticks used to eat food, have been part of Japanese culture for

___*a*___ (a. many centuries b. many century c. a lot of century d. plenty centuries). _____ (a. Some
  0.   **1.**

historian b. A few historian c. Some historians d. A little historians) believe that the Japanese began using

chopsticks in the 7th century. At _____ (a. any meals b. a meal c. the meal d. some meals) the
                                         2.

Japanese also use spoons. But they often drink soup from bowls, so spoons are not always

necessary. In Japan it is considered polite to take food from a serving dish with the ends of your

chopsticks that you do not put in your mouth. This shows _____ (a. any respect b. many respects
                                                                        3.

c. a great deal of respect d. a lot of respects) for your dinner companions.

If you don't have _____ (a. a lot b. any c. many d. a few) experience using chopsticks, it may
                            4.

take _____ (a. enough try b. a few try c. any try d. several tries) to learn to use them correctly. At
         5.

first you might only be able to pick up _____ (a. a little food b. little food c. a few foods d. few foods)
                                              6.

at a time. But after learning, _____ (a. a great deal of people b. many peoples c. any people d. a lot of
                                      7.

people) find that eating with chopsticks helps them experience a more authentic Japanese meal.

3 | TEX-MEX FOOD

Complete this information about Tex-Mex food. Circle the correct words or phrases. (Note: Ø means that you don't need a word.)

Tex-Mex food refers to dishes that include a combination of typical ingredients from the

southwestern American state of Texas and from Mexico. The word is a combination of the

words *Texan* and *Mexican*. There are (many) / any / a great deal of different Tex-Mex dishes,
                                                       0.

including tacos, nachos, and burritos. Many restaurants serve rice and a little / some / few
                                                                1.

beans along with the main dish. Although a little / some / any dishes can be quite spicy,
                                                    2.

a few / a great deal of / a Tex-Mex food is mild.
              3.

Tex-Mex food was first developed hundreds of years ago, but the type of Tex-Mex food that

<u>a lot of / any / much</u> Americans love is actually a 20th century creation. The word "Tex-Mex"
4.

was first used in <u>the / some / many</u> 1940s. At that time, <u>the / several / a little</u> Tex-Mex
5.   **6.**

restaurants appeared in <u>the / a / any</u> southwestern part of the United States, especially Texas,
7.

where many Mexicans lived. Tex-Mex gradually became very popular. Nowadays it's popular in

<u>much / many / the</u> parts of the United States, not just Texas and the Southwest. Some Tex-Mex
8.

restaurants are very elegant, but <u>a great deal of / a lot of / a few</u> them are casual.
9.

If you like Mexican food and you like southwestern American food, you probably can't get

<u>enough / any / some</u> Tex-Mex food!
10.

| 4 | MISS MANNERS: TABLE MANNERS |

Complete this letter about table manners in the United States. Circle the correct words or
phrases. (Note: Ø means that you don't need a word.)

Dear Miss Manners,

I am going to <u>the /ⓐ/ Ø</u> formal dinner at my boss's house next week with some co-workers,
0.

and I'm nervous. I have pretty good table manners, but I have <u>some / a little / a great deal of</u>
1.

concerns. First of all, when I eat at <u>the / a / Ø</u> friend's house, I always sit at <u>the / some / Ø</u> table
2.   **3.**

and pick up <u>the / a / Ø</u> wrong silverware. When I'm with friends I don't worry too much, but I
4.

don't want to make <u>the / a / Ø</u> mistake like that with my boss and co-workers. Also, I always
5.

seem to have <u>an / the / Ø</u> extra fork when dinner is over. How do I know which fork to use
6.

when? Another thing—do I have to put <u>the / some / Ø</u> napkin on my lap? Last, I will probably
7.

spill <u>a / any / Ø</u> drink or <u>an / any / a</u> appetizer on <u>the / a / Ø</u> floor—that always happens to me.
8.   **9.**   **10.**

What should I do? Laugh and make <u>the / a / Ø</u> joke? I want to make <u>the / an / Ø</u> impression,
11.   **12.**

but I want to make <u>the / a / Ø</u> *good* one. I need <u>a / the / Ø</u> help!
13.   **14.**

Sincerely,

Worried in Ohio

Name _____ **Date** _____

*Complete Miss Manners's answer. Use **a, an,** or **the**. Use **Ø** if you don't need an article.*

Dear Worried in Ohio,

Don't be nervous! Simply follow ___*the*___ tips below.
0.

There are several rules about eating. _____ good general rule is that you should never do
1.

anything until _____ host, or person who has invited you, does it first. This means don't sit
2.

or begin to eat before your boss does.

When you sit down, there will be a plate in front of you. _____ plate is yours. There will
3.

be a napkin on or near your plate. Take _____ napkin off your plate and place it on your
4.

lap. You'll also probably have three pieces of silverware at your place: a fork, a knife, and a

spoon. _____ fork will be on your left, and _____ knife and spoon will be on your right.
5. 6.

If there is more than one fork, then use one fork for each course. Start with _____ one that
7.

is on _____ outside, or far left. After that, use the next fork for the next course.
8.

If you have a slice of bread, don't butter _____ whole piece at once. Put a little butter on
9.

your bread plate. That will be the small plate on _____ left, above your silverware. Then put
10.

a small amount of that butter on a bite of bread.

Make polite conversation during dinner. Ask people _____ questions about themselves.
11.

But don't ask anything too personal. If you meet someone for _____ first time, a good way
12.

to start is by asking, "What do you do for a living?" If you've met a person before, try to

remember something about him or her and talk about that.

If you drop food on _____ floor, just pick it up and continue as if nothing had happened.
13.

If _____ accident happens and you spill something, be calm and apologize.
14.

Remember that _____ practice makes perfect. After a few dinners like this one, you'll feel
15.

confident enough to join people at a formal dinner any time.

Good luck!

Miss Manners

6 | EDITING: SOUTH AFRICA OYSTER FESTIVAL

Read this diary entry about Tom's trip to the Oyster Festival in South Africa. There are eight mistakes in the use of quantifiers and articles. The first mistake is already corrected. Find and correct seven more. (Note: There can be more than one way to correct a mistake.)

July 5

    My trip to South Africa has been ~~many~~ *a lot of* fun so far! This is a great place. The past few days I've been participating in much activities at Oyster Festival. The festival is amazing celebration. It's the ten-day party! I've eaten several kinds of oysters, and I didn't eat some kinds I didn't like! I've had so many wonderful things, but I still haven't tried an enough food. I'm glad I have a little more days left.

PART VI Diagnostic Test

1 | LISTENING: JOB FAIR

A. 🎧 *Listen to this radio announcement about a job fair. Complete the announcement by writing the words that you hear. You will hear the recording two times.*

The 23rd annual job fair is _____*almost*_____ here, and it will be the best job fair this
                   0.

town has ever had! The purpose of the fair is to bring together job candidates and companies

with open positions. If you come, you'll have the chance to talk to representatives of many

companies and learn more about the open positions they have.

Job opportunities in some fields are growing the fastest that they ever have! And here's some

more good news: This job expansion is lasting _____ of any in the past 20 years.
                                        1.

Now is the time to make a career change!

There are lots of reasons to consider changing jobs or careers. Maybe your current job

doesn't pay you _____ you should be paid. Maybe you're working the hardest of
                           2.

anyone in your office, and you're tired of it. Or maybe you want more of a challenge. The reason

doesn't matter. Life is too short to be _____. Come discover hundreds of jobs at
                               3.

the most exciting job fair around! This is the biggest opportunity of the year. Find the best jobs

for you, this Saturday from 9:00–4:00 at the Gables Conference Center. Get a job you love and

start living _____!
                4.

*B. These sentences are based on the listening. Write **ADJ** if the underlined word or phrase is the superlative form of an adjective and **ADV** if it is the superlative form an adverb.*

__ADJ__ 0. The job fair will be <u>the best</u> the town has ever had.

_____ 1. Job opportunities in some fields are growing <u>the fastest</u> that they ever have!

_____ 2. Maybe you're working <u>the hardest</u> of anyone in your office, and you're tired of it.

_____ 3. This job fair will be <u>the most exciting</u> job fair around.

_____ 4. The job fair is <u>the biggest</u> opportunity of the year.

PART V

2 | JOB DISSATISFACTION

Wade isn't happy with his job. Read this entry in his blog, or online journal. Find two adjectives, two adverbs, two comparative adjectives, and three superlative adjectives. Write them in the table below. An example is given.

I heard an announcement on the radio today for a job fair. It sounds good, and I want to go. My job is boring, and the hours pass so slowly! I'm just not interested in it. Plus, it doesn't pay well. It's not the worst job that I've ever had, but I want to find something else. What job would be the most satisfying for me? I still don't know. I've been thinking about changing jobs, but now it's time to start doing something about it. I want to find the most rewarding job I can. The more pleasant the job, the more content I'll be.

ADJECTIVES	ADVERBS	COMPARATIVE ADJECTIVES	SUPERLATIVE ADJECTIVES
0. *good*	1. _____	1. _____	1. _____
1. _____	2. _____	2. _____	2. _____
2. _____			3. _____

3 | JOB FAIR ATTRACTS HUNDREDS

Complete this newspaper article about the job fair. Circle the correct words or phrases.

The city's 23rd annual job fair was held on Saturday, and the organizer, Laura Williams, called it one of the successfulest /(the most successful)/ as successful as fairs so far. Hundreds of people
                                                                        0.
attended. The conference center filled suddenly / more suddenly / suddenlier when it opened at
                                                                                        1.
9:00, and it remained filled with people long after the official closing time of 4:00. A local

mariachi band performed, making this job fair at least the liveliest / as lively as / livelier past
                                                                                    2.
fairs. In fact, Williams commented, "This was the most liveliest / the liveliest / more lively job
                                                                                    3.
fair ever, both in terms of its great / greatly / more greater attendance, and also in terms of its
                                        4.
general / generally / generalest atmosphere."
            5.

Paula Mendez, one of the many people who attended the fair, was pleased. "The job

opportunities are amazed / amazing / amaze this year," Mendez said. "Last year's job fair was
                        6.

good, but I got more results from the fair this year. They just keep getting better and

best / good / better!"
    7.

    When you go to a job fair, you can apply to many jobs and have several interviews on the

same day. This system of interviewing is about efficient / more efficient / as efficient as it can be!
                                                     8.

Said Williams, "A lot of people at the fair find a job pretty faster / fast / more fast."
                                                            9.

4 | COMPARING COMPANIES

Wade has received job offers from two companies, Epicenter Group and Agicor Direct.
Complete his thoughts about the companies. Use the adjective or adverb forms of the
words in the box.

big	loud	~~rare~~	silent	useful
good	mean	risky	small	usual
long	nice	serious		

0. I _____*rarely*_____ have problems making decisions, but this time I'm really having a hard
    time. I can't decide which job to take—the one at Epicenter Group or the one at Agicor Direct.

1. I need to consider both options _____. This is an important decision.

2. Epicenter is a _____ company. They're so large that they have lots of offices all
    over the world.

3. I think a job at Agicor might be _____. Epicenter is a well-established company,
    but Agicor is pretty new. If the company fails, I'll lose my job.

4. There's one big disadvantage to the job with Epicenter. The office is far away, so it would be a
    _____ distance to travel every day.

5. But Epicenter sells things that are _____ to everyone. Its products are very
    practical.

6. Salespeople at Agicor _____ sell their products in person. They do about 90
    percent of their sales this way.

7. The interviewer from Agicor was really _____ and friendly. He was easy to talk
    to, and I liked him a lot.

8. I think I could get along really _____ with the people at Agicor. Everyone there
    is great.

5 | COMPARING JOBS

*Wade is still trying to decide between Epicenter Group and Agicor Direct. Complete the sentences. Use the words in parentheses with **as ... as** or the comparative or superlative form. Add **the, than, more,** or **less** where necessary. Some items may have more than one right answer.*

0. Epicenter has existed _____*longer than*_____ Agicor. It's been around for 20 years,
   (long)

   while Agicor has only been around for half that amount of time.

1. Agicor is _____ Epicenter. It's only about 10 years old.
   (new)

2. But with seven offices, Epicenter is _____ employer in the city.
   (big)

3. Agicor is _____ Epicenter. It has only three offices.
   (small)

4. At Agicor, I might have to work _____ at Epicenter. I might have to
   (hard)

   work 50 hours each week instead of 40 hours.

5. At Epicenter, I would travel _____ I would with Agicor. Both
   (frequent)

   companies require the same amount of travel.

6. It might be _____ to sell Agicor's products than Epicenter's. Agicor
   (difficult)

   sells things that people don't really need, but Epicenter's products are necessities.

7. Both companies have been making lots of changes. But Epicenter hasn't been making

   changes as _____ Agicor has. Epicenter announces all their plans,
   (quiet)

   but Agicor doesn't say much about theirs.

8. Agicor is the third _____ company in the state.
   (rich)

9. Agicor has a great training program. With this training, its employees are working more and

   _____.
   (skillful)

10. Agicor has _____ website I've ever seen.
    (cool)

11. Agicor's salary is _____ Epicenter's salary. Agicor is offering a lot
    (high)

    more money than Epicenter.

12. Also, there are opportunities to make extra money at Agicor. The

    _____ you work, the more generously they reward you.
    (well)

PART VI

13. Lately, Epicenter hasn't been _____ Agicor in sales. Agicor's sales
    (successful)

    have been much higher.

14. Agicor has _____ environment of all the companies I looked at.
    (relaxed)

15. I interviewed with a man at Agicor and a woman at Epicenter. The interviewer from Agicor

    dressed _____ the interviewer from Epicenter; he looked very casual,
    (formal)

    but she looked formal.

16. The interviewer from Epicenter seemed _____ the interviewer from
    (knowledgeable)

    Agicor. She knew a lot, and he didn't know much at all.

17. The woman from Epicenter spoke _____ the man from Agicor. She
    (professional)

    was very professional, but he was very informal.

---

6 | EDITING: WADE'S NEW JOB

*Read Wade's e-mail to his friend Kerem about his new job at Epicenter Group. There are ten
mistakes in the use of adjectives and adverbs. The first mistake is already corrected. Find
and correct nine more.*

Hi Kerem,

    I wanted to catch up a little. I just started a ~~newly~~ job at Epicenter Group! I have a quiets
        new

office, and everything is very nicer. It's a lot interesting than my last job. Epicenter is one the best

employers in the state. I think it will be better here that at Agicor, which is another company

that offered me a job. I applied for both jobs at the local job fair, and both companies called

pretty quickly me after that. The mostest enjoyable part of my new job is that I feel like I've

accomplished something at the end of the day. I use my time much more efficient here than I did

at my other job, and my new co-workers encourage more frequently me. So I think I chose the

right job.

Talk to you later!

Wade

Unit 23 Achievement Test

| 1 | LISTENING: UPCOMING CONCERT |

A. 🎧 *Listen to the radio announcement about a concert by the band Dot Matrix. Complete the announcement by writing the words that you hear. You will hear the recording two times.*

DJ 1: That was the _____ *new* _____ release from Dot Matrix, "Don't Let Me Down."
                              0.

DJ 2: Isn't that a great song? Dot Matrix is one of my _____ groups. The lead
                                                          1.

singer has an incredible voice.

DJ 1: Yeah, I always enjoy listening to Marlene Rivera. And I understand she's a really friendly

person. But the other band members are great too.

DJ 2: Yes, Dot Matrix is an exceptional group of musicians. And they'll be in town for a show

this Friday night.

DJ 1: That's right. Everyone is excited because this is their first show here in Pleasantville.

They're going to perform in the beautifully restored Bravado Hall.

DJ 2: Well, that should be an _____ evening.
                                  2.

DJ 1: Yeah, it'll be a lot of fun. Listeners, you'd better buy your tickets now, because they're

going awfully quickly! Call our ticket hotline at 555-WXLR. That's 555-9957. Now we'll

take a short break and when we return, more non-stop hits from the bands you love.

DJ 2: I can _____ wait!
                   3.

B. *These sentences are based on the radio announcement about Dot Matrix. Write **ADJ** if the underlined word is an adjective and **ADV** if the underlined word is an adverb.*

ADJ 0. "Don't Let Me Down" is a <u>great</u> song.

_____ 1. Dot Matrix's lead singer is a <u>friendly</u> person.

_____ 2. DJ 1 <u>always</u> enjoys listening to Marlene Rivera.

_____ 3. Dot Matrix is an <u>exceptional</u> group of musicians.

_____ 4. The people of Pleasantville are <u>excited</u> about Dot Matrix's concert on Friday.

_____ 5. They restored Bravado Hall <u>beautifully</u>.

2 | THE CONCERT

Complete the sentences about the Dot Matrix concert. Circle the correct words or phrases.

0. The Dot Matrix show was great! I (always wanted)/ wanted always to see them.

1. They played some new songs, as well as some of their ones old / old ones.

2. One of their new songs is a lovely song / song lovely about Marlene Rivera's mother.

3. Rivera dressed beautiful / beautifully.

4. She looked great / greatly. Her clothes were gorgeous.

5. Rivera always sounds fantastic. She sings never / never sings her songs poorly.

6. Dot Matrix always gives wonderful shows / shows wonderful.

7. Dot Matrix has a new guitarist. He played very good / well.

8. Bravado Hall was the perfect / perfectly place to hold the concert.

9. There was a largely / large audience.

10. The audience was fascinating / fascinated by every song.

11. They cheered happy / happily after each one.

12. Some audience members danced energetically / energetic in the front.

3 | HISTORY OF THE BAND

Complete this paragraph from an Internet article about the history of Dot Matrix. Use the correct adjective or adverb form of each word.

Marlene Rivera knew _____*early*_____ in life that she wanted to be a professional

                   0. (early)

singer. When she was young she sang with her school choir. Her teachers, family, and friends

were _____ by her voice. After high school, Rivera put an ad in her local
     1. (amaze)

newspaper to organize a band. She got several responses _____. She chose
                                         2. (quick)

four _____ musicians, and they started playing together. The group practiced
   3. (serious)

_____ for a few years, and in 2002 they recorded their _____
4. (regular)   **5. (first)**

album. It became a hit very _____, receiving positive reviews from critics and
                 6. (fast)

selling over 500,000 copies.

---

4 | EDITING: ALBUM REVIEW

*Read this review about the new Dot Matrix album. There are five mistakes in the use of
adjectives and adverbs. The first mistake is already corrected. Find and correct four more.*

     Music has been a little ~~bored~~ ^{boring} for me this year. Most bands aren't coming up with new ideas.

A lot of what I hear is disappointing. But I've just discovered an excellently album, Dot Matrix's

This Way to Freedom. I bought the album recent, and I haven't stopped listening to it. The album

isn't just well, it's great! It's hardly to compare to any other music. The band has many different

influences, from classic rock and roll to rhythm and blues. You should definitely check it out!

Unit 24 Achievement Test

1 | LISTENING: THE COUNTRY INN

A. 🎧 *Listen to the restaurant review on a local radio program. Complete the review by writing the words that you hear. You will hear the recording two times.*

The Country Inn has just reopened under new management, and they've made some great

changes. The dining room looks _____*bigger*_____, and the lighting is better too.
           0.

The dishes are a little _____ they were, but the food is as good as
           1.

ever. The only exception is the breadsticks, which are even tastier than before. The desserts

are _____ you can imagine. The homemade pies are
           2.

_____ you can get, and the chocolate soufflé is lighter than air.
           3.

    Apparently a lot of people like the changes at The Country Inn. Every time I go for dinner,

it seems _____ to get a table! Try lunch for a quieter meal.
           4.

B. *Reread the restaurant review. Then read each statement and circle* **T** *(true) or* **F** *(false).*

T **Ⓕ** 0. The lighting in The Country Inn is worse than before.

T **F** 1. The Country Inn's food is worse than before.

T **F** 2. The Country Inn's breadsticks are getting less and less tasty.

T **F** 3. The Country Inn's chocolate soufflés are light.

T **F** 4. Dinner at The Country Inn is as quiet as lunch.

2 | WHAT'S THE DIFFERENCE?

Complete this Internet discussion board about two brands of rice. Use the words in the box.

more nutritious	less money	as expensive as	saltier
~~better~~	the higher	less time	as hot as
unhealthy than	higher	the faster	

Q: What's the difference between Rice Right and Best Rice? I hear they're both good brands.

A: I think Best Rice is slightly _____*better*_____ than Rice Right. The quality of
                                        0.

Best Rice is _____ than the quality of Rice Right. And Best Rice is
              1.

_____ than Rice Right, so it's generally popular with people who are
2.

careful with their diets. The big advantage to Rice Right is the amount of cooking time. Rice

Right is considered "instant" rice because it takes only five minutes to prepare. Many people

like it because they think "_____, the better." People have less and
                              3.

_____ these days, so a lot of them buy Rice Right. In terms of price,
4.

Rice Right is _____ Best Rice.
               5.

3 | FACTS ABOUT RICE

*Complete this article from a health food magazine about different kinds of rice. Use the
words in parentheses and the comparative form,* **as** *+ adjective +* **as,** *or* **the** *+ comparative
adjective +* **the** *+ comparative adjective.*

An individual piece of rice is called a grain. Rice is divided into different types—long grain,

medium grain, and short grain—depending on the size of the grain.

When long-grain rice is cooked, it is _____*drier*_____ than medium- and short-
                                        0. (dry)

grain rice. Its grains are also _____, and they stay separated. Long-grain
                                 1. (light)

rice is _____ than other types in foods such as curries, pilafs, and salads.
        2. (typical)

Medium-grain and short-grain rice are _____ than long-grain rice;
                                       3. (sticky)

their grains stick together. They are _____ than the long-grain variety
                                       4. (good)

for desserts such as rice pudding. Both short-grain rice and medium-grain rice are

_____ in Asia than they are in other parts of the world. But now they
5. (common)

are becoming more and _____ in some other regions as well.
6. (known)

   You need to know a few things before you cook rice. The procedure isn't

_____ it first seems. A few extra minutes of cooking can make
7. (easy)

a big difference in the end result. _____ the cooking time,
8. (long)

_____ the rice becomes. But you don't want it to become too soft.
9. (soft)

Some people think there is nothing _____ than rice that is too soft.
10. (bad)

Properly cooked rice is also _____ in flavor and contains more nutrients
11. (rich)

than overcooked rice.

   Here's another nutritional fact about rice. White rice is not _____
12. (healthy)

brown rice because many of its nutritious vitamins are removed during processing.

---

4 | EDITING: RICE PUDDING

*Russ ate at The Country Inn after hearing the review on the radio. Read his conversation
with the waiter about ordering a dessert. There are six mistakes in the use of comparisons.
The first mistake is already corrected. Find and correct five more. (Note: There can be more
than one way to correct a mistake.)*

RUSS: What do you recommend for dessert—the ice cream or the rice pudding?

WAITER: It depends on what you're looking for. The ice cream is ~~more cold~~ *colder*, of course. And it's

   also sweeter that the rice pudding.

RUSS: Hmmm. I see that the ice cream is just expensive as the rice pudding.

WAITER: Well, yes, all of our desserts are the same price. We added rice pudding to our menu last

   month, so it's not as popularer as the ice cream yet, but it's becoming more than more

   popular.

RUSS: I want to try the rice pudding, but I usually like sweeter desserts. Is there anything on

   the rice pudding?

WAITER: If you'd like, I can make the rice pudding more livelier by adding some whipped cream.

   Some customers think it tastes more flavorful that way.

RUSS: OK, I'll try that.

Unit 25 Achievement Test

1 | LISTENING: PHONE MESSAGES ON VALENTINE'S DAY

A. 🎧 *In many parts of the world, Valentine's Day is a holiday to celebrate love. Paul is leaving some messages on his girlfriend Marlene's answering machine on Valentine's Day. Listen to the messages. Complete the messages by writing the words that you hear. You will hear the recording two times.*

MACHINE: You have five new messages. Message one. 12:30 P.M.

PAUL: Hi, Marlene! It's Paul. Happy Valentine's Day. I was just thinking about you, and I

wanted to tell you that you're _____*the nicest*_____ girl in the world. You're
                                   0.

also one of _____ people I've ever met. I'm so lucky you're
                            1.

my girlfriend. I'm so excited to see you tonight. Talk to you then!

MACHINE: Message two. 12:35 P.M.

PAUL: Oh, hi. It's me again. I forgot to tell you that you're also the cutest girl I know. You

have _____ eyes I've ever seen. I'm such a lucky guy. OK. Bye.
                      2.

MACHINE: Message three. 12:45 P.M.

PAUL: Hi again. You know, I can't stop thinking about you. You're the kindest woman I

have ever dated. And intelligent! You're the most intelligent person I know! You're

_____ person ever!
                3.

MACHINE: Message four. 12:50 P.M.

PAUL: Marlene, I'm not sure I've told you this before, but you're

_____ people in the world. In fact, I don't think there's
                4.

anyone better, anywhere! You're the most amazing girl on Earth!

MACHINE: Message five. 12:55 P.M.

PAUL: Seriously. You are so great! You've made me the happiest guy alive. Happy Valentine's

Day! I can't wait to see you later.

B. *Reread Paul's phone messages for Marlene. Find four superlative adjectives. Write them below. (Note: Only use words that are given in the phone messages. Do not use any words that you wrote.) An example is given.*

0. _the cutest_____

1. _____

2. _____

3. _____

4. _____

2	AD FOR A CHOCOLATE STORE

Complete the Valentine's Day advertisement for a chocolate store, Emery Row Chocolate Factory. Circle the correct words or phrases.

Valentine's Day is here again—the most sweet / (the sweetest) / the most sweetest
                                                    0.

day of the year. Have you gotten a gift for that "special someone" yet? There's still

time, but you'd better hurry! Come to Emery Row Chocolate Factory for

the most delicious / the deliciousest / the deliciouser selection of Valentine's Day sweets.
                            1.

We're the second most large / the largest second / the second largest chocolate company
                                            2.

on / in / ever the country, and we make all our chocolates in our store. We have the best
  3.

chocolate you're ever tasted / you've ever tasted / you're ever tasting. Don't waste any time.
                            4.

Come in today!

3 | VALENTINE'S DAY CARDS

Paul is trying to choose a Valentine's Day card for Marlene. Complete his thoughts about each card. Use the superlative form of each adjective. Some items may have more than one right answer.

0. I can't decide which card is _____*the best*_____ one to get Marlene for
   0. (good)

   Valentine's Day.

1. This shop has _____ selection of cards I've ever seen.
   1. (great)

2. I want to get Marlene a perfect card, one that really shows how I feel. I'm going to get her

   _____ card they have.
   2. (fantastic)

3. This is _____ card I've ever read. But do I want to get her a funny
   3. (funny)

   card?

4. I like this card, but it's _____ one of all. It's a really nice card, but I
   4. (expensive)

   don't think cards should cost so much.

5. This is _____ card in the store. They just got it today.
   5. (new)

6. This is _____ card they sell, but it isn't very nice.
   6. (inexpensive)

7. Here's another inexpensive card, but it's not as cheap as the other one. I guess it's the second

   _____ card in the store.
   7. (cheap)

8. This card is really romantic. It has _____ message of all of them, but
   8. (romantic)

   I don't like the picture.

9. This card is _____ one I've seen today, but the poem is kind of
   9. (gorgeous)

   strange.

10. This is one of _____ cards I've ever seen. Who would buy it?
    10. (bad)

11. This is _____ card I've ever seen. You can hardly read the print!
    11. (small)

12. These cards are _____ ones they sell. They are so delicate and
    12. (fancy)

    beautiful.

13. There are lots of nice cards with flowers, but this card has _____
    13. (lovely)

    flowers of all. I think I'll get this one.

PART VI

4 | EDITING: MARLENE'S DIARY

Read Marlene's diary about Valentine's Day. There are six mistakes in the use of superlatives.
The first mistake is already corrected. Find and correct five more.

                                                                        nicest

    I love Valentine's Day. It's the best day of the year! Paul left the ~~most nice~~ messages on my

answering machine today. He said so many wonderful things. We went out to dinner tonight,

and he gave me the most pretty card that I ever seen. He also gave me the most biggest box of

chocolates. They're very fancy, and they taste delicious. They're definitely the best chocolates

town! It was the most fabulous night of my life. Paul is so great. He's the most specialest guy I

know. I'm the luckiest girl in the world!

Unit 26 Achievement Test

| 1 | LISTENING: CHOOSING A NEW MANAGER |

A. 🎧 *Denise is the president of a small book company called Amboso. Listen to her conversation with her co-worker, Olivia. Complete the conversation by writing the words that you hear. You will hear the recording two times.*

OLIVIA: Hi, Denise. Here's the report you asked for. It didn't take nearly

_____ *as long as* _____ the last one to complete.
              0.

DENISE: Oh, well, I'm glad you finished so quickly. Listen, I want to ask you something. Who do

you think we should select as the new general manager of the Chicago office?

OLIVIA: Well, all three of the candidates are great. Marty probably works

_____. But that doesn't necessarily mean he's the best person for
                1.

the job.

DENISE: What do you mean?

OLIVIA: Well, all their strengths are different. For example, Albert is definitely quicker than

Marty in his work.

DENISE: Hmmm, that's true. Marty doesn't work as efficiently as Albert does. But he's improving.

The longer Marty stays here, _____ he works. So, what about
                                           2.

Sidney?

OLIVIA: The other candidate? Well, of the three of them, Sidney speaks the most confidently, so

she has the potential to be a strong leader. But I think there are some other things to

consider, too.

DENISE: Yeah? Like what?

OLIVIA: Well, on their last evaluations, Marty scored just _____ Albert
                                                                            3.

did in sales. But Sidney did better _____ either of them in
                                                  4.

overall customer satisfaction.

DENISE: You're right. Those are important things to consider. I'll have to think this over a bit

more.

PART VI

*B. Reread the conversation. Then read each statement and circle **T** (true) or **F** (false).*

T **(F)** 0. It took Olivia a longer time to finish this report than the last one.

T **F** 1. Marty works more quickly than Albert.

T **F** 2. Marty is as efficient as Albert.

T **F** 3. Albert is the most confident speaker of the three candidates.

T **F** 4. Albert and Marty have similar selling skills.

2 | THE COMPANY

Complete the paragraph about the book company. Circle the correct words or phrases.

Amboso has grown (the quickest)/ the most quicker / quicker of all bookselling
0.

organizations in the United States over the past 10 years. They have increased sales

as steadily as / more steadily / the most steadily than the top sales organizations in the
1.

country. The longer / The longest / As long as the organization is in business, the more rapidly
2.

the profits increase. And as a result, all Amboso employees are well paid. In fact, the company

pays middle-level employees the best / the most good / as well as some companies pay their
3.

managers and directors. Compared to other sales organizations, Amboso cooperates

most effective / the most effectively / as effectively as with health care providers to offer
4.

its workers outstanding health benefits. In general, people regard the company

more highly / as high as / the most highly than other employers in the industry.
5.

3 | COMPARING THE CANDIDATES

*Complete Denise's thoughts about the candidates for general manager at Amboso's Chicago office. Use the words in parentheses with **as ... as** or the comparative or superlative forms. Add **the** or **than**, and choose between **more** or **less** where necessary.*

0. This week Olivia and I are working _____*the most aggressively*_____ we ever have to
   (aggressively)

   choose the best general manager for the Chicago branch of Amboso.

1. Albert has worked at the company _____ of all the
   (long)

   candidates. He's been here for 32 years.

2. Sidney has risen in position _____ of the three candidates.
   (fast)

   In just three years she has gone from a salesperson to director of sales.

3. Marty works _____ of the three candidates. He can work
   (cooperatively)

   with anyone.

4. Co-workers seem to treat Marty _____ they treat Albert;
   (respectfully)

   they respect Marty and Albert equally.

5. Marty has changed jobs _____ Sidney has; Marty has
   (often)

   changed jobs only twice, and Sidney has changed jobs four times.

6. Sidney arrives to work on time _____ of the candidates.
   (regularly)

   She's almost always on time, but Marty and Albert often arrive late.

7. But Sidney misses work _____ Marty and Albert do. She
   (frequently)

   called in sick several more times than Marty and Albert did last year.

8. Albert is introducing new sales techniques more and _____.
   (often)

9. Marty can use a computer _____ of anyone at work.
   (skillfully)

10. Marty generally learns things _____ the other two
    (slowly)

    candidates. It takes him more time to learn things, but he usually learns them very well.

11. And Marty usually does his work _____ the other two do.
    (accurately)

    His work is always the best.

12. The sooner Olivia and I choose a general manager, _____
    (quickly)

    the new manager can start the position.

PART VI

4 | EDITING: THE NEW MANAGER

Denise and Olivia have interviewed the candidates. Read their conversation about their final selection for the position. There are six mistakes in the use of adverbs. The first mistake is already corrected. Find and correct five more.

OLIVIA: So, what do you think?

DENISE: Well, honestly, I think Marty is the best one for the position. He's simply more ~~higher~~ *highly* qualified than the others.

OLIVIA: I agree. He scored better on his quality evaluations than they did. And although he's a little slower than the others with certain tasks, he's been learning things more and more quick as time passes.

DENISE: Yes. He also works more carefuller than Sidney and Albert, so he doesn't have to redo his work. And he has worked more aggressively than the others to improve his sales record. No one has worked as hard he has. That really impressed me.

OLIVIA: Me too. I also thought that Marty answered more professionally my questions during the interview.

DENISE: Well, all the candidates were quite professional during their interviews with me. But I think Marty will be able to perform the duties of general manager more effective than anyone else could.

PART VI Achievement Test

| 1 | **LISTENING: HOMES FOR SALE** |

A. 🎧 *Property development companies make money by buying land and building homes or other buildings on it. Listen to this television ad for a property development company. Complete the ad by writing the words that you hear. You will hear the recording two times.*

Red Sky Developers' 12th Annual Home Expo is _____*almost*_____ here, and it'll
0.

be the best expo ever! Face it: You're probably not saving money _____
1.

you could be because your monthly house payments are too high. Did you know that you can live

_____ in a better home for the same amount of money you're paying
2.

now? You might even pay less! Come see our _____ homes at the most
3.

exciting home expo we've ever had.

Only the most carefully trained professionals work at Red Sky. We work

_____ of all the developers in the area to make sure you get outstanding
4.

service.

Don't miss the greatest opportunity of the year to find the best home for you, this Saturday

from 10:00 to 5:00. Come and get to know the homes of the most highly rated property

development company in the area: Red Sky Developers.

B. *These sentences are based on the television ad. Write* **ADJ** *if the underlined word or phrase is the superlative form of an adjective and* **ADV** *if it is the superlative form an adverb.*

ADJ **0.** The 12th Annual Home Expo will be <u>the best</u> one ever.

_____ **1.** It will be <u>the most exciting</u> home expo we've ever had.

_____ **2.** Only <u>the most carefully</u> trained professionals work at Red Sky.

_____ **3.** Come and get to know the homes of <u>the most highly</u> rated development company in the area.

_____ **4.** The home expo is <u>the greatest</u> opportunity of the year to find a home.

2 | SOPHIA'S HOUSE

Sophia wants to move her family to a new house. Read her diary entry. Find two adjectives, two adverbs, two comparative adjectives, and three superlative adjectives. Write them in the correct categories below. An example is given.

I saw an ad today about a home expo. It sounds interesting. The house we're in now is surprisingly old. The development company presented nice houses in their ad, and I want one. I know that I'd live happily in one of those places. I'd like to have one of the biggest houses in town, but they're probably the most expensive ones. I'd better go to the expo. I want the most wonderful house I can afford, and the more aggressive I am about searching, the more likely I will be to find one.

ADJECTIVES	ADVERBS	COMPARATIVE ADJECTIVES	SUPERLATIVE ADJECTIVES
0. _interesting_	1. _____	1. _____	1. _____
1. _____	2. _____	2. _____	2. _____
2. _____			3. _____

3 | HOME EXPO A SUCCESS

Complete this newspaper article about the home expo. Circle the correct words or phrases.

Saturday's 12th Annual Home Expo, sponsored by Red Sky Developers, was a success. Red Sky owner Rebecca Park called it one of the most outstandinger / most outstandingest / **(most outstanding)** expos so far. The Expo Center quickly / as quick as / more quicker filled up as soon as the doors were opened. There was entertainment by a local rock band, which made this expo as lively as / lively / livelier a concert. According to Park, "This was lively / livelier / the liveliest expo ever, not only because of the large / largest / as large as number of people who came, but also because of the wonderful / more wonderful / as wonderful as music here today."

Ji-Eun Lee, one person at the expo, was happy. "The houses are as gorgeous as / gorgeous / more gorgeous than," Lee said. "And Red Sky provides better and good / better / best service each year." Others agreed that the service was as good as / good / better Red Sky had promised in their ads. Said Park, "Most people find a house pretty easily / as easy as / most easy with Red Sky because we really pay attention to clients' needs."

4 | COMPARING HOUSES

Sophia likes two different houses. Complete her thoughts about the two houses. Use the adjective or adverb forms of the words in the box.

bad	close	friendly	~~happy~~	quick	unusual
big	famous	good	lovely	small	usual

0. I'm _____*happy*_____ because I've found two houses that my family likes. But now I have

   to decide between them. I'll call them House A and House B.

1. House B is a _____ house. There are five bedrooms!

2. House B has a great yard with _____ trees. I guess they're a kind that's not very

   common around here.

3. The kitchen in House A is _____. I really like the way it looks.

4. Everything in that kitchen is top quality. With that fancy stove, I could cook really

   _____.

5. I think the people in the neighborhood of House B are _____ and would make

   good neighbors, but I'm not sure about the people in the neighborhood of House A.

6. House B is far from work. But House A is _____ to work. It's only about a

   10-minute drive.

7. There is _____ a lot of traffic going through Neighborhood A. It's common to

   hear cars all day.

8. I must decide _____ which house I'll buy. Other people are very interested in

   them, too. Someone else might buy one if I don't hurry.

5 | COMPARING HOUSES AND NEIGHBORHOODS

*Sophia is still trying to decide between House A and House B. Complete the sentences. Use the words in parentheses with **as . . . as** or the comparative or superlative form. Add **the, than, more,** or **less** where necessary.*

0. House B has been around _____*longer than*_____ House A. House B was built
    (long)

    two years ago, and House A was just built this year.

1. House B is _____ house in the neighborhood. No other houses
    (incredible)

    are nicer.

2. House A is _____ House B. It has only three bedrooms, and
    (small)

    House B has five.

3. But House A is _____ House B. It costs thousands of dollars less.
    (cheap)

4. In other words, House B is _____ House A. It actually costs a lot
    (expensive)

    more.

5. But House B has _____ view I've ever seen.
    (pretty)

6. From the outside, House A looks _____ House B. House A is brand
    (beautiful)

    new, but House B needs some repairs.

7. Both houses were painted recently. But the painters of House A worked

    _____. The paint on House B looks pretty bad in comparison.
    (professional)

8. Both houses are nice inside. I think House A has _____ living room
    (attractive)

    of all the houses we saw at the expo.

9. House A is located _____ House B. It is only two miles from my
    (convenient)

    workplace, but House B is 20 miles away.

10. House A's neighborhood is _____ House B's neighborhood. The
    (new)

    homes in House A's neighborhood were built this year.

11. House A's neighborhood is the third _____ neighborhood in the city.
    (large)

12. In contrast, House B's neighborhood isn't growing as _____ House
    (fast)

    A's neighborhood.

13. It only takes 10 minutes to get to work from House A, but it takes 30 minutes from House

B. So, it would take _____ to get to work from House B.

(long)

14. The children in House B's neighborhood play _____ than the

(quiet)

children in House A's neighborhood. I can hardly hear the kids in House B's neighborhood.

15. I think that the schools in House A's neighborhood are not as _____

(good)

the schools in House B's neighborhood.

16. And House B's neighborhood is very safe. I wouldn't need to watch my children as

_____ I would in House A's neighborhood.

(careful)

17. The _____ I think about buying a new house, the more desperately

(serious)

I want one.

---

6 | EDITING: SOPHIA'S NEW HOUSE

*Read Sophia's e-mail to her friend Naomi about her new house. There are ten mistakes in
the use of adjectives and adverbs. The first mistake is already corrected. Find and correct
nine more. (Note: There can be more than one way to correct a mistake.)*

Hi Naomi,

                 new

We finally moved in to our ~~newly~~ house! I'm sitting in our living room, looking out the

larges windows at the beautiful garden. The neighborhood is very calmer here. It's a lot peaceful

than my old house. This is one the best neighborhoods in the city. I think I'll be happier here that

at my old house. The grass here grows more tall than at my other house, and I'm more skillfully

working in the garden than ever before. This house doesn't have the most convenient location,

but everything else is perfect. I saw many wonderful houses at the Red Sky Home Expo, but I

decided this one was the best. I liked immediately this house. The mostest wonderful part is that

we have more room for all our things. Finally, we have a place we will be happy in for a long

time!

Come visit!

Sophia

PART VII Diagnostic Test

---

1 | LISTENING: THRIFT STORES

A. ⌒ *Machiko and Tamara are new roommates. Listen to their conversation about shopping. Complete the conversation by writing the words that you hear. You will hear the recording two times.*

MACHIKO: I need _____*to get*_____ some things at the store today. Actually, I'm planning on
   0.

going to the thrift store to look for a skirt. Are you interested in coming with me?

TAMARA: To a thrift store? Do you mean a place that sells used things?

MACHIKO: Yes.

TAMARA: I don't know. Why do you shop at thrift stores instead of at the mall?

MACHIKO: To save money. Things are expensive at the mall. I _____ shop there,
   1.

but not anymore. I'm _____.
   2.

TAMARA: Not having money doesn't mean you can't buy things. You can use your credit card.

MACHIKO: But you shouldn't buy things with your credit card when you don't have any money!

That's a terrible habit.

TAMARA: Well, I don't shop at thrift stores _____ I don't want old, worn-out
   3.

things.

MACHIKO: It's easy for people to think that everything at thrift stores is in bad condition, but you

can actually find some very nice things there. Sometimes people donate to thrift stores

_____ get rid of stuff they don't use, even if it's in good condition.
   4.

Come with me. You'll see.

TAMARA: Well . . . OK.

B. *Reread the conversation. Find two gerunds and two infinitives. Write them in the table below. (Note: Only use words that are given in the conversation. Do not use any words that you wrote.) Two examples are given.*

GERUNDS	INFINITIVES
0. *going* _____	0. ___*to look for*_____
1. _____	1. _____
2. _____	2. _____

2 │ MACHIKO'S BLOG

Complete Machiko's blog, or online journal, about going with Tamara to the thrift store. Use the words in the box. Some items may have more than one right answer. Some words can be used more than once.

buying	getting	shopping	to come	~~to go~~	to stay
coming	going	staying	to feel	to see	to watch
feeling	seeing	to buy	to get	to shop	watching

It was funny _____*to go*_____ shopping with Tamara today. I asked her if she'd like
                    0.

_____ with me to the thrift store. _____ at thrift stores is totally
        1.   **2.**

normal for me, but she avoids _____ to them. She prefers _____ at
                                          3.   **4.**

the malls. She went with me, but she was planning _____ in the car. She was afraid
                                                              5.

of _____ someone that she knew there. I had to persuade her _____
         6.   **7.**

out of the car and go in with me. She finally agreed to come in. Eventually, she stopped

_____ so nervous. It was interesting _____ her attitude change. She
        8.   **9.**

ended up _____ some pants and a shirt.
                  10.

3 | SHOPAHOLISM

Shopaholism *is the problem of shopping too much. Complete these sentences from an Internet article about shopaholism. Circle the correct words or phrases.*

0. People who suffer from shopaholism need (to buy)/ buy / buying things.

0. Some sources say that up to 8 percent of all Americans are obsessed with (buying)/ buy / to buying things.

1. Shopaholics are people who are addicted to spend / spending / to spending money.

2. Shopaholics will say, "Let's go to shop / shop / shopping" even when they don't need anything or don't have the money.

3. Shopaholics often buy things that are too expensive to afford / too expensive affording / expensive enough to afford.

4. Credit cards make it too easy not to spend / too easy overspending / easy enough to overspend.

5. The friends and family of shopaholics can't get used to watch / watching / to watching them waste their money on unnecessary things.

6. Some husbands and wives of shopaholics become too frustrated not / frustrated enough / too frustrated to seek a divorce.

7. Shopaholics usually shop fulfill / fulfilling / to fulfill some kind of need that they have.

8. Some people may shop proving / to prove / prove to themselves that they are "worth it."

9. Spending / To spending / Spend too much money often gives people feelings of guilt.

10. If you think you have a problem, don't postpone to get / getting / get help.

11. Shopaholics usually find it too difficult / enough difficult / difficulty enough to change on their own. They need help.

4 | TAMARA'S BLOG

Complete Tamara's blog about shopping with Machiko. Use the gerund or infinitive forms of the verbs in the box. Some items may have more than one right answer. Some words can be used more than once.

ask	buy	get	insist	see	think
be	do	go	look	shop	walk

Today I finished _____*doing*_____ my homework. Then Machiko invited me
0.

_____ to a thrift store with her. I considered _____ to thrift stores
1. **2.**

to be strange. _____ at thrift stores was never something that I did. I remember
3.

_____ into a thrift store several years ago, but everything there seemed
4.

_____ old and ugly. I really resisted _____ into the store with
5. **6.**

Machiko today, but she really wanted me to. At first, I was kind of annoyed with her for

_____ that I go into the store. I was nervous about _____ someone
7. **8.**

who knew me. What would they think?! But I finally relaxed, and I started looking around. They

had some really nice things! I decided _____ a shirt and some pants. They're nice,
9.

and I saved money! Now I'm thinking about _____ for a purse there.
10.

5 | MALE SHOPPERS

Complete these sentences from an Internet article about how to market to male shoppers. (To market is to try to persuade someone to buy a product by advertising it in a particular way.) Use the gerund or infinitive form of each verb in parentheses. Some items may have more than one right answer.

0. If you're in sales and want _____*to increase*_____ your profits, think about targeting men.
   (increase)

0. Men are famous for _____*being*_____ difficult to sell to.
   (be)

1. In the past, _____ to men has been profitable only with certain products, such
   (market)

   as sports drinks and steaks.

2. Many men claim that they can't stand _____.
   (shop)

3. But that isn't stopping many marketing firms that would like _____ more male
   (attract)

   shoppers.

4. These marketing firms are attempting _____ out what makes men spend
   (find)

   money.

5. Finally, they are beginning _____ more about men's shopping habits.
   (understand)

6. Nearly 50 percent of married men say that they go shopping only when their wives persuade

   them _____.
   (go)

7. Only 7 percent of men say that they enjoy _____ clothes.
   (buy)

8. Most men do not stop _____ at things unless they already planned to buy them.
   (look)

9. The secret to _____ men is to do it before they come into the store.
   (target)

10. The marketing firms are offering _____ retailers attract more male customers.
    (help)

11. For more information on _____ to men, click <u>here</u>.
    (market)

6 | EDITING: SMART SHOPPERS

*Read Tamara's article in the school newspaper about being a smart shopper. There are
eleven mistakes. The first mistake is already corrected. Find and correct ten more.*

Are you a smart shopper? When is the last time you went to the mall in order ^to buy a sweater,

look for gifts, or eating lunch? If you do these things regularly, you're wasting your money. Smart

shoppers prefer to not spend more money than necessary. I quit to go to malls because the stores

there charge way too much. Besides, I got sick of to spend a lot of money on something, and then

hearing my roommate say that she found something similar at a thrift store for only a dollar or

two. I've learned that it's OK to check thrift stores first in order to not pay more money than

necessary. I believe on looking nice and fashionable, but not if I have to spend all my money to

do it. For instance, I needed buying a dress, and I found one for $70 at the mall. I regretted to

buy it the very next day when I found an even nicer dress at a thrift store for $10. If you are

enough rich to buy things without going into debt, go right ahead. After all, smart shoppers like

us need you buy things at full price so that we can have them later for much less money.

Unit 27 Achievement Test

---

1 | LISTENING: TIME TO PRACTICE

A. 🎧 *Phillip doesn't like practicing the violin. Listen to his conversation with his mother. Complete the conversation by writing the words that you hear. You will hear the recording two times.*

PHILLIP: Mom, I finished _____*doing*_____ my homework. Can I go out and play?
0.

MRS. SMITH: Not yet. You need to practice playing your violin first.

PHILLIP: Aw, Mom! _____ the violin is a waste of time. I can't stand
1.

practicing. I don't want to play the violin anymore. Can't I please go

skateboarding?

MRS. SMITH: You know I don't mind _____ you skateboard, but I want you to
2.

practice first. Quitting is not an option.

PHILLIP: But Mom, I miss hanging out with my friends. They keep _____ me
3.

where I am.

MRS. SMITH: Practice first, or you'll risk _____ your allowance this week.
4.

B. *Reread the conversation. Find one subject gerund and three object gerunds in the conversation. Write them in the table below. (Note: Only use words that are given in the conversation. Do not use any words that you wrote.) An example is given.*

SUBJECT GERUND	OBJECT GERUNDS
1. _____	0. _*playing*_____
	1. _____
	2. _____
	3. _____

2 | PHILLIP'S REQUEST FOR ADVICE

Phillip is asking for advice from a help columnist at a newspaper. Complete his letter. Use the gerunds in the box. Some items may have more than one right answer.

being	looking	~~practicing~~	skateboarding	telling
doing	making	seeing	staying	

Dear Greg,

    I need your help! I dislike _____*practicing*_____ the violin, but my mom won't stop
                                      0.

_____ me to practice! I enjoy _____ a lot more
        1.   **2.**

than I like the violin. Not _____ able to skateboard with my friends very
                                  3.

much is no fun. The weather outside is perfect, and _____ inside to
                                                                4.

practice is driving me crazy! It seems like my mom considers practicing the most important thing

in the world. Please tell me, what do you advise _____ to convince my
                                                              5.

mom to quit _____ me play the violin?
                   6.

Going Crazy

3 | GREG'S ADVICE

Complete Greg's letter of advice to Phillip. Use the correct gerund form of each verb.

Dear Going Crazy,

    When I was little, I resisted _____*learning*_____ to play the piano, too. I understand that
                                        0. (learn)

_____ inside to practice an instrument is not most kids' idea of fun, but you
        1. (stay)

should avoid _____ with your mother. Have you considered _____
                  2. (argue)   **3. (explore)**

other ways to deal with the problem? I suggest _____ out what you spend most of
                                                        4. (figure)

your time doing. Do you watch a lot of TV? _____ TV takes time away from
                                                    5. (watch)

doing other things that you enjoy. If you usually watch TV before you do your homework, you

could stop _____ TV, do your homework, and then use the extra time to
                6. (watch)

skateboard and practice the violin! _____ better ways to use your time should
                                            7. (find)

allow you to go skateboarding with your friends AND make your mom happy. Good luck!

4 | EDITING: NO MORE TV!

*Read Phillip's journal entry. There are ten mistakes in the use of gerunds. The first mistake is
already corrected. Find and correct nine more.*

Last month, the newspaper printed Greg's response to my letter for help. He had a great idea.

He suggested ~~to watch~~ *watching* less TV so that I could have more time to skateboard. I admit feel at first

like he was wrong. I denied waste my time. I considered to watch TV an important time for me

to relax before starting my homework. But Greg was right! I always avoided start my homework

until after I watched *two hours* of TV! At first, I missed watches my favorite shows. But I made

it a goal to finish do my homework at the school library before coming home. Now, think about

how much time I used to waste on TV makes me sick! Practice the violin is still not great fun, but

no practicing was worse because it made my mom mad, and it made me feel guilty!

PART VII

Unit 28 Achievement Test

30 Items
Score: _____

1 | LISTENING: APPLYING TO THE UNIVERSITY

A. 🎧 *Luz is applying to a university. Listen to her conversation with Sandy. Complete the conversation by writing the words that you hear. You will hear the recording two times.*

SANDY: Have you heard anything from the University of Greendale yet?

LUZ: No, but I plan on _____*contacting*_____ them if I don't hear from
0.

them soon. They've been really slow at letting me know their decision. I look forward to

finding out if I've been accepted or not. I'm so _____ rejected.
1.

SANDY: What will you do if you don't get in?

LUZ: I'm not sure. I could go back to Mexico, but I'm used _____ in
2.

the States now. I'm just annoyed with the admissions office for taking so long to let me

know their decision. I have to wait to hear from them before making any plans.

SANDY: So what are you interested in studying if you're accepted?

LUZ: Well, I've thought about getting a degree in physical therapy.

SANDY: Oh, really? I have an aunt who used _____ a physical therapist.
3.

She says they need people in that field. Don't worry too much about hearing from the

school. I'm sure you'll be accepted.

LUZ: Thanks. I hope so!

B. *Reread the conversation. Find six phrases with prepositions and gerunds. Write them below. (Note: Only use words that are given in the conversation. Do not use any words that you wrote.) An example is given.*

0. _*at letting*_____

1. _____

2. _____

3. _____

4. _____

5. _____

6. _____

2 | WAITING

Complete Luz's journal entry. Use the correct words in the box.

~~about not getting~~	on getting	to work	not getting
about receiving	of waiting	for taking	to waiting
to calling	about being	of waiting	before going

I'm concerned _____*about not getting*_____ a letter from the University of Greendale
                                    0.

yet. I've never been so excited _____ a piece of mail in my life! I'm
                                                    1.

afraid of _____ in. I'm sick _____! I'm not
                    2.   **3.**

used _____ so long for an answer. I used _____
                    4.   **5.**

in a college admissions office, so I know it doesn't need to take so long. It's been so long that

maybe I should resort _____ the admissions office instead
                                        6.

_____ for the letter. That way, I could insist _____
            7.   **8.**

an answer.

3 | GOOD NEWS!

*The University of Greendale has accepted Luz. Complete the paragraph. Use the gerund or
infinitive form of each verb.*

When I got my letter yesterday, I was so nervous about _____*opening*_____ it! I'm so
                                                            0. (open)

happy about _____ accepted to Greendale! I can't believe that I succeeded in
                    1. (be)

_____ in. I'm excited about _____ school. Greendale is famous for
    2. (get)   **3. (start)**

_____ an excellent physical therapy program. It's amazing that my English is good
    4. (have)

enough to study at a university! I used _____ very little English. I'm a little worried
                                        5. (know)

about _____ everything in the classroom. I'm used _____ English,
        6. (understand)   **7. (study)**

but not other subjects *in* English! I need to work on _____ to classroom talk.
                                                        8. (listen)

Maybe I could improve my listening by _____ in on some summer classes before
                                            9. (sit)

my physical therapy classes begin.

PART VII

4 | EDITING: E-MAIL TO A PROFESSOR

Read Luz's e-mail to a professor of physical therapy at the University of Greendale. There are five mistakes in the use of prepositions and gerunds. The first mistake is already corrected. Find and correct four more.

Dear Professor Hunt:

    I will be a new student at Greendale in the fall, and I'm interested ~~to observe~~ *in observing* some of your classes. I am from Mexico, and I used study in an English language program. If you are not opposed to have an observer, I would like to come to your classes so that I can get used to listen to classroom lectures before I start school in the fall. I look forward to hear from you.

Sincerely,

Luz Maria Lerma

Unit 29 Achievement Test

1 | LISTENING: RADIO CALL-IN SHOW

A. 🎧 *Camilla has a teenage daughter. Listen to Camilla's conversation with a radio talk show host. Complete the conversation by writing the words that you hear. You will hear the recording two times.*

TINA: You're listening to the *Tina Monroe Show*. Our next caller is Camilla in New Jersey.

Hi, Camilla.

CAMILLA: Hi, Tina. I need some advice on handling my teenage daughter.

TINA: OK.

CAMILLA: I expect her _____ *to hang out* _____ with her friends a lot, but it seems like
0.

she's *never* home.

TINA: Tell me more.

CAMILLA: Well, for instance, she'll promise to spend an evening with me, but if her friends call,

she'll go out with them instead. I ask her _____ out so much,
1.

but she does it anyway.

TINA: Are you worried about the friends she spends time with?

CAMILLA: A little bit. I just _____ who her friends are, but she refuses to
2.

bring them over. I encourage her to bring her friends home once in a while, but she

always decides to go somewhere else. I even _____ her friends
3.

to celebrate her birthday at a restaurant last month, but she planned her own party. I

don't think I'm being unreasonable, do you?

TINA: Stay on the line, Camilla. We need to take a short break, but I'll

_____ you when we come back. You're listening to the *Tina*
4.

Monroe Show.

PART VII

B. *Reread the conversation. Find three verbs followed by an infinitive and one verb followed by an object and an infinitive. Write them in the table below. (Note: Only use words that are given in the conversation. Do not use any words that you wrote.) An example is given.*

VERB + INFINITIVE	VERB + OBJECT + INFINITIVE
0. *promise to spend*	1. _____
1. _____	
2. _____	
3. _____	

---

2 | TINA'S ANSWER

Complete the rest of Tina and Camilla's conversation. Use the correct words in the box.

~~wants to meet~~	need to take	not to bring	to introduce
learn to trust	decides to go	fails to bring	choose to
to meet	promises	need to allow	come back

TINA: You're listening to the *Tina Monroe Show*. We have Camilla from New Jersey on the

line, and she _____*wants to meet*_____ her daughter's friends, but her daughter
        0.

prefers _____ them home. Is that right, Camilla?
        1.

CAMILLA: Yes, that's right.

TINA: Let me tell you, Camilla, you can't force your daughter _____
                                                                        2.

her friends to you. If your daughter _____ her friends
                                            3.

home, it isn't necessarily because her friends are bad. Teenagers value privacy,

so you _____ your daughter to have some privacy. If
            4.

you'd like _____ her friends, then you must
                5.

_____ your daughter. If she feels that you really trust
        6.

her, she might _____ bring her friends home on her own.
                        7.

3 | IN SUMMARY

Read the short conversations. Then use the information to help you complete the summary statement for each conversation. Use the correct forms of the verbs from the box, followed by an infinitive or an object + infinitive. Some items may have more than one right answer.

advise	choose	learn	remind	~~urge~~
agree	forget	plan	think	volunteer
ask	learn	promise		

0.　　SON: I don't know which college to apply to.

　　FATHER: I encourage you to apply to both. You never know who will accept you.

　　SUMMARY: The father _____ *urged his son to apply* _____ to both colleges.

1. MOTHER: Will you call me as soon as you arrive at the airport?

　　SON: OK, I will.

　　SUMMARY: The son _____ when he arrives at the airport.

2.　　MOTHER: Would you please clean your room before you go swimming?

　　DAUGHTER: Sure.

　　SUMMARY: The daughter _____ her room.

3.　　FATHER: I need someone to help clear the table.

　　DAUGHTER: I'll do it!

　　SUMMARY: The daughter _____ clear the table.

4.　　MOTHER: Don't forget to take your lunch to school.

　　DAUGHTER: I won't forget.

　　SUMMARY: The mother _____ her lunch.

5. MOTHER: Would you rather have hamburgers or chicken tonight?

　　SON: Let's have hamburgers!

　　SUMMARY: The son _____ hamburgers.

6.　　FATHER: Did you remember to lock the car door?

　　SON: No, I didn't. Oops!

　　SUMMARY: The son _____ the car door.

7. DAUGHTER: I don't know what to do. Should I get a job now or finish school first?

   FATHER: I think you should definitely finish school first.

   SUMMARY: The father _____ school first.

8. MOTHER: Will you be home for dinner tonight?

   DAUGHTER: Not tonight. I'm going to Elena's birthday party.

   SUMMARY: The daughter _____ to Elena's party.

9. SON: Dad, can I borrow the car to go to a movie this afternoon?

   FATHER: Sure.

   SUMMARY: The son _____ the car.

---

4 | EDITING: PLANNING A PARTY AT HOME

Read Camilla's daughter's journal. There are seven mistakes in the use of verbs, infinitives, and objects. The first mistake is already corrected. Find and correct six more. (Note: There may be more than one way to correct a mistake.)

                          to

My mom seems be relaxing about my friends. I think she trusts me more these days. I told

her today that I wanted to have some friends over for a party this weekend. She said, "OK, that's

fine." I thought she'd be much more excited. Anyway, she's going to help me to cleaning the

house. I also asked to make her famous homemade ice cream. I hope to invites a lot of people. I

managed to talked to about 10 people so far. I persuaded Mark come. He's so cute! And I also

told Bridget to bringing her CDs because she has a fabulous CD collection.

Unit 30 Achievement Test

30 Items
Score: _____

---

1 | LISTENING: INTERNET USE

A. 🎧 *Listen to this news report about why people use the Internet. Complete the report by writing the words that you hear. You will hear the recording two times.*

REPORTER: When the Internet first appeared, some thought that people would use it

_____*to buy*_____ everything they needed and that people would never have to
      0.

leave their homes to shop in stores again. Although that's not the case yet, online

shopping is definitely popular. According to a recent survey by the American Sales

Association (ASA), about 50 percent of Americans use the Internet to purchase items.

Many companies now use the Internet _____ their products, and every
      1.

day many more individuals and companies make their products available online in

order not to lose business.

    The ASA conducted this study _____ they wanted information
      2.

about how people were using the Internet. Results show that shopping is not the only

popular online activity. Forty-three percent of Americans use the Internet to e-mail

people. Thirty-five percent log on to find information. I'm at the local library now

asking a few people why they're using the Internet . . .

    Excuse me, Sir. Why are you using the Internet right now?

MAN: _____ the news. I figure, why pay for a paper when I can find the same
      3.

information for free online?

REPORTER: That's an interesting point. And why are you using the Internet, Ma'am?

WOMAN: _____ games. I'm always here playing games.
      4.

REPORTER: And there you have it. This is Janelle Williams, Network News Radio, Washington.

B. *Reread the news report. Find three affirmative infinitives of purpose and one negative infinitive of purpose. Write them in the table below. (Note: Only use words that are given in the report. Do not use any words that you wrote.) An example is given.*

AFFIRMATIVE INFINITIVES OF PURPOSE	NEGATIVE INFINITIVE OF PURPOSE
0. _to shop_	1. _____
1. _____	
2. _____	
3. _____	

2 | HOW PEOPLE USE THE INTERNET

Complete the paragraph about how people use the Internet. Use the words in the box.

because	in order to	to find	to look	to teach
e-mail	make	to give	to study	~~to use~~
in order not to	to do	to go		

There are some really interesting ways _____to use_____ the Internet. Many teachers go
0.

online _____ up information for their lesson plans, and some even use the Internet
1.

in their classrooms _____ certain lessons. Then there are students who use the
2.

Internet _____ a language or _____ homework. Of course, students
3.   4.

need to be careful how they use the Internet _____ steal someone else's ideas.
5.

Students can get in a lot of trouble for using another person's ideas without permission. Some

people search the Internet _____ songs and _____ CDs. Finally,
6.   7.

people use the Internet _____ it is often the fastest way to communicate with
8.

people.

3 | MESSAGE BOARD

Complete these sentences from an online message board about how people are using the Internet. Use the correct form of each verb.

0. I go online _____*to check*_____ how much money I have in my bank account.
   0. (check)

1. I've searched the Internet _____ out when to plant my tomatoes.
   1. (find)

2. I made my own Web page in order _____ old friends a way to find me.
   2. (give)

3. I search the Internet _____ directions before I drive somewhere for the first time.
   3. (get)

4. I use the Internet _____ the snow report on the mountain before I go skiing.
   4. (read)

5. I got rid of my old dictionary and use the Internet _____ new words online.
   5. (look up)

6. I've never used the Internet _____ groceries. I prefer to see the food before I
   6. (order)
   buy it.

7. I go online _____ the weather before I plan anything outdoors.
   7. (check)

8. I don't write letters anymore, and I prefer to use the Internet _____ my friends.
   8. (e-mail)

9. I look for things I want to buy on the Internet first in order _____ more than I
   9. (not / pay)
   need to.

4 | EDITING: STUDENT ERRANDS

Read the conversation between two college students. There are six mistakes in the use of expressions of purpose. The first mistake is already corrected. Find and correct five more.

PHILLIP: I just went to the bookstore in order to ~~bought~~ *buy* my books, but the line was so long!

GREG: I know. I went online buy my books a couple of days ago. I usually buy my books

online not in order to stand in line at the bookstore and cause the prices are usually

better than in the bookstore.

PHILLIP: That's a good idea. Hey, I need to go out again to eat lunch, get a newspaper, and

sending a letter. Do you want to come?

GREG: Thanks, but I can't. I need to read this article now order to finish it before class.

Unit 31 Achievement Test

1 | LISTENING: TOO BUSY

A. 🎧 *Listen to the conversation between Eduardo and his psychologist Dr. Packard. Complete the conversation by writing the words that you hear. You will hear the recording two times.*

EDUARDO: Doctor, I'm so busy all the time. When I was young, I was

_____*calm enough to relax*_____, and I didn't feel like I had to rush everywhere.
0.

Now, unscheduled moments are too short to enjoy and too few to remember. And

when I do have a free moment, I'm usually too tense to relax.

DR. PACKARD: Do you ever schedule time to relax?

EDUARDO: No, I'm _____. The days aren't long enough to do
1.

everything that I need to do. How can I add relaxing to my schedule?

DR. PACKARD: How does it feel when you can't get everything done that you need to do?

EDUARDO: I feel mad enough to scream!

DR. PACKARD: It makes you _____ to go crazy, doesn't it?
2.

EDUARDO: Absolutely!

DR. PACKARD: You know, sometimes we schedule our days too tightly to do everything we need

or want to do and that can be upsetting. I want you to read this book about

something called the "Slow Movement." Will you read it and return it to me next

week?

EDUARDO: Sure, it looks _____.
3.

B. *Reread the conversation. Find three phrases with* **too** *+ adjective / adverb + infinitive and two phrases with adjective +* **enough** *+ infinitive. Write them in the table below. (Note: Only use words that are given in the conversation. Do not use any words that you wrote.) An example is given.*

TOO + ADJECTIVE / ADVERB + INFINITIVE	ADJECTIVE + *ENOUGH* + INFINITIVE
0. *too short to enjoy*	1. _____
1. _____	2. _____
2. _____	
3. _____	

---

2 | FASTER IS NOT ALWAYS BETTER

Complete the following sentences from the book about the Slow Movement. Use the phrases in the box.

~~fast enough to do~~	~~too productive to enjoy~~	too busy to do
good enough to make	too hard to be	too full to allow
well enough to stay	too late to make	too fast to be
rare enough to count	relaxed enough to sleep	too bad to count
too long to have time	stressed enough to be	too good to be
long enough to spend	productive enough to get	too stressed to be

0. People can't seem to move _____ *fast enough to do* _____ everything that they want.

0. Sometimes people try to be _____ *too productive to enjoy* _____ what they are doing.

1. People feel _____ the things that are important to them.

2. They are trying _____ productive.

3. Many people's schedules are simply _____ them to accomplish everything.

4. People often feel that their best isn't _____ them successful.

PART VII

5. It is never _____ changes that will improve your life.

6. People often drive _____ safe.

7. Relaxing moments in a year are _____ on one hand.

8. At night, people are often not _____ well.

9. Parents are often not home _____ time with their kids.

10. I feel guilty if I'm not _____ everything done that I plan.

11. People often do not eat _____ healthy because they think

it takes too much time.

12. People are at work _____ for other meaningful things.

13. Many people become _____ healthy.

3 | DR. PACKARD'S NOTES

Complete Dr. Packard's notes about his meeting with Eduardo. Use **too** *or* **enough** *and the words provided.*

Eduardo is often _____*too stressed to function*_____ normally. He says that
　　　　　　　　　　0. (stressed / function)

work is _____ him seriously consider quitting. He
　　　　　　1. (stressful / to make)

wakes up _____ rested. He comes home
　　　　　2. (early / feel)

_____ dinner with his family. He says that sometimes
3. (late / eat)

he feels _____ for two whole days.
　　　　4. (tired / sleep)

4 | EDITING: A NEW LIFE

*Read Eduardo's journal. There are six mistakes in the use of **too** and **enough**. The first mistake is already corrected. Find and correct five more.*

I've decided to simplify my life! I quit my job because I was too anxious~~be~~ to be valuable to the

company anymore. After meeting with Dr. Packard, I felt that my happiness was enough

important to fight for. I was getting too frustrated to handling the stress. Now I have a new job.

It pays less, but it's too relaxing me to complain about the money. Besides, the salary is enough

high to pay the bills. Before, my time at home was to short to play with my kids. Now I have the

time to play with them, and it's wonderful!

Unit 32 Achievement Test

30 Items
Score: _____

1 | LISTENING: THE "PRINCE OF CLEAN"

A. 🎧 *Listen to part of a radio program called* The Pablo Show. *Pablo is interviewing Nick Politz, the "Prince of Clean." Complete the interview by writing the words that you hear. You will hear the recording two times.*

PABLO: We're back. I'm Pablo Jimenez. Our next guest is cleaning expert Nick Politz, who calls

himself the "Prince of Clean." We have an e-mail from Elena in Michigan. She writes, "I

don't mind _____*cleaning*_____, but I never seem to have the time." Nick, what do you
                      0.

do if it's difficult _____ time for housework?
                          1.

NICK: Well, keeping your house clean doesn't have to take a lot of time. The problem is that

many people don't clean for a long time, and then they end up _____ a lot
                                                                      2.

of time and effort after weeks of neglect. You should plan to spend a little bit of time

cleaning each week. It's easier to keep the house clean if you can remember

_____ a little bit each week.
       3.

PABLO: Nick Politz, the "Prince of Clean," thank you for being on our show today.

NICK: You're most welcome, Pablo. I appreciated being here.

PABLO: If you'd like _____ pictures of the "Prince of Clean" as he was cleaning
                           4.

our studios, visit our website at www.thepabloshow.org.

B. *Reread the program. Find two phrases with gerunds and two phrases with infinitives. Write them in the table below. (Note: Only use words that are given in the program. Do not use any words with that you wrote.) Two examples are given.*

PHRASES WITH GERUNDS	PHRASES WITH INFINITIVES
0. *keeping your house clean*	0. *seem to have*
1. _____	1. _____
2. _____	2. _____

2 | WHAT'S YOUR CLEANING PERSONALITY?

Complete some people's statements about their cleaning personalities. Circle the correct words or phrases.

0. When I finish (cleaning)/ to clean / to cleaning, I feel satisfied.

0. I intend (to keep)/ to keeping / keeping my house clean, but I usually don't have time.

1. I can't stand to scrubbing / to scrub / scrubbing the toilet.

2. I enjoy to have / to having / having a clean house.

3. I prefer not clean / to cleaning / to clean, but I'll do it if the house is dirty.

4. I rarely delay wash / to wash / washing my dishes after a meal.

5. I would have a housecleaner if I could afford to hire / hiring / hire one.

6. I usually choose cleaning / clean / to clean the house on the weekends.

7. If I fail to keeping / keeping / to keep my house clean, I feel guilty.

8. I usually put off cleaning / clean / to cleaning my house until I know that someone is coming over.

9. If I see something out of place, I stop to putting / to put / putting it away immediately.

10. Sometimes I forget to throw / throw / throwing out old food that is in the refrigerator.

11. I look forward to clean / cleaning / be cleaning my house.

12. Just about anything is more fun than clean / to clean / cleaning the house.

3 | THE PABLO SHOW WEBSITE

Complete this paragraph from The Pablo Show *website about the "Prince of Clean." Use the gerund or infinitive form of each verb. Some items may have more than one right answer.*

When Nick Politz, also known as the "Prince of Clean," was here, he offered

_____ *to give* _____ our cleaning staff some advice about cleaning the studios. In this picture, he
0. (give)

began _____ the floor. Politz suggested _____ a new vacuum cleaner.
1. (vacuum)   **2. (buy)**

He arranged _____ his favorite one sent to us and warned us not to forget
3. (have)

_____ it after each use. In this picture, he was showing the cleaning staff his
4. (empty)

method of _____. One member of our cleaning staff, Ernie, said he has been
5. (dust)

cleaning buildings for 25 years and regrets not _____ about the prince's dusting
6. (know)

technique earlier. Politz promised _____ again soon to see how the staff is doing.
7. (visit)

4 | EDITING: E-MAIL TO NICK POLITZ

Read this e-mail to Nick Politz, the "Prince of Clean." There are four mistakes in the use of gerunds and infinitives. The first mistake is already corrected. Find and correct three more.

Dear Nick,

    I usually avoid ~~to clean~~ *cleaning* at all costs, but I realized that I can't postpone to do housework all my

life. This year, I've promised myself being better about cleaning, but it's hard for me making the

change. Can you recommend anything for people like me?

Sincerely,

Kara Peterson

PART VII Achievement Test

60 Items
Score: _____

---

1 | LISTENING: MOVING

A. 🎧 *Marisol and Theo are married. They're moving to a new house. Listen to their conversation. Complete the conversation by writing the words that you hear. You will hear the recording two times.*

MARISOL: I'm going to the store. We need _____*to buy*_____ some boxes, and I plan on getting

      0.

      some extra tape too. Are you interested in going with me?

THEO: Why do you want to buy boxes? We can get them for free at the grocery store.

MARISOL: Yeah, but then they won't be all the same size. I _____ free boxes, but

      1.

      couldn't stack them very easily. Besides, grocery store boxes are _____.

      2.

THEO: Not having boxes that are all the same size is no problem. We can just pack them well.

      I don't think we should buy boxes _____ I don't want to waste money.

      3.

      We can get them for free!

MARISOL: But it's easy for the boxes to fall and for things to get damaged if they don't stack well

      in the truck. Believe me, I used grocery store boxes _____ save money

      4.

      once, but then I spent money to replace the things that got broken.

THEO: OK . . . let's go see how much they cost.

B. *Reread the conversation. Find two gerunds and two infinitives. Write them in the table below. (Note: Only use words that are given in the conversation. Do not use any words that you wrote.) Two examples are given.*

GERUNDS	INFINITIVES
0. *getting*	0. *to fall*
1. _____	1. _____
2. _____	2. _____

PART VII

2 | MARISOL'S JOURNAL

Complete Marisol's journal about going with Theo to buy moving boxes. Use the words in the box. Some items may have more than one right answer. Some words can be used more than once.

being	going	spending	to buy	to let	to spend
buying	letting	thinking	to get	to move	to watch
getting	moving	to be	to go	~~to pack~~	watching

It was interesting _____*to pack*_____ our things today. I told Theo that I'd like
                              0.

_____ some packing boxes. Theo didn't like that idea. In general, he avoids
          1.

_____ money, and he prefers _____ things for free whenever
          2.   **3.**

possible. He said there were free boxes at the supermarket we could use. I'm also afraid

_____ too much money during our move, but _____ is something
          4.   **5.**

that I recognize costs some money. I had to persuade him _____ me buy the boxes.
                                                                    6.

He finally agreed _____ with me, I think because he wanted to see how expensive
                         7.

the boxes were. Well, the moving company had a bunch of grocery store boxes stacked up to

show how difficult they are to move with. When he saw that, he stopped _____ so
                                                                              8.

nervous about spending the money. It was interesting _____ his attitude change
                                                              9.

when he saw the display. We ended up _____ some great boxes that will all stack
                                              10.

very nicely.

3 | TOO FRUGAL

A frugal person does not like to spend money, and sometimes that can be a problem. Complete these sentences from a magazine article about being extremely frugal. Circle the correct words or phrases.

0. Some sources say that around 5 percent of Americans are obsessed with not

   (spending)/ spend / to spend money.

0. People who are very frugal sometimes feel guilty about spending money, even if they need

   buy / buying /(to buy) something, like food.

1. Overly frugal people are addicted to save / saving / to saving.

2. They refuse to go to shop / shopping / to shopping even if they have money to spend.

3. Sometimes they are too frugal / too frugal not / frugal enough to buy things they need.

4. They think that everything is too expensive not / too expensive / expensive enough to be

   worth the price.

5. They can't get used to spend / to spending / spending money on things they consider

   unnecessary.

6. Sometimes their husbands and wives become too frustrated / too frustrated not /

   frustrated enough to file for divorce.

7. Extremely frugal people usually try fulfill / to fulfilling / to fulfill some kind of need that

   they have by saving money.

8. They try not to spend money to proving / proving / to prove to themselves that they can

   live simply.

9. Walking / To walking / Walk into a store is something they rarely do.

10. If you think you are too frugal, don't postpone to get / to getting / getting help.

11. Extremely frugal people usually find it too hard / too hard not / enough hard to change on

    their own.

4 | THEO'S JOURNAL

Complete Theo's journal about buying boxes with Marisol. Use the gerund or infinitive forms of the verbs in the box. Some words may be used more than once. Some items may have more than one right answer.

admit	buy	get	help	look	waste
ask	finish	go	insist	spend	work

We're getting close to _____*finishing*_____ our packing. Marisol asked me

_____**0.**_____ with her to buy boxes. I considered _____**2.**_____ boxes to be a

1.

waste of money because there are free boxes everywhere, and _____**3.**_____ money is

something that *I* never do. I remember _____**4.**_____ some neighbors move one time.

Their boxes were all free, and they seemed _____**5.**_____ just fine. I really resisted

_____**6.**_____ that it was OK to spend money on boxes. At first, I was kind of

annoyed with Marisol for _____**7.**_____ that we buy them. I was nervous about

_____**8.**_____ a lot of money. I finally relaxed when I saw in the store how unstable the

free boxes were, and I decided _____**9.**_____ all our boxes there. Maybe we didn't buy

enough, and I'm thinking about _____**10.**_____ back to buy some more.

5 | NOMADS

Nomads are people who don't have permanent homes and move according to the seasons. Complete these sentences from an Internet article about nomads. Use the gerund or infinitive form of each verb in parentheses.

0. If you have too much stuff and want _____*to get*_____ rid of things, think like a nomad.
   (get)

0. Nomads are known for _____*being*_____ able to survive without very much.
   (be)

1. Nomads are good travelers, stopping only _____. They can even eat while
   (sleep)

   traveling.

2. _____ for a nomad simply means taking whatever you or your animals can
   (move)

   carry.

3. Nomads avoid _____ houses or land.
   (own)

4. But that doesn't mean that nomads don't need _____ money.
   (make)

5. A group of researchers is attempting _____ about the role of nomads in the
   (learn)
   economy of Indian towns and cities.

6. Finally, they are beginning _____ more about nomads' financial habits.
   (discover)

7. The problem with _____ about nomads is that it requires living like them too.
   (learn)

8. Because nomads avoid _____ property, they usually do not have voting rights.
   (buy)

9. Some groups are encouraging lawmakers _____ the impact of new land laws
   (consider)
   on India's nomads.

10. The researchers are offering _____ their findings with everyone who is
    (share)
    interested.

11. If you're interested in _____ more about nomads' economic influence in India,
    (read)
    click here.

---

6 | EDITING: SMART MOVERS

*Read Theo's blog about being a smart mover. There are eleven mistakes. The first mistake is
already corrected. Find and correct ten more.*

    Are you a smart mover? The last time you needed ^to^ move, did you take the time to ask for

help, tell others you were packing, or talking to professional movers? Smart movers prefer to not

do it alone. I used to move alone because I thought it was my own responsibility. But I quit to try

to move all by myself because I got sick of to spend so much time and energy, and other people

were happy to help. I've learned that it's OK to ask people to help in order to not waste my time

and energy. I believe on helping other people, so why shouldn't I let them help me? For instance,

I needed putting my refrigerator onto a moving truck. I did it by myself, but I later realized to do

that was a mistake. I was so sore the next day that I couldn't get out of bed! If you are enough

strong to move a refrigerator by yourself, feel free. But smart movers like me need people like

you help us sometimes!

PART VIII Diagnostic Test

60 Items
Score: _____

---

1 | LISTENING: LATE FOR THE PICNIC

A. 🎧 *Listen to this telephone conversation between two friends. Complete the conversation by writing the words that you hear. You will hear the recording two times.*

LISA: Hello?

MELISSA: Hi Lisa! It's Melissa. How are things going?

LISA: OK. I have to go to a picnic for my co-workers and their families this afternoon.

I _____ *'m supposed to* _____ help with the kids' activities.
         0.

MELISSA: When _____ leave?
                        1.

LISA: I was supposed to leave 20 minutes ago, but I lost my keys.

MELISSA: They _____ there somewhere. Or maybe your son has them.
                      2.

LISA: I'm not sure. Actually, now that I think about it, he must have them. They can't be in

this house. I've looked everywhere!

MELISSA: _____ he'll be back soon?
                    3.

LISA: I hope so! He wasn't supposed to be gone for very long. In fact, he

_____ back by 3:00, but it's already 4:00 now!
              4.

MELISSA: Do you need a ride?

LISA: That would be great if it's not too much trouble. But my son might get back before you

get here. If he does, I'll call your cell phone.

MELISSA: OK.

B. *Reread the conversation. Then read each statement and circle* **T** *(true) or* **F** *(false).*

T **Ⓕ** 0. Lisa doesn't need to go to the picnic.

T **F** 1. Lisa was planning to leave 20 minutes ago.

T **F** 2. Lisa is almost 100 percent certain that her son has the keys.

T **F** 3. Lisa's son had plans to be gone for a long time.

T **F** 4. Lisa is almost 100 percent certain that her son will return before Melissa gets there.

2 | TRAFFIC JAM

Read Melissa and Lisa's conversation in the car. Write each underlined verb phrase in the correct category below. An example is given.

MELISSA: I can't believe this traffic! There <u>must be</u> a faster way to the park.

LISA: <u>I'd rather not walk</u> all the way there, but it might be faster than driving!

MELISSA: I know! Originally they <u>were going to finish</u> construction on this road six months ago. I can't believe they're still working on it.

LISA: I can't either.

MELISSA: I <u>was going to get</u> on Stanley Avenue, but I think we <u>have to take</u> a different route. Stanley Avenue is closed.

LISA: That's too bad. It's the fastest way to get there.

MELISSA: I know. OK . . . I <u>have got to change</u> lanes. This one is too slow. And we <u>must get</u> in front of this truck. I can't see anything when we're behind it. Oh, let's take this street here.

LISA: Be careful! You <u>can't turn</u> there. It's a one-way street.

MELISSA: Oops! Sorry. <u>Do you think</u> 22nd Street will be faster? We <u>could try</u> it and see.

LISA: No, <u>I'd rather take</u> the freeway. It's <u>got to be</u> faster than 22nd Street.

EXPRESSES A PREFERENCE	EXPRESSES A NECESSITY	EXPRESSES PROHIBITION	EXPRESSES A PAST EXPECTATION	EXPRESSES A POSSIBILITY	EXPRESSES A CONCLUSION
1. _____ _____	1. _____ _____	1. _____ _____	1. _____ _____	1. _____ _____	0. *must be* _____
2. _____ _____	2. _____ _____		2. _____ _____	2. _____ _____	1. _____ _____
	3. _____ _____				

3 | LOOKING FOR THE PICNIC

Read another conversation between Lisa and Melissa in the car. Complete the conversation with the correct words or phrases. Write the letter of the best answer on each line.

LISA: I'm starving! I ___c___ (a. 'm supposed b. must c. 'd like d. 'd rather) to eat as soon as I
0.
get there!

MELISSA: _____ (a. Are they going to b. May they c. Are they supposed d. Might they) have hamburgers
1.
and hot dogs?

LISA: They might. I usually _____ (a. 'd rather b. 'd prefer c. prefer d. rather) hot dogs.
2.

MELISSA: Really? I prefer having a hamburger _____ (a. than b. or c. to d. of) eating a hot dog
3.
any day.

LISA: Well, the guy who is cooking them is a chef, so I think everything _____ (a. will must
4.
be b. could be c. mustn't be d. maybe) really good.

MELISSA: So, you're in charge of the kids' activities?

LISA: Yeah. When I get there, I _____ (a. 've got to b. might c. 'd prefer d. 'd rather) set up
5.
everything right away. I was supposed to do it earlier. I hope I'm not too late.

MELISSA: Maybe someone has already set up and you _____ (a. may not b. couldn't c. don't have to
6.
d. must not) do it. Anyway, you _____ (a. don't have to b. must not c. might not d. can't)
7.
arrive right on time to a picnic. Everyone knows it's not really necessary.

LISA: I don't know. You _____ (a. would b. 're supposed to c. would rather d. may) be right.
8.

MELISSA: Oh, there are a bunch of people over there getting out of cars. I'm not sure, but that
_____ (a. might b. 's going to c. has to d. is supposed to) be them.
9.

LISA: Yeah, I see people wearing shirts with the company name. That _____ (a. may
10.
b. 's going to c. 's supposed to d. 's got to) be them. No one else has those shirts.

MELISSA: That's good. You _____ (a. can't b. don't have to c. would rather not d. aren't supposed to)
11.
be too late if other people are still arriving. Hey, do you want a ride home?

LISA: Maybe. If my son doesn't call me in the next few hours, then he _____ (a. can't
12.
b. 'd rather c. might d. is supposed to) be busy, and I'll call you.

4 | AT THE PICNIC

*Complete these sentences from conversations at the picnic. Use the correct forms of **would rather, would prefer, have to, be supposed to, may, might, could,** or **can't**. Some items may have more than one right answer.*

0. Sorry I'm late. I _____*was supposed to*_____ get here a while ago. At least that was my plan, but I lost my keys.

1. In the end my friend _____ give me a ride. I didn't have any other way to get here.

2. If you don't live too far, maybe Steve _____ take you home. But you should ask him, because I don't know for sure.

3. I _____ eat than play volleyball. I'm hungry!

4. Everyone _____ eat a hot dog at a picnic. It's a tradition.

5. We _____ have a barbecue without hot dogs! It's impossible!

6. I _____ have a hot dog than a hamburger. I don't really like hamburgers.

7. I _____ set up the kids' activities. I need to do it because I said I would.

8. I called Seth's house, but he didn't answer. He _____ be on his way here, but I don't know for sure.

9. Kim isn't here yet, either. She _____ be with Seth, I guess. I really don't know.

10. I _____ start the games now than wait for Seth.

11. I can't stay at the picnic too late because I made plans with Koko. I _____ take her home early.

5 | HOW TO BARBECUE

To barbecue *means to cook food on a metal frame over a fire outdoors. People often barbecue at picnics. Complete this Internet article about how to barbecue. Use the correct words or phrases. The first letter of each word or phrase is provided. Some items may have more than one right answer.*

Most people would r___ather___ eat barbecued meat t_____ meat cooked just about any
               0.   **1.**

other way. So why don't people barbecue more? Here are a few possible reasons. It m_____
                                                                          2.

be because they don't have a grill. Or maybe they think that barbecuing h_____ to take a
                                                                 3.

long time. But you d_____ have to wait until you're invited to a picnic to enjoy a barbecue.
                     4.

You can do it yourself pretty easily. Here's how:

First, you've g_____ to have a nice piece of meat. If the meat is tough, soaking it in
                            5.

vinegar is s_____ to make it tender. You can add some salt before you cook it, or if you'd
                     6.

p_____ to add barbecue sauce, that works, too.
7.

If you don't have a grill, you m_____ find one. You can't barbecue without a grill! Public
                                            8.

parks sometimes have them. The fire must n_____ be too hot, or the meat will burn on the
                                          9.

outside, and it m_____ be raw on the inside. That's not a very tasty possibility! Watch the
                     10.

meat carefully to be sure it doesn't cook too much. When it's ready, eat and enjoy!

6 | EDITING: BACK HOME

Lisa is back home talking to her son Nelson. There are nine mistakes in the conversation. The first mistake is already corrected. Find and correct eight more. (Note: There can be more than one way to correct a mistake.)

LISA: I was going ~~take~~ *to* take the car today, but I couldn't find the keys. Do you have them?

NELSON: Oh, sorry. I guess I took them by accident.

LISA: You must to remember to leave them by the door. And I prefer know when you're going to be home.

NELSON: I know. Hey, I was going use the car tomorrow at 2:30. Is that OK?

LISA: Sorry, but I need it then. I have an appointment at 3:00.

NELSON: But I have an appointment too. And I can't to miss it. It's a job interview at Fiamont.

LISA: Oh! That's suppose to be a good company. You must being really excited.

NELSON: I am!

LISA: Well, I can try to change my appointment, but I mayn't be able to. Or, I maybe able to take the bus. I would rather take the bus than make you miss this opportunity. I'll go check the bus schedule.

NELSON: Thanks a lot, Mom. I appreciate it.

Unit 33 Achievement Test

30 Items

Score: _____

1 | LISTENING: HOUSE HUNTING

A. 🎧 *A real estate agent helps people buy, rent, and sell homes. Listen to this telephone conversation between Arlene and a real estate agent. Complete the conversation by writing the words that you hear. You will hear the recording two times.*

AGENT: Thank you for calling ABC Realty. How can I help you?

ARLENE: Well, my husband and I are looking for a place to rent. We ___*'d prefer*___
0.
a house to an apartment. Also, we'd rather not spend more than $800 a month.

AGENT: Well, there are some nice houses for rent in the West End.

ARLENE: Actually, we prefer to live on the North Side—closer to our jobs at the university.

AGENT: OK. There are some good one- and two-bedroom places available there.

ARLENE: _____ two bedrooms.
1.

AGENT: All right. I know of a nice house around there for $750 a month. Would you be

interested in seeing it?

ARLENE: Sure. But I prefer to see places with my husband. Oh, are pets allowed there?

AGENT: I'm sorry, but the landlord _____ to people with pets.
2.

ARLENE: That's too bad. We have a cat, so that won't work. What else do you have?

AGENT: Well, there's an apartment on Center Street. It's very close to the university. And there's

another house that's a little bigger, but it's further away from campus.

ARLENE: Well, my husband would rather walk to work than drive. But I'd rather rent a big house

_____ a small apartment. So I guess we should see both.
3.

AGENT: Great. How about taking a look at them tonight? _____
4.

because places in that neighborhood are going fast.

ARLENE: OK. Sounds good.

B. *Reread the conversation. Find four verb phrases that express preference. Write them below. (Note: Only use words that are given in the conversation. Do not use any words that you wrote.) An example is given.*

0. _____ 'd rather not spend _____

1. _____

2. _____

3. _____

4. _____

---

2 | MOVING IN

Arlene and her husband TJ have found a house to rent. Now they are talking about organizing things in their new house as they move in. Complete these sentences from their conversation. Circle the correct words or phrases.

0. I'd prefer to putting /(to put)/ put the bookshelves on the wall opposite the window.

1. I prefer / rather / 'd rather move the bookshelf into the master bedroom.

2. I rather / 'd rather / prefer putting the couch in front of the fireplace.

3. I prefer organizing one room at a time than / to / or unpacking all the boxes at once.

4. I 'd rather / prefer / 'd prefer keep the silverware in the top drawer.

5. I prefer keep / to keeping / to keep the towels in the closet.

6. I'd rather not putting / not to put / not put the plates in the cupboards until after I clean them.

7. I'd prefer eating early than / and / to waiting until after we finish unpacking.

8. I'd rather order out than to cook / cook / cooking since the kitchen is a mess.

3 | WHERE DOES IT GO?

Arlene and TJ are still moving in. Complete these sentences from their conversation. Use
prefer, rather, rather not, than, *or* **to.**

0. I'd _____*prefer*_____ to put the mirror in the bathroom.

1. I'd _____ hang that picture in the living room.

2. I'd _____ put the CDs in a drawer. Let's leave them out instead.

3. I'd _____ cover the crack in the floor with a rug.

4. I _____ white towels in the small bathroom.

5. I'd _____ to keep the computer in the corner.

6. I'd _____ put that lamp in here. Let's put it in the living room instead.

7. I'd _____ to move the boxes off the table so we have a place to eat.

8. I'd prefer blue curtains _____ green ones.

9. I'd prefer keeping the plants in the kitchen _____ putting them in the garage.

10. I'd rather clean the blinds _____ replace them.

4 | EDITING: HOUSEWARMING PARTY

*Arlene and TJ have finished moving in and decorating. Read their conversation. There are
five mistakes in the use of* **prefer** *and* **would rather.** *The first mistake is already corrected.
Find and correct four more. (Note: There can be more than one way to correct a mistake.)*

ARLENE: We should have a party so our friends can come see how the house looks.

TJ: Great idea. Would you rather ~~sending~~ ^{send} invitations or just call people?

ARLENE: I rather would call people.

TJ: I agree. I'd rather not to send invitations because it's too much work. When would you

prefer to have the party, on a Saturday or a Sunday?

ARLENE: Well, I generally would prefer parties on Saturday evenings. But if we want people to

see the house during the day, then a Sunday afternoon would be nice. So I guess I would

rather have it on a Sunday afternoon.

TJ: Sounds good. We could do it this weekend or next weekend.

ARLENE: I'd prefer next weekend than this one.

Unit 34 Achievement Test

1 | LISTENING: THE APPLICATION PROCESS

A. 🎧 *Listen to this conversation about applying for a job. Complete the conversation by writing the words that you hear. You will hear the recording two times.*

KIRSTEN: Clifton General Hospital. This is Kirsten. How can I help you?

TERESA: Hi, I'm calling about the nursing position advertised in the Sunday paper. Can you give me some more information about the application process?

KIRSTEN: Sure. Go to our website. It's www.cliftongeneralhospital.com. There's an application form there. You _____*have to complete*_____ it and send it back to us.
0.

TERESA: OK. Do I have to send my résumé with it too? I've had to do that for some other jobs I've applied for.

KIRSTEN: Yes. In fact, you've got to read the application instructions carefully and send everything we need. We _____ all the information
1.
together to evaluate your application.

TERESA: All right. And _____ all the information?
2.

KIRSTEN: You can, but you can use regular mail too, or you can fax it. But we

_____ it by May 31st. It can't be late. If we receive
3.

your application after the deadline, we can't accept it.

TERESA: OK. Where _____ the completed application?
4.

KIRSTEN: The e-mail address, street address, and fax number are all on the website.

TERESA: Great. Thanks for your help.

KIRSTEN: You're welcome.

B. *Reread the conversation. Find two verb phrases that express necessity and two verb phrases that express prohibition. Write them in the table below. (Note: Only use words that are given in the conversation. Do not use any words that you wrote.) An example is given.*

PHRASES THAT EXPRESS NECESSITY	PHRASES THAT EXPRESS PROHIBITION
0. *Do I have to send* _____	1. _____
1. _____	2. _____
2. _____	

2 | REQUIREMENTS AND RESPONSIBILITIES

Read these sentences about nurses' requirements and responsibilities. Complete the sentences with the correct words or phrases. Write the letter of the best answer on each line.

0. Students _____c_____ (a. got b. can c. must d. have got) have good grades to get into nursing school.

1. If you want to be a nurse, you _____ (a. will have to b. got to c. must to d. can) finish nursing school. It's a requirement for becoming a nurse.

2. Nurses _____ (a. must not b. can't c. don't have to d. must) spend as much time in school as doctors do. Doctors are usually required to spend several more years in school than nurses.

3. Nurses in the United States _____ (a. don't have to b. must not c. can't d. must) have a nursing license for the state where they want to work. A license is required.

4. Nurses _____ (a. have to b. got to c. can d. must not) know and follow all the hospital's rules. If they don't, they'll lose their jobs.

5. They _____ (a. don't have to b. have to c. had to d. can) wash their hands before visiting each patient. This is a very important rule.

6. Nurses _____ (a. don't have to b. mustn't to c. can't d. must) prescribe medication to patients. Only doctors are allowed to prescribe medication.

7. They _____ (a. must to b. have got c. had to d. 've got to) make sure patients' records are accurate. This is one of their responsibilities.

8. They _____ **(a. must not b. can c. don't have to d. haven't got to)** cause any harm to patients. Their job is to protect the patients from harm.

9. They _____ **(a. have b. have got to c. must not d. can)** communicate well with doctors. Good communication is extremely important.

10. It is very important to give each patient special attention. Nurses _____ **(a. don't have to b. can't c. mustn't to d. haven't got to)** forget that each patient is an individual and that he or she deserves the best care possible.

---

3 | HOSPITAL RULES FOR VISITORS

Complete these rules for visitors to a hospital. Use the correct form of **(not) have to, have got to, must (not),** *or* **can't**. *Some items may have more than one right answer.*

0. Visitors to the hospital _____*must*_____ follow these rules. The rules are necessary for the health and safety of all patients.

1. Visitors _____ sign in at the front desk. You will not be allowed to visit guests until you sign in.

2. Children _____ be with an adult at all times. They are not permitted to enter the hospital without an adult.

3. Visitors _____ use cell phones in patients' rooms. Cell phones may interfere with some medical equipment, and this could be dangerous for patients.

4. But visitors _____ turn off their cell phones. They may keep them on and use them in public areas.

5. Visitors _____ bring animals into the hospital. Animals are not permitted because they could carry diseases that might harm patients.

6. Visitors who are sick _____ wear a mask. Masks are required because they help prevent spreading sickness to patients.

7. For security reasons, visitors _____ spend the night in waiting areas. If you stay at the hospital overnight, you need to be in a patient's room.

PART VIII

8. Large numbers of people _____ visit a patient in small groups. There is a limit of three guests per patient at one time.

9. If you visit a patient after 11:00 P.M., you _____ use the Emergency Room entrance to the hospital. The other entrances are closed.

4 | EDITING: E-MAIL TO SARAH

Read this e-mail from Teresa to her sister Sarah. There are four mistakes in expressing necessity. The first mistake is already corrected. Find and correct three more.

Hi Sarah,

    I can't believe that I've been out of nursing school for a month already! I have $\overset{to}{\wedge}$ get a job soon!

I'm applying for a position at Clifton General Hospital. Yesterday I have to fill out an application.

I must to send it in today because the deadline is tomorrow.

    What have you been up to? We have to get together soon so we can catch up on everything.

    Well, I just wanted to say hi. I've got go mail my application. Wish me luck!

Love,

Teresa

Unit 35 Achievement Test

1	LISTENING: NEW YEAR'S EVE

A. 🎧 *Listen to Luisa and Javier's conversation about New Year's Eve. Complete the conversation by writing the words that you hear. You will hear the recording two times.*

LUISA: What did you do last night for New Year's Eve?

JAVIER: Nothing. A friend and I _____*were going to go*_____ to a party, but he couldn't come
                                    0.

pick me up. I went to bed just before midnight.

LUISA: What? Everyone is supposed to stay up until midnight, at least! You're supposed to count

the seconds until midnight and then make a lot of noise.

JAVIER: I know. I _____ up, but I was really tired. How about you?
                            1.

What did you do?

LUISA: Well, there _____ fireworks downtown. Some friends and I were
                            2.

going to go, but then it started raining. So we decided to stay home and celebrate there.

It's too bad, though, because it was supposed to be a great show.

JAVIER: Yeah, I heard last night that they _____ the show since the weather
                                                    3.

was so bad. I guess they weren't supposed to light the fireworks in the rain. But they also

said that they _____ the fireworks off another night instead.
                        4.

LUISA: Really? Cool. If the weather's good, then I'll go. I don't care if it's actually New Year's

Eve or not.

B. Reread the conversation. Find four verb phrases that express expectations. Write them below. (Note: Only use words that are given in the conversation. Do not use any words that you wrote.) An example is given.

0. _____*is supposed to stay up*_____

1. _____

2. _____

3. _____

4. _____

PART VIII

2 | JAVIER'S JOURNAL

Complete Javier's journal entry about New Year's Eve. Circle the correct words or phrases.

January 1

It's New Year's Day, and it's (supposed to be)/ supposed be / supposed to a good day. But so
                                                                    0.

far this year isn't off to a good start. I guess I will be / 'm / was going supposed to make a
                                                           1.

decision to change something in my life in the new year, so this year I've decided to buy a car.

George was suppose / was supposed / is supposed to come over and pick me up last night to
            2.

do something for New Year's Eve. We were / was / are going to go to a party at Collin's house,
                                         3.

and it will suppose / was supposed / supposed to be really fun. But George's car broke down,
            4.

and he couldn't pick me up. So I called Collin. He was supposed send / going to send /
                                                              5.

going to supposed to send someone to pick me up, but no one ever came. Then I was / am / did
                                                                                      6.

going to take a taxi to Collin's place, but it was already getting late. People are supposed

to spending / spends / to spend New Year's Eve with friends, but I was home alone. And it was
        7.

all because I don't have my own car. This year I'm going to change that!

3 | NEW YEAR'S CELEBRATIONS AND CUSTOMS IN JAPAN

*Complete these sentences about New Year's celebrations and customs in Japan. Use the
correct forms of the words in parentheses. Some items may have more than one right
answer.*

0. In Japan, people _____ are supposed to clean _____ their houses before New Year's Day.
                          (be / supposed / clean)

1. On New Year's Eve, people _____ buckwheat noodles in
                                      (be / supposed / eat)

   order to live a long life.

2. Children _____ money on New Year's Day.
                  (be / supposed / receive)

3. Many stores are closed from January 1–3, and families _____
                                                                (be / supposed / spend)

   time together.

4. In the past, the first days of the year _____ a time of rest,
                                                  (be / supposed / be)

   although today some stores open on January 2 so the kids can spend their money.

5. The first dream a person has in the new year _____ true.
   (be / supposed / come)

6. I _____ to remember my dream when I woke up this
   (be / going / try)
   morning, but I forgot it.

7. People _____ the new year if someone in the family has
   (be / not / supposed / celebrate)
   died in the past year.

8. I _____ a New Year card to my friend in Japan, but then I
   (be / going / send)
   remembered that her grandfather had died this past year, so it wasn't appropriate.

9. I _____ Japan during the new year, but I couldn't save
   (be / going / visit)
   enough money.

4 | EDITING: AT THE NEW YEAR'S EVE PARTY

Read this conversation at Collin's New Year's Eve party. There are seven mistakes in the use of **be supposed to** *and* **was / were going to**. *The first mistake is already corrected. Find and correct six more.*

GEORGE: Sorry I'm late. I know I was supposed get here a while ago. I had car trouble.
         to

COLLIN: No problem. But where's Javier? You were supposing to pick him up, right?

GEORGE: Yeah, we are going to come together, but since my car wouldn't start, I took a taxi

         instead. I going to call him and tell him to take a taxi too, but I didn't. I feel bad. I was

         supposed to pick him up an hour ago.

COLLIN: That's OK. I'll call him right now.

HARU: Hey, George! Did you just get here?

GEORGE: Yeah, just now. I was going be here earlier, but I had car trouble.

HARU: Well, get something to eat. And don't forget the pork and cabbage.

GEORGE: Why? Are they traditional New Year's foods?

HARU: Well, Collin said we supposed to eat them. They're supposed to bring good luck and

      money through the year.

GEORGE: I've heard that you're supposed to eating something round so you'll live through the

        year.

HARU: Yeah, I think I've heard that too.

PART VIII

Unit 36 Achievement Test

30 Items
Score: _____

1 | LISTENING: PRESIDENTIAL CANDIDATES TO DEBATE

A. 🎧 *Listen to this radio broadcast about an upcoming presidential debate. Complete the broadcast by writing the words that you hear. You will hear the recording two times.*

RAQUEL: Tomorrow is the first presidential debate between candidates Senator Jackson from Connecticut and Governor Crowley from Texas. Political analyst Will Pelton joins us now to talk about what might happen at tomorrow's debate. Welcome, Will.

WILL: Thank you, Raquel.

RAQUEL: Will, Senator Jackson has been ahead in the polls for the past month. Is it possible that Governor Crowley will change his position in the polls tomorrow?

WILL: He might. Some voters are still not sure of how they'll vote. Now, will all those undecided votes go to Governor Crowley? _____*They could*_____, but they

0.

probably won't.

RAQUEL: Do you think Governor Crowley will announce anything new?

WILL: _____, but he probably won't change his message.

1.

RAQUEL: What about Senator Jackson?

WILL: Senator Jackson could say something new. His message has continued to develop over time. Some people have said that he _____ the election with

2.

this strategy. But you never know. He may be the next president.

RAQUEL: And of course everyone is talking about Governor Crowley and the budget.

_____ announce a plan to balance it?

3.

WILL: He may. However, if he's planning that, it's not official.

RAQUEL: How about Senator Jackson?

WILL: _____ mention the budget tomorrow as well. But again, we're

4.

not sure.

RAQUEL: Thank you, Will.

WILL: You're welcome, Raquel.

B. Reread the broadcast. Find two verb phrases that express future possibility and two short answers to questions about possibility. Write them in the table below. (Note: Only use words that are given in the broadcast. Do not use any words that you wrote.) An example is given.

VERB PHRASES THAT EXPRESS FUTURE POSSIBILITY	SHORT ANSWERS TO QUESTIONS ABOUT POSSIBILITY
0. _might happen_	1. _____
1. _____	2. _____
2. _____	

2 | WHAT WILL THEY SAY?

Complete these sentences about possible topics for the presidential debates. Circle the correct words or phrases.

0. Senator Jackson (could talk)/ could to talk / could talking about lowering taxes.

1. If someone asks him about how he has changed positions, he might discussing / might discuss / might be discuss it.

2. Senator Jackson may / may be / maybe comment on creating jobs.

3. He couldn't / maybe / might describe his plan for his first year as president.

4. He could say / maybe say / mayn't say that he has a plan to improve education.

5. Senator Jackson maybe talk / may talk / may be talk about health care.

6. He might not speak / mayn't speak / couldn't speak about his service in the war.

7. Governor Crowley maybe tell / might to tell / may tell people that he won't raise taxes.

8. He may be / could to / might argue for giving more money to technology research.

9. Governor Crowley could / could not / couldn't comment that he is the best person to become president.

10. He may not / mayn't / mightn't answer every question directly.

11. He could not mention / could mention / could to mention how he has made Texas better.

12. He mayn't / might not / maybe not want to discuss his private life.

13. He might say / might be / might be say he's going to win.

3 | PLANS FOR THE EVENING

Lillian and Kanya belong to a reading club. Complete the conversation. Use the correct forms of the words in parentheses. Put the words in the correct order.

KANYA: Are you going to the reading club tomorrow night?

LILLIAN: I'm not sure yet. I _____*may decide*_____ to stay home and watch the
                  0. (decide / may)

       presidential debate on TV. How about you?

KANYA: I _____ either. I'm probably going to watch the debate.
           1. (not / go / might)

LILLIAN: I really want to go to the reading club though . . . I _____
                                            2. (go / could)

       for a little while and leave early. Or I _____ the debate.
                              3. (might / record)

KANYA: Oh, recording it is a good idea. I _____ that instead.
                                   4. (do / may)

4 | EDITING: DEBATES FOCUS ON BUDGET

*Read this article about the debates. There are six mistakes in the use of **may, might,** and* **could.** *The first mistake is already corrected. Find and correct five more.*

    This presidential race is very close, and either candidate could ~~winning~~ *win*. Here's a look at their

positions on one issue:

    Senator Jackson may raises taxes. He says he doesn't want to, but it maybe necessary. He

could expand education programs with that extra money. He says, "The government could to

spend more on education. We have to make it a priority."

    Governor Crowley, on the other hand, says he won't raise taxes. However, according to his

plans, there mightn't be enough money in the budget to increase education spending. Parents and

educators may not like that idea very much, so Governor Crowley might be need to find

additional support from other groups of voters.

Unit 37 Achievement Test

1 | LISTENING: MYSTERIES

A. 🎧 *Listen to the conversation between two roommates, Veronica and Colleen. Complete the conversation by writing the words that you hear. You will hear the recording two times.*

VERONICA: That new TV show *Mysteries* is on in a few minutes. It _____*might be*_____ good.
0.
Do you want to watch it?

COLLEEN: *Mysteries*? That sounds like it might be interesting. What's it about?

VERONICA: UFOs. You know, unidentified flying objects—the space ships that aliens travel in.

COLLEEN: What?! Those things _____ real. I mean, there's no proof that they
1.
really exist.

VERONICA: They've got to be real! Just think of all the people who say they've seen them! Could
all of them be wrong?

COLLEEN: Well, they _____. Their stories can't be true.
2.

VERONICA: They could be. You don't know. Would you believe in UFOs if you saw proof of their
existence?

COLLEEN: _____, I guess. I don't really know.
3.

VERONICA: Well, people see strange things in the sky all the time. If they're not UFOs, then what
_____?
4.

COLLEEN: I don't know. They might be airplanes or something.

VERONICA: All right, the show's starting. Let's watch it, and you'll see!

B. *Reread the conversation. Then read each statement and circle* **T** *(true) or* **F** *(false).*

T **(F)** 0. Colleen is almost 100 percent certain that the show is interesting.

T **F** 1. Veronica is almost 100 percent certain that UFOs exist.

T **F** 2. Colleen is almost 100 percent certain that stories about UFOs aren't true.

T **F** 3. Veronica thinks that stories about UFOs are impossible to believe.

T **F** 4. Colleen is almost 100 percent certain that UFOs are really just airplanes.

2 | UFOS

Read these sentences about UFOs from the TV show Mysteries. *Circle the verb phrases that express conclusions.*

0. Part of the population thinks that aliens (might want) to contact us.

1. A recent poll suggests that 45 percent of Americans believe that UFOs must be real.

2. Some people believe UFOs have to exist. They think there's no other explanation for their sightings.

3. Some people feel strongly about UFOs and aliens. They think they have got to exist.

4. But others don't agree. They think a person who reports seeing a UFO must be crazy.

5. Despite many reports of UFO sightings, there still may not be enough evidence to say that they are real.

6. Photographs and video recordings might not provide enough proof of their existence.

7. If you try to photograph a UFO, the object might not come out clearly in the photo.

8. Some video recordings of UFOs may be fake.

9. For example, the UFO in this home video might be a bird or an airplane.

10. Some people who say they've seen a UFO could be making up the story for attention.

3 | PEOPLE'S THOUGHTS ON UFOS AND ALIENS

Complete these quotes from people who saw the Mysteries *TV show about UFOs. Use* **must, have to, have got to, may (not), might (not), could,** *or* **can't** *and the words in parentheses. Some items may have more than one right answer. Use each modal at least once.*

0. "I'm not sure whether I believe in UFOs or not. I guess they _____*could exist*_____."

(exist)

1. "How could these stories be true? They're impossible to believe. People

    _____ them for fun. That's the only explanation."

(create)

2. "If humans can build spaceships, then creatures on other planets _____

(know)

    how to build them too. Even though we don't know for sure, it's always possible."

3. "That isn't an airplane, and it's certainly not a bird. There's only one possible explanation: It

    _____ a UFO."

(be)

4. "You don't know for sure what's in the sky. You _____ an airplane or
   (see)

   a helicopter or a UFO when you look up. You never know."

5. "We don't have enough information to say for sure whether UFOs exist or not. They

   _____ around all the time. No one really knows."
   (fly)

6. "UFOs are impossible. Aliens _____ to Earth in spaceships! I just
   (travel)

   don't believe those stories."

7. "I absolutely believe in UFOs. They _____."
   (exist)

8. "I don't know why aliens don't try to communicate with humans. I guess they

   _____ to make contact with us."
   (want)

9. "I strongly believe in intelligent life in other parts of the universe. Intelligent creatures

   _____ in places besides Earth. There's no doubt in my mind."
   (live)

---

4 | EDITING: AFTER THE SHOW

*Read this conversation between Colleen and Veronica after the TV show. There are four
mistakes in the use of **must, have (got) to, may, might, could,** and **can't**. The first
mistake is already corrected. Find and correct three more. (Note: There can be more than
one way to correct a mistake.)*

VERONICA: So what do you think now? Do you believe in UFOs?

                                    can't
COLLEEN: Not at all! I strongly feel they ~~may not~~ exist. Do you still believe in them?

VERONICA: Absolutely. I could be wrong, but I just think that so many people have seen them

           that they must to be real.

COLLEEN: But may some people be mistaken?

VERONICA: A few of them might, but not all of them. Some of them have to be telling the truth.

COLLEEN: Well, maybe they're just unsure about what they saw.

PART VIII Achievement Test

1 | LISTENING: LATE FOR PRACTICE

A. 🎧 *Listen to this conversation between two neighbors. Complete the conversation by writing the words that you hear. You will hear the recording two times.*

MATEO: Hey, Leonard! My wife sent me to borrow some salt. Do you have any?

LEONARD: Sure . . . here you go.

MATEO: Are you OK?

LEONARD: I'm fine, but I _____ *have to take* _____ my son to basketball practice. And
0.

   I was supposed to leave 15 minutes ago, but my daughter has our truck.

MATEO: Oh, no. How frustrating.

LEONARD: Yeah. I was supposed to get there early to help the coach with a few things. He

   _____ wondering if I'm going to show up.
   1.

MATEO: Could your daughter be on her way home now?

LEONARD: I don't know. She's not answering her cell phone. She might be home soon, but I'm

   not sure. She wasn't supposed to take the truck without telling me.

MATEO: Well, she can't be too far. _____ you'll wait for her to get
   2.

   back?

LEONARD: I guess I don't have much choice. I _____ her friend's house
   3.

   and see if she's there, but I can't find the number.

MATEO: Well, I'd be happy to give you both a ride if you like.

LEONARD: _____ out anyway? If it's not too much trouble, that'd be
   4.

   great. Let me just leave a note for my daughter.

MATEO: OK.

B. *Reread the conversation. Then read each statement and circle* **T** *(true) or* **F** *(false).*

Ⓣ **F** 0. Leonard planned to leave 15 minutes ago.

T **F** 1. Leonard was planning to get to practice early.

T **F** 2. Leonard is almost 100 percent certain that his daughter will be home soon.

T **F** 3. Leonard's daughter had permission to take the truck without telling him.

T **F** 4. Mateo thinks that Leonard's daughter isn't very far.

---

2 | STUCK IN TRAFFIC

Read Mateo and Leonard's conversation in the car. Write each underlined verb phrase in the correct category below. An example is given.

MATEO: There's so much traffic! There <u>must be</u> some road work or something. I <u>have to change</u> lanes. This one is closed up ahead.

LEONARD: Yeah, that sign says all traffic <u>must use</u> the right lane.

MATEO: I wonder if they're putting in a traffic light at the next intersection. They <u>were going to do</u> it a while ago, but for some reason they never did.

LEONARD: I hope that's what they're doing. You <u>have to be</u> really careful there.

MATEO: Uh-oh. I <u>was going to take</u> Washburn Avenue, but we <u>can't turn</u> here. The street is closed. We <u>could take</u> Broadway instead.

LEONARD: <u>Is it possible</u> that the traffic will be better on the freeway? I think <u>I'd rather take</u> that because you can drive faster.

MATEO: That's fine. I <u>would rather not stay</u> on this road any longer than we have to.

LEONARD: Any street <u>has got to be</u> faster than this one.

EXPRESSES A PREFERENCE	EXPRESSES A NECESSITY	EXPRESSES PROHIBITION	EXPRESSES A PAST EXPECTATION	EXPRESSES A POSSIBILITY	EXPRESSES A CONCLUSION
1. _____ _____	1. _____ _____	1. _____ _____	1. _____ _____	1. _____ _____	0. *must be* _____
2. _____ _____	2. _____ _____		2. _____ _____	2. _____ _____	1. _____ _____
	3. _____ _____				

PART VIII

3 | LOOKING FOR THE GYM

Read another conversation between Leonard and Mateo in the car. Complete the conversation with the correct words or phrases. Write the letter of the best answer on each line.

LEONARD: It's so hot! I ___*c*___ (a. 'd prefer b. would rather c. 'd like d. must) some water. I don't
         0.
enjoy the heat. I _____ (a. 'd rather b. got to prefer c. prefer d. rather) cold weather.
         1.

MATEO: Yeah, me too. I prefer staying inside _____ (a. than b. to c. or d. of) being outdoors
         2.
when it's like this. So, does the team usually practice at this school?

LEONARD: No, actually we've never been to this school before, so when we get there,

we _____ (a. 'd prefer b. might c. 'd rather d. 've got to) look for the gym. I hope we get
         3.

there soon. I _____ (a. mustn't b. don't have to c. have to d. 'm not supposed to) do a lot
         4.

of stuff this afternoon.

MATEO: Maybe somebody already did everything for you and you _____ (a. may not b. don't
         5.
have to c. can't d. must not) do it.

LEONARD: You _____ (a. must not b. don't have to c. may d. might not) be right. In fact, you
         6.

probably are. I just really hate to be late.

MATEO: Hey, you shouldn't worry about things you can't control. It _____ (a. would rather
         7.
give b. had to give c. could give d. must give) you a heart attack, you know.

LEONARD: I know. Anyway, we _____ (a. can't be b. aren't supposed to c. mayn't be d. don't have to)
         8.

be *too* late. It's probably not even 3:30 yet.

MATEO: All right . . . here's the school. There are some kids over there. I'm not sure, but that

_____ (a. is supposed to b. can c. might d. has got) be the gym.
         9.

LEONARD: Yeah, that _____ (a. 's has to b. 's got to c. 's supposed to d. may not) be the gym if that's
         10.

where the kids are.

MATEO: Will you need a ride home?

LEONARD: I _____ (a. could be b. maybe c. 'm supposed to d. could). I'll call my daughter later. If she
         11.

doesn't answer, then I _____ (a. can't b. 'd rather c. might d. am supposed to) call you.
         12.

MATEO: OK. No problem.

4 | AT THE GYM

Complete the conversation between Leonard and the coach. Use the correct forms of **would rather, prefer, have to, be supposed to, may, might, could,** *or* **can't.** *Some items may have more than one right answer.*

LEONARD: Sorry I'm late, Coach. My daughter took off with the car, so I

_____*couldn't*_____ get here any earlier. My neighbor
       0.

_____ drive me. It was the only way I could get here.
    1.

COACH: No problem. I can give you a ride home after practice. I have to go downtown, and I

know you live near there. Your house _____ be close to
         2.

where I'm going. I don't know, but I guess it's not too far.

LEONARD: Thanks. Sounds good. So, what should I do now?

COACH: OK, we have a few things that we _____ take care of today.
       3.

And it's really important to do them right away. Let's see . . . Oh, we

_____ wait another day to find out about the new uniforms.
  4.

We must do that today. All the kids _____ wear the same
      5.

thing for the first game on Friday. It's a rule and a tradition!

LEONARD: What's the problem with the uniforms?

COACH: They _____ get here yesterday, but they didn't. I called the
   6.

company, and they said they don't have our order.

LEONARD: That _____ be right. I sent it myself.
    7.

COACH: This _____ be a disaster if we don't fix the problem soon.
    8.

LEONARD: Don't worry about it. I'll find out what's going on.

COACH: That's great. I _____ focus on the team than worry about that.
    9.

LEONARD: No problem. That's my preference too. I _____ not have to
        10.

control all those kids! I _____ organizing to coaching any day!
    11.

Name _____ Date _____

5 | NEWSLETTER TO THE PARENTS

A newsletter is a short written report of news about a club or organization. Complete this paragraph from a basketball newsletter. Use the correct words or phrases. The first letter of each word is provided. Some items may have more than one possible answer.

According to a recent poll, most people would r_____*ather*_____ watch basketball
0.

t_____ play it. So make sure that you come out to watch your kids' basketball
1.

practices and games this season. You m_____ feel that you're too busy, or
2.

that you h_____ to do other things while your children are playing. But you
3.

c_____ send your kids to basketball practice and games without ever coming to
4.

watch them! That's not right! You d_____ have to attend every basketball game.
5.

But, as parents, we're s_____ to support our kids, so we've g_____
6.   **7.**

to see some parental involvement. In fact, it's necessary. We m_____ show
8.

them our support, and we can do that by coming to their practices and games. If you'd

p_____ to participate even more, you m_____ consider being an
9.   **10.**

assistant coach. If you're interested, e-mail Coach Skaggs at lskaggs@fog.com.

6 | EDITING: AT HOME

Leonard is back home talking to his daughter Nelly. There are nine mistakes in the conversation. The first mistake is already corrected. Find and correct eight more.

LEONARD: I was going ^to use the truck to take your brother to basketball practice this afternoon.

You must to talk to me before taking it. If you'd rather not discuss your plans

with me, then you can take the bus.

NELLY: No! I prefer drive. Let's talk about our schedules. I was go to use the truck tomorrow.

It's my first day of volleyball practice.

LEONARD: Oh, that's right. You must being excited. But you can't have the truck. I need it.

NELLY: Dad, I can't missing the first practice! If I'm not there, I'll get in trouble.

LEONARD: Look, I might am able to drop you off, but I maybe not able to pick you up. Can you

find a ride home?

NELLY: Yeah, I'm sure I can. Everyone on the team is suppose to help each other out.

Audioscript

PART I Diagnostic Test

CARLA: What are you doing?

SHEILA: I'm getting ready to go out.

CARLA: Oh, yeah? Where are you going?

SHEILA: I'm going out to lunch and then to a geography lecture. Hand me my purse, please.

CARLA: Sure. Here you go. So, who are you going with?

SHEILA: I'm going with this guy Ray. I met him at Virginia's party last night.

CARLA: What's he like?

SHEILA: He's really cool. He used to live in Madagascar, just like me. And he speaks French!

CARLA: Wow! Well, let me know how it goes.

SHEILA: OK. I'll tell you as soon as I get home.

Unit 1 Achievement Test

STEVE: And now some local news. Eileen Hill is at Arkansas General Hospital with an interesting story. Eileen, what's happening?

EILEEN: Kevin, I'm standing outside General Hospital, where Mary Griffith just gave birth to five babies. Mary is doing fine, but doctors are watching the quintuplets carefully. We've been told that the father, John Griffith, is preparing for a press conference . . . Wait a minute, it looks like he's starting to talk now!

JOHN: First, I want to thank the nurses and doctors. Mary and I appreciate all of their hard work. Thanks to them, we believe the five babies will be just fine.

EILEEN: How is Mary doing?

JOHN: Well, she's tired, of course. Right now she's resting, but she's doing well.

EILEEN: Do you have all the help that you need?

JOHN: Obviously, we need a lot of help, but fortunately we have some wonderful friends and neighbors who are helping us. That's all for now. I need to get back to Mary. Thank you.

Unit 2 Achievement Test

OK, everybody. Get ready! First we're going to stretch. We're going to try to touch our toes. Bend over slowly, and stay in that position for three counts. One, two, three, and come up. Good! We'll try it again. Now, as you're stretching, you should feel a stretch in the back of your legs and in your lower back. Don't bend your knees, if possible. If you bend your knees, your muscles won't stretch as much. Relax your neck so that your head hangs straight down. This will help stretch the muscles in your neck. Breathe deeply. Your body needs a lot of oxygen, so don't hold your breath. Concentrate on your breathing. One, two, three, and stand up. Exhale! Whoo!

Unit 3 Achievement Test

ROBERTO: When did you arrive in the United States?

LUCILLE: I came two years ago. How about you? When did you come here?

ROBERTO: Three years ago.

LUCILLE: Were you married at that time?

ROBERTO: No, I met my wife Marcela in 2003 at the restaurant where we worked. We also lived in the same apartment complex, but we didn't realize that until after we started dating. We got married two years later.

LUCILLE: And when did you become an engineer?

ROBERTO: Last year. I started my studies in Mexico. That was in 2001. I completed my studies here in the States.

LUCILLE: Did I hear that you're going to be a father soon?

ROBERTO: Well, actually, I already am. I became a father yesterday.

LUCILLE: Congratulations!

Unit 4 Achievement Test

OFFICER: Were you sitting at your desk at 10:20, when the robber came into the office?

ARTHUR: Yes, I was.

OFFICER: What were you doing?

ARTHUR: I was working on a report.

OFFICER: I find it strange that you didn't hear anything. Were you talking on the telephone?

ARTHUR: No, not at that time.

OFFICER: Were you listening to the radio?

ARTHUR: No.

OFFICER: So what were you doing that stopped you from hearing while the robber was moving through the office?

ARTHUR: Well, while I was sitting at my desk, I was listening to the news over the Internet.

OFFICER: Why were you listening to the news while you were working?

ARTHUR: Well, sometimes the work I do doesn't require much thought. This morning I was entering numbers into the computer. Listening to the news doesn't distract me with that kind of work.

OFFICER: I see.

Unit 5 Achievement Test

LESLIE: Isn't it hard to believe some of the crazy things we used to do to be cool?

HILLARY: I know. Just think about jeans. Remember how tight we used to wear them?

LESLIE: I sure do. Did you use to sit with your new jeans on in hot bath water to make them shrink?

HILLARY: No, I never used to do that. I just used to buy jeans that were already too small for me.

LESLIE: Didn't it hurt to wear them?

HILLARY: It did at first, until I got used to wearing them.

LESLIE: Why did we use to do that to ourselves?

HILLARY: Because it was cool, I guess.

LESLIE: Oh, and whenever I got new sneakers, I used to get them dirty on purpose.

HILLARY: Me too! Now I try hard to keep my shoes clean.

LESLIE: I know. I'm glad we don't do that anymore. But we had fun, didn't we?

HILLARY: We sure did.

Unit 6 Achievement Test

TANYA: Did you hear about the new mall they're going to build? They say it's going to create a lot of jobs.

VICTOR: Really? I didn't hear anything about it. Where will it be?

TANYA: It'll be right across the street from us.

VICTOR: Oh, no! Is there going to be more traffic?

TANYA: Probably, but now we won't need to drive so far to go shopping.

VICTOR: I suppose, if you shop at malls. But I'm probably not going to shop there. Everything is too expensive at malls. Hey . . . will our houses decrease in value?

TANYA: That's a good question. I don't know.

VICTOR: When are they starting construction?

TANYA: I think they start soon.

VICTOR: Well, I'll look online. There must be some more information there.

Unit 7 Achievement Test

Looking for a job? Unhappy at work? Still in school? Where will you go when you decide to change jobs? What will you do when you graduate? Here at Jobs Are Us Employment Agency, we can help you find a great job. As soon as you give us some basic information, we'll look hard for the right job for you. Before you know it, an exciting new job will be yours. After you sign up with us, you'll realize that Jobs Are Us Employment Agency is the best way to find the work you love. Call or stop by today!

Unit 8 Achievement Test

INTERVIEWER: Well, Kathy, tell me: Why do you want to become an actress?

KATHY: Well, I was in a few theater performances here in town, and I loved them.

INTERVIEWER: Where did you perform?

KATHY: At the Little Black Theater downtown. I had the lead role in our last production.

INTERVIEWER: Really? Whom did you play?

KATHY: I played Hannah in *Denial Is a River*.

INTERVIEWER: That sounds familiar. Who wrote that play?

KATHY: Emil Sher. There was a good review of my performance in the local newspaper. There's a copy of it in my portfolio.

INTERVIEWER: Oh? Who wrote the review?

KATHY: A reporter named Jim Carlotta. He saw the play on closing night.

INTERVIEWER: How many performances did you have?

KATHY: Twelve. And then in May came my biggest break yet.

INTERVIEWER: What happened in May?

KATHY: I had a small part in an independent film. That was fun.

INTERVIEWER: Which kinds of characters do you prefer to play?

KATHY: I like to play smart, confident women. I played a lawyer in the film.

INTERVIEWER: I see. And whose scripts do you relate to the most?

KATHY: Well, I really like scripts by Scott Hathaway.

INTERVIEWER: Oh? I haven't heard of him. What did he write?

KATHY: His most famous play is called *Elsewhere*. Do you know it?

INTERVIEWER: I'm afraid I don't. Well, Kathy, now I'd like you to read a script for me. . . .

PART I Achievement Test

CARRIE: What are you doing?

SHARON: I'm getting ready to go out for dinner.

CARRIE: Really? Where are you eating?

SHARON: I'm going to the new Mexican restaurant downtown. And afterwards I'm going to a magic show. Give me my wallet, please. It's on the bedside table.

CARRIE: Sure. Here you go. So who are you going with?

SHARON: A guy named Reggie. I met him at Veronica's party last night.

CARRIE: Oh yeah? What's he like?

SHARON: He's really nice. I found out that he used to live in the Philippines, just like I did. And he speaks Tagalog.

CARRIE: Wow! Well, tell me all about what happens.

SHARON: OK. I'll tell you as soon as I get home.

PART II Diagnostic Test

LUISA: How's your apartment search going?

JUAN: Not too well. It's got me talking to myself. I'm having trouble figuring out if I should get a roommate or not. My parents want me to, but I'm not sure.

LUISA: That's really a decision you need to make for yourself.

JUAN: I know. I want to live by myself, but I can't afford to do that right now. I'm finding out that apartments are more expensive than I thought.

LUISA: Then maybe you should find yourself a roommate.

JUAN: You're probably right. I did meet a guy in chemistry class the other day who's looking for a roommate. His name is Bob. He's living by himself right now, but he can't afford to pay the rent. He suggested that I move into the extra room in his apartment.

LUISA: So what did you tell him?

JUAN: I told him I needed to think about it. We gave each other our phone numbers and said we'd talk on Friday.

LUISA: That's tomorrow.

JUAN: Yes, I know, but I have some other things on my mind, too. I have a job interview today. I hope I get the job. I'm nervous about the interview.

LUISA: Just be yourself. I'm sure you'll get the job. Then you can afford your own apartment.

Unit 9 Achievement Test

TOM: What do you think it means to be an optimistic person? To me, optimistic people see themselves and the world around them in a positive way.

SARA: I think being an optimistic person means looking for the positive in the situation itself, whether it's good or bad.

TOM: I think so too. My sister describes herself as an optimistic person, but I don't think she is.

SARA: Why not?

TOM: Well, for example, she's always complaining that her boss doesn't like her. She says that's the reason she didn't get a promotion last year.

SARA: Hmmm. I see what you mean. How about you? Would you describe yourself as an optimistic person?

TOM: Yes, I do describe myself as optimistic. When my car broke down last week, I had to take the bus. It took longer than driving, but I decided to enjoy the trip and read the newspaper.

SARA: Well, people can learn from one another. Maybe you should talk to your sister about what it means to be an optimistic person.

TOM: Good idea. We could help each other deal with life's problems.

Unit 10 Achievement Test

PABLO: I'll pick up the movie on my way to your place. What time do you want me to get there?

CARMEN: Oh, I don't know. I still have some work to do. I need to write up my lab report and hand it in. Then I have to figure out how much time I need to study for my chemistry test tomorrow.

PABLO: Do you think you'll be finished by 8:00?

CARMEN: Probably. I just need to look over my notes. That's enough studying for me to get by.

PABLO: OK. Do you care what kind of movie I pick out?

CARMEN: Get something funny or something romantic.

PABLO: How about an old classic movie like *Casablanca*? I can't pass that movie up!

CARMEN: Sounds good. Listen, can you drop off the movie tomorrow while I'm taking my test?

PABLO: Sure. I'm going to the library now to look up some information for a paper I have to write. I'll call you when I get back from there to find out if you're done studying.

CARMEN: Great. I'll talk to you then.

PART II Achievement Test

JOHN: I have to write myself a note.

LISA: Why?

JOHN: I signed up to meet with my anthropology professor tomorrow, and I'm afraid I might forget about it.

BILL: Then yes, you'd better write yourself a note. What's your meeting about?

JOHN: My professor is setting out to make a documentary, and he's looking for two students to help him carry out the project.

LISA: What's the documentary about?

JOHN: The culture of a small village in South America. He spent last summer studying it.

LISA: Did he live with the villagers?

JOHN: No, he lived by himself just outside the village.

LISA: Hmmm. What kind of qualifications do the students need to have?

JOHN: Well, the students must see themselves as optimistic and flexible people. And they have to be prepared to work long hours.

LISA: Is your professor only looking for anthropology students?

JOHN: Oh, no. The positions are open to any students.

LISA: The project sounds interesting. I can see myself working on it. Since we know each other, you could recommend me for the job, couldn't you?

BILL: That's a great idea, Lisa. You promised yourself a fun and challenging job this summer. It sounds like this could be it.

JOHN: Lisa, I don't know why I didn't think of that myself. Of course I'll recommend you, and I'll bring you an application to fill out.

PART III Diagnostic Test

ANDY: Look at all that wood left over from building the house. They shouldn't throw it out like that. Hey, *we* should use it for something.

TAYLOR: I know! Can we make a treehouse out of that kind of wood?

ANDY: I think so. Actually, that's a great idea! Should we build it in the tree by the fence?

TAYLOR: I don't know if Mom and Dad will let us. Let's go ask Dad. We can convince him.

ANDY: OK. . . . Dad!

MOM: Could you please shut the door?

ANDY: Sorry, Mom. Dad! May we build a treehouse in the tree by the fence, please?

DAD: Well, a treehouse sounds like a good idea. But there's one problem. The tree by the fence won't be able to hold the weight of a treehouse.

TAYLOR: Could we please build it in a different tree then?

DAD: Sure. You should build it in the tree on the side of the house. That one can hold the weight.

ANDY: Thanks, Dad! This is going to be great.

DAD: I think so, too. I always wanted a treehouse when I was a kid, but I couldn't have one.

Unit 11 Achievement Test

ESTELLA: Thanks for seeing me today, Greg. I'm sorry I had to cancel my appointment last week.

GREG: No problem. A lot of people are looking for an actor like you. I just need to ask you a few questions. I have a client who is looking for someone to play a small part in a television series. Are you able to work next month?

ESTELLA: Absolutely. I can work anytime.

GREG: OK, great. Now, I have another client who needs some singers for a musical comedy. Can you sing?

ESTELLA: Well, actually, no, I can't sing very well.

GREG: That's OK. Are you able to dance?

ESTELLA: I've taken a lot of lessons, and yes, I can dance pretty well.

GREG: Great. Can you play the role of an old woman?

ESTELLA: Well, I've never done it before. But I'm sure I can do it.

GREG: OK. Are you able to do comedy?

ESTELLA: Yes. In fact, most of my work has been in comedy.

GREG: Great. I'll make sure that people look at your résumé, OK?

ESTELLA: Thanks! Again, I'm sorry I couldn't come in last week.

GREG: Oh, that's OK. We should have some work for you soon.

Unit 12 Achievement Test

DAMIAN: Excuse me. Could we sit here next to you?

STAN: Yes, of course you can. I'm Stan, and this is Becky. We work in the art department.

BECKY: Hi.

DAMIAN: Nice to meet you both. I'm Damian, and this is my daughter, Jody. I'm in sales. I just started on Monday.

STAN: Welcome to the company.

DAMIAN: Thanks. Hey, Stan, could I ask you a favor?

STAN: Certainly.

DAMIAN: Could I borrow your cell phone? I need to call my wife and give her directions to get here, but my battery's dead.

STAN: I'm sorry, but my phone's in the car.

BECKY: Here, you can use mine.

DAMIAN: Thanks so much. Oh, do you mind if my daughter plays her video game? It's a little noisy.

STAN: No, not at all.

JODY: Hey, Dad. Can I please go get something to eat? I'm hungry.

DAMIAN: Sure. The food is right over there. I'll call Mom, and I'll meet you there in a minute.

Unit 13 Achievement Test

JACKIE: Hello?

GABE: Hi, honey. What are you up to?

JACKIE: I'm checking my e-mail. We got a message from our landlord, but I haven't read it yet.

GABE: Oh, really? Can you open it now?

JACKIE: Yeah, hold on a minute . . . OK. It says, "Hi, Gabe and Jackie, I'm going out of town next week. Could you water the flowers in front of the apartment building? I'll take $50 off your rent for the month. Would you please let me know as soon as possible? Thanks!" Do you want to do it?

GABE: Sure. It won't be much work. Would you e-mail him back?

JACKIE: No problem.

GABE: Great. Listen, I'm about ready to leave the office. Is there anything you need me to get on the way home?

JACKIE: Yes, can you buy some milk and cheese, please?

GABE: Sure. Do you need anything else from the grocery store?

JACKIE: No, but would you mind stopping by the bank to get some cash?

GABE: Not at all. Anything else?

JACKIE: Just one more thing. Can you please rent a movie to watch tonight?

GABE: I'm sorry, I can't. I don't have my video rental card. They won't let me rent a movie without it.

JACKIE: Too bad. Oh well. See you in a little bit.

Unit 14 Achievement Test

CINDY: We're back with *Money Matters*. I'm Cindy Hall. What should you do if your wallet is lost or stolen? Russ Severson is here today to give us the answer. According to him, you ought to do several things in that situation. Russ, let's say my wallet is missing. Should I call the police?

RUSS: Yes!

CINDY: When should I call them?

RUSS: You had better call as soon as you realize your wallet is missing. Thieves can act fast.

CINDY: Should I cancel my credit cards right away?

RUSS: Absolutely. You ought to do that right after you call the police. By the way, you'd better write down the numbers of your cards or make a photocopy of them now, *before* you lose them. Then you'll have all the information you need to give the credit card companies.

CINDY: When should I get new ID cards?

RUSS: That isn't as important as calling the police and your credit card companies, but you should get new ID cards within a few days.

CINDY: Russ Severson, great to have you on the show. I think we all had better pay attention to your excellent advice.

RUSS: Thank you, Cindy.

Unit 15 Achievement Test

TAYLOR: Why don't we do something fun this weekend? Let's have a barbecue. We can cook some food outside and invite some people to come over.

GABRIELLA: Good idea! Why not invite the new neighbors, Matt and Anita?

TAYLOR: OK. We'll need to buy a few things. Why don't we get meat for hamburgers?

GABRIELLA: I think there's a sale on steak. Maybe we could have steak instead.

TAYLOR: Well, only if it's not too expensive. Let's not spend too much money.

GABRIELLA: OK, I agree. We shouldn't spend a lot. Why not buy hot dogs? They're cheap.

TAYLOR: I don't know. That doesn't sound very good. How about sausage instead?

GABRIELLA: Mmm! That sounds great! Let's get some chips too. Do we have anything for dessert?

TAYLOR: I think we have soda, and we have ice cream. How about having ice cream sodas?

GABRIELLA: Great idea!

PART III Achievement Test

AMBER: Look at this assignment. Mr. Vargas shouldn't make us work so hard! I don't even understand the project.

TANISHA: I don't really either. I just know that we have to build a rocket—you know, like those things that travel into space.

AMBER: That sounds really complicated. He should at least give us more time. Can we do it in only four days?

TANISHA: Well, of course ours won't really go into space. We'll just make a really simple version of a rocket. But I think we need to start working on it. I can come over tonight.

AMBER: That's a good idea. Should we ask Mr. Vargas now for a little help? I think he's still in his classroom.

TANISHA: OK. Let's go.

MR. VARGAS: Yes?

TANISHA: Excuse me, can we please talk to you for a minute?

MR. VARGAS: Sure. What's up?

AMBER: Could you please tell us more about the project? We couldn't understand everything when you explained it in class.

MR. VARGAS: I think you should wait until tomorrow. I'll explain the project more to the whole class then. After that, you'll be able to complete it with no problems.

TANISHA: OK. But if we still have questions, may we come talk to you again?

MR. VARGAS: Of course. But don't worry. You can get a good grade on this project. It won't be too hard.

PART IV Diagnostic Test

CONNIE: Donna! What a surprise to see you! I haven't seen you since high school!

DONNA: Hi, Connie! Wow, you haven't changed a bit since then!

CONNIE: Thanks! What are you doing in Boston? Do you live here?

DONNA: Yeah, I've been living here since I graduated. How about you?

CONNIE: I lived in Wisconsin for a few years, but I've recently moved here. I remember that you wanted to open your own hair salon. Did you?

DONNA: Yes, I've worked in the beauty business for a while now, and I opened my first salon a few years ago. Actually, I've recently opened a second one.

CONNIE: Wow! That's exciting! I heard something else about you. Someone told me that you've been writing a book. Is that right?

DONNA: Yes. Actually, I've recently finished it. It's called *Becoming Beautiful: Beauty Tips for Women.*

CONNIE: I'd love to read it! Hey, are you busy right now?

DONNA: No. Do you want to get some coffee?

CONNIE: Sure. I haven't had a chance to relax for days.

DONNA: I know the perfect coffee shop.

Unit 16 Achievement Test

TRICIA: I heard that you've designed some websites.

SCOTT: Yes, I've done a few for friends, but nothing professionally. I've built five or six websites since I started studying computer science. I'm interested in becoming a website designer.

TRICIA: Oh, really? How long have you studied computer science?

SCOTT: For two years.

TRICIA: Do you know Gerald West?

SCOTT: The guy who used to go to school here? He graduated, right?

TRICIA: Yeah, with a degree in Web design. He's created hundreds of websites for businesses. That's all he's done since he graduated. I think he's made a lot of money. You ought to e-mail him and talk to him about his experiences.

SCOTT: That's a good idea.

Unit 17   Achievement Test

LORI: Would you like a glass of orange juice?

DAVID: Thanks, but I've already had three glasses.

LORI: Have you looked at today's paper yet? I bought you a copy.

DAVID: Oh, thanks, but I've read two papers and three magazines this morning already.

LORI: OK. Have you seen the movie *Playing by Ear* yet? I hear it's available on DVD now.

DAVID: Yep, I've already seen it.

LORI: Is there anything you haven't done yet?

DAVID: Well, I haven't taken a nap yet, but I think I'm ready for one.

LORI: OK. I'll leave you alone, then. Have a good nap.

Unit 18   Achievement Test

LIZ: Are you looking forward to Mother's Day?

BETH: Oh, sure. I've always enjoyed Mother's Day. My children have done some wonderful things for me over the years to celebrate.

LIZ: Oh, really? Like what?

BETH: They've often written me lovely notes. They've taken me out to dinner several times. And they've sent me flowers twice.

LIZ: That's nice. Have they ever forgotten Mother's Day?

BETH: No, never. I'm a lucky woman!

Unit 19   Achievement Test

ACTRESS: Have you tried the new variety of Barry's Cookies?

ACTOR: No, I haven't! I bought a box earlier today, but I haven't eaten any yet. Are they good?

ACTRESS: Oooo, are you kidding? They're delicious! I ate a whole box yesterday! As for today, I've had five already . . . and I'm going to have more after dinner!

ACTOR: Hmmm, sounds dangerous.

ACTRESS: Not at all! This new variety is low fat.

ACTOR: Low fat? And they taste good?

ACTRESS: Yes! Barry has done it again! He always makes great-tasting cookies.

ACTOR: Well, maybe I'll try one right now . . . Hey, what happened to my box of cookies? It's disappeared!

ACTRESS: Oh . . . you left your cookies here? Er . . . I thought they were my cookies . . .

ANNOUNCER: Barry's Cookies: They're America's favorite!

Unit 20   Achievement Test

Daniel Meyers has released his twentieth album. That's right, his twentieth. Meyers has been one of Britain's most productive musicians for quite some time. He's been writing music for 20 years, which means that he's been putting out an average of an album per year. But more amazing than the quantity of his work is the quality. Many critics say that every one of his albums has been worth buying. He's studied the masters of classical, blues, rock, jazz, pop, and world music, and he's picked up new musical skills with every album. He's even lived in different musical hotspots around the world to find inspiration for each new album. This past year, he's been living on Corfu, a Greek island in the Mediterranean Sea, where he has been playing and recording with local musicians. You can hear some of Meyers's latest music on our website at worldradionews.net. This is Hannah Phillips, World Radio News, Washington.

PART IV   Achievement Test

CARLOS: Hey, Doug! How are you doing? I haven't seen you since we played football together in high school!

DOUG: I know! It's been a long time.

CARLOS: So have you moved to Los Angeles, or are you just visiting?

DOUG: I've been living here since we graduated. What about you?

CARLOS: I've just moved here. So, what did you end up studying at school?

DOUG: I studied criminology, and then I completed my master's degree in criminal justice.

CARLOS: Cool! If I remember correctly, you always wanted to become a detective. Did you?

DOUG: Well, I started a private investigator firm a few years ago, and my plan was to open up about a dozen offices around the state. I've already opened ten of them—they're in all the major cities and towns.

CARLOS: Wow! I bet you've been working really hard all these years.

DOUG: Yes, I have. On top of everything else, I've been teaching a course on professional investigation techniques.

CARLOS: I'd like to hear more about that. Have you eaten dinner yet?

DOUG: No, I haven't even had lunch—I'm pretty hungry.

CARLOS: Why don't we get something to eat now?

DOUG: All right, let's go!

PART V Diagnostic Test

PAUL: Hey, have you decided what to write about for your history report?

MARA: No, I don't have any ideas, but I haven't given it much thought. Have you?

PAUL: Yeah, I think I'm going to write about the history of baseball and the World Series.

MARA: Will you be able to find enough information?

PAUL: Yeah, I don't think that will be a problem. I have a lot of sports magazines, and I'm sure there's a lot of stuff on the Internet, so I think I'll be able to find enough material. If you have a hard time thinking of a topic, I can give you some help.

MARA: Well, if you have a few extra ideas, I would be happy to hear them!

Unit 21 Achievement Test

CHRIS: Did you watch the TV show about Wangari Maathai last night?

NOEL: No. Who's that?

CHRIS: She was the winner of the 2004 Nobel Peace Prize. She's from Kenya.

NOEL: Really? What did she do?

CHRIS: She started an environmental movement there in 1976. She organized women to plant trees. Since then, thousands of women have planted more than 30 million trees in Kenya.

NOEL: That's impressive!

CHRIS: Yeah, and she's been very active in politics too. She has been in prison for fighting against cutting down trees and for demanding an end to corruption. She helped get rid of the Kenyan dictator, Daniel Moi, and she helped bring peace to the country.

NOEL: Wow, she did all that? It sounds like she really had a lot of courage!

CHRIS: Yeah, I was impressed. And she's also really respected for her intelligence. In fact, she was the first woman from the region to get a Ph.D.

NOEL: So what's she doing now?

CHRIS: A lot! She's a member of the Kenyan parliament, and she's the Assistant Minister in the Ministry of Environment, Natural Resources, and Wildlife. In 2005, she also became the first president of the African Union's Economic, Social and Cultural Council. So she's still doing a lot of work for the environment and for democracy.

NOEL: Too bad I missed the program. She sounds amazing.

Unit 22 Achievement Test

ASHLEY: What do you feel like having for dinner?

SHARI: I don't know. I'd like something interesting. . . . Do you have an international cookbook?

ASHLEY: No, but we could go to the store to look for one.

SHARI: Or we could look for a recipe on the Internet.

ASHLEY: That's a good idea. I'll go online, and we can look right now.

SHARI: Do you want to try a dish from Asia?

ASHLEY: Sure, how about an Indian dish? A friend of mine made an amazing curry once. I remember that it was a chicken curry, and it had potatoes, tomatoes, and lots of spices.

SHARI: Well, why don't we try a beef curry this time?

ASHLEY: Let's see what we can find. . . . How about this one?

SHARI: Oh, that looks like an excellent recipe. It doesn't look too hard.

ASHLEY: I think we'll have to go to the supermarket to buy some things, though. Actually, there's a great international market not too far from here. They have spices and things from around the world.

SHARI: That sounds great. Why don't we write down the ingredients and go?

PART V Achievement Test

JANET: Hey, what are you doing?

SAM: I'm planning my class schedule for next semester, but I still need one more class. How do you like your cultural studies class?

JANET: It's really good. I've learned a lot of new things about cultures around the world.

SAM: Do you have much homework in that class?

JANET: Well, we really don't have many assignments to hand in, but there is a lot of reading. The good part is that the professor doesn't give us any boring things to read. And there's just one big project: We have to write a research paper about a custom from a culture other than our own.

SAM: That sounds interesting. Do you have some ideas of what you'll write about?

JANET: Well, I have a few ideas, but I haven't decided yet. I may write about customs related to food. I'm going to the library tomorrow to do a little research on the topic.

PART VI Diagnostic Test

The 23rd annual job fair is almost here, and it will be the best job fair this town has ever had! The purpose of the fair is to bring together job candidates and companies with open positions. If you come, you'll have the chance to talk to representatives of many companies and learn more about the open positions they have.

Job opportunities in some fields are growing the fastest that they ever have! And here's some more good news: This job expansion is lasting the longest of any in the past 20 years. Now is the time to make a career change!

There are lots of reasons to consider changing jobs or careers. Maybe your current job doesn't pay you as well as you should be paid. Maybe you're working the hardest of anyone in your office, and you're tired of it. Or maybe you want more of a challenge. The reason doesn't matter. Life is too short to be unhappy. Come discover hundreds of jobs at the most exciting job fair around! This is the biggest opportunity of the year. Find the best jobs for you, this Saturday from 9:00–4:00 at the Gables Conference Center. Get a job you love and start living more happily!

Unit 23 Achievement Test

DJ 1: That was the new release from Dot Matrix, "Don't Let Me Down."

DJ 2: Isn't that a great song? Dot Matrix is one of my favorite groups. The lead singer has an incredible voice.

DJ 1: Yeah, I always enjoy listening to Marlene Rivera. And I understand she's a really friendly person. But the other band members are great too.

DJ 2: Yes, Dot Matrix is an exceptional group of musicians. And they'll be in town for a show this Friday night.

DJ 1: That's right. Everyone is excited because this is their first show here in Pleasantville. They're going to perform in the beautifully restored Bravado Hall.

DJ 2: Well, that should be an enjoyable evening.

DJ 1: Yeah, it'll be a lot of fun. Listeners, you'd better buy your tickets now, because they're going awfully quickly! Call our ticket hotline at 555-WXLR. That's 555-9957. Now we'll take a short break, and when we return, more non-stop hits from the bands you love.

DJ 2: I can hardly wait!

Unit 24 Achievement Test

The Country Inn has just reopened under new management, and they've made some great changes. The dining room looks bigger, and the lighting is better too. The dishes are a little more expensive than they were, but the food is as good as ever. The only exception is the breadsticks, which are even tastier than before. The desserts are as delicious as you can imagine. The homemade pies are as fresh as you can get, and the chocolate soufflé is lighter than air.

Apparently a lot of people like the changes at The Country Inn. Every time I go for dinner, it seems harder and harder to get a table! Try lunch for a quieter meal.

Unit 25 Achievement Test

MACHINE: You have five new messages. Message one. 12:30 P.M.

PAUL: Hi, Marlene! It's Paul. Happy Valentine's Day. I was just thinking about you, and I wanted to tell you that you're the nicest girl in the world. You're also one of the most interesting people I've ever met. I'm so lucky you're my girlfriend. I'm so excited to see you tonight. Talk to you then!

MACHINE: Message two. 12:35 P.M.

PAUL: Oh, hi. It's me again. I forgot to tell you that you're also the cutest girl I know. You have the most beautiful eyes I've ever seen. I'm such a lucky guy. OK. Bye.

MACHINE: Message three. 12:45 P.M.

PAUL: Hi again. You know, I can't stop thinking about you. You're the kindest woman I have ever dated. And intelligent! You're the most intelligent person I know! You're the most wonderful person ever!

MACHINE: Message four. 12:50 P.M.

PAUL: Marlene, I'm not sure I've told you this before, but you're one of the greatest people in the world. In fact, I don't think there's anyone better, anywhere! You're the most amazing girl on Earth!

MACHINE: Message five. 12:55 P.M.

PAUL: Seriously. You are so great! You've made me the happiest guy alive. Happy Valentine's Day! I can't wait to see you later.

Unit 26 Achievement Test

OLIVIA: Hi, Denise. Here's the report you asked for. It didn't take nearly as long as the last one to complete.

DENISE: Oh, well, I'm glad you finished so quickly. Listen, I want to ask you something. Who do you think we should select as the new general manager of the Chicago office?

OLIVIA: Well, all three of the candidates are great. Marty probably works the hardest. But that doesn't necessarily mean he's the best person for the job.

DENISE: What do you mean?

OLIVIA: Well, all their strengths are different. For example, Albert is definitely quicker than Marty in his work.

DENISE: Hmmm, that's true. Marty doesn't work as efficiently as Albert does. But he's improving. The longer Marty stays here, the faster he works. So, what about Sidney?

OLIVIA: The other candidate? Well, of the three of them, Sidney speaks the most confidently, so she has the potential to be a strong leader. But I think there are some other things to consider, too.

DENISE: Yeah? Like what?

OLIVIA: Well, on their last evaluations, Marty scored just as highly as Albert did in sales. But Sidney did better than either of them in overall customer satisfaction.

DENISE: You're right. Those are important things to consider. I'll have to think this over a bit more.

PART VI Achievement Test

Red Sky Developers' 12th Annual Home Expo is almost here, and it'll be the best expo ever! Face it: You're probably not saving money as well as you could be because your monthly house payments are too high. Did you know that you can live more comfortably in a better home for the same amount of money you're paying now? You might even pay less! Come see our beautiful homes at the most exciting home expo we've ever had.

Only the most carefully trained professionals work at Red Sky. We work the most consistently of all the developers in the area to make sure you get outstanding service.

Don't miss the greatest opportunity of the year to find the best home for you, this Saturday from 10:00 to 5:00. Come and get to know the homes of the most highly rated property development company in the area: Red Sky Developers.

PART VII Diagnostic Test

MACHIKO: I need to get some things at the store today. Actually, I'm planning on going to the thrift store to look for a skirt. Are you interested in coming with me?

TAMARA: To a thrift store? Do you mean a place that sells used things?

MACHIKO: Yes.

TAMARA: I don't know. Why do you shop at thrift stores instead of at the mall?

MACHIKO: To save money. Things are expensive at the mall. I used to shop there, but not anymore. I'm too poor.

TAMARA: Not having money doesn't mean you can't buy things. You can use your credit card.

MACHIKO: But you shouldn't buy things with your credit card when you don't have any money! That's a terrible habit.

TAMARA: Well, I don't shop at thrift stores because I don't want old, worn-out things.

MACHIKO: It's easy for people to think that everything at thrift stores is in bad condition, but you can actually find some very nice things there. Sometimes people donate to thrift stores in order to get rid of stuff they don't use, even if it's in good condition. Come with me. You'll see.

TAMARA: Well . . . OK.

Unit 27 Achievement Test

PHILLIP: Mom, I finished doing my homework. Can I go out and play?

MRS. SMITH: Not yet. You need to practice playing your violin first.

PHILLIP: Aw, Mom! Playing the violin is a waste of time. I can't stand practicing. I don't want to play the violin anymore. Can't I please go skateboarding?

MRS. SMITH: You know I don't mind letting you skateboard, but I want you to practice first. Quitting is not an option.

PHILLIP: But Mom, I miss hanging out with my friends. They keep asking me where I am.

MRS. SMITH: Practice first, or you'll risk losing your allowance this week.

Unit 28 Achievement Test

SANDY: Have you heard anything from the University of Greendale yet?

LUZ: No, but I plan on contacting them if I don't hear from them soon. They've been really slow at letting me know their decision. I look forward to finding out if I've been accepted or not. I'm so afraid of being rejected.

SANDY: What will you do if you don't get in?

LUZ: I'm not sure. I could go back to Mexico, but I'm used to living in the States now. I'm just annoyed with the admissions office for taking so long to let me know their decision. I have to wait to hear from them before making any plans.

SANDY: So what are you interested in studying if you're accepted?

LUZ: Well, I've thought about getting a degree in physical therapy.

SANDY: Oh, really? I have an aunt who used to be a physical therapist. She says they need people in that field. Don't worry too much about hearing from the school. I'm sure you'll be accepted.

LUZ: Thanks. I hope so!

Unit 29 Achievement Test

TINA: You're listening to the *Tina Monroe Show*. Our next caller is Camilla in New Jersey. Hi, Camilla!

CAMILLA: Hi, Tina! I need some advice on handling my teenage daughter.

TINA: OK.

CAMILLA: I expect her to hang out with her friends a lot, but it seems like she's *never* home.

TINA: Tell me more.

CAMILLA: Well, for instance, she'll promise to spend an evening with me, but if her friends call, she'll go out with them instead. I ask her not to go out so much but she does it anyway.

TINA: Are you worried about the friends she spends time with?

CAMILLA: A little bit. I just want to know who her friends are, but she refuses to bring them over. I encourage her to bring her friends home once in a while, but she always decides to go somewhere else. I even invited her friends to celebrate her birthday at a restaurant last month, but she planned her own party. I don't think I'm being unreasonable, do you?

TINA: Stay on the line, Camilla. We need to take a short break, but I'll try to help you when we come back. You're listening to the *Tina Monroe Show*.

Unit 30 Achievement Test

REPORTER: When the Internet first appeared, some thought that people would use it to buy everything they needed and that people would never have to leave their homes to shop in stores again. Although that's not the case yet, online shopping is definitely popular. According to a recent survey by the American Sales Association (ASA), about 50 percent of Americans use the Internet to purchase items. Many companies now use the Internet to sell their products, and every day many more individuals and companies make their products available online in order not to lose business.

The ASA conducted this study because they wanted information about how people were using the Internet. Results show that shopping is not the only popular online activity. Forty-three percent of Americans use the Internet to e-mail people. Thirty-five percent log on to find information. I'm at the local library now asking a few people why they're using the Internet . . .

Excuse me, Sir. Why are you using the Internet right now?

MAN: To read the news. I figure, why pay for a paper when I can find the same information for free online?

REPORTER: That's an interesting point. And why are you using the Internet, Ma'am?

WOMAN: To play games. I'm always here playing games.

REPORTER: And there you have it. This is Janelle Williams, Network News Radio, Washington.

Unit 31 Achievement Test

EDUARDO: Doctor, I'm so busy all the time. When I was young, I was calm enough to relax, and I didn't feel like I had to rush everywhere. Now, unscheduled moments are too short to enjoy and too few to remember. And when I do have a free moment, I'm usually too tense to relax.

DR. PACKARD: Do you ever schedule time to relax?

EDUARDO: No, I'm too busy. The days aren't long enough to do everything that I need to do. How can I add relaxing to my schedule?

DR. PACKARD: How does it feel when you can't get everything done that you need to do?

EDUARDO: I feel mad enough to scream!

DR. PACKARD: It makes you angry enough to go crazy, doesn't it?

EDUARDO: Absolutely!

DR. PACKARD: You know, sometimes we schedule our days too tightly to do everything we need or want to do, and that can be upsetting. I want you to read this book about something called the "Slow Movement." Will you read it and return it to me next week?

EDUARDO: Sure, it looks short enough.

Unit 32 Achievement Test

PABLO: We're back. I'm Pablo Jimenez. Our next guest is cleaning expert Nick Politz, who calls himself the "Prince of Clean." We have an e-mail from Elena in Michigan. She writes, "I don't mind cleaning, but I never seem to have the time." Nick, what do you do if it's difficult to find time for housework?

NICK: Well, keeping your house clean doesn't have to take a lot of time. The problem is that many people don't clean for a long time, and then they end up spending a lot of time and effort after weeks of neglect.

You should plan to spend a little bit of time cleaning each week. It's easier to keep the house clean if you can remember to do a little bit each week.

PABLO: Nick Politz, the "Prince of Clean," thank you for being on our show today.

NICK: You're most welcome, Pablo. I appreciated being here.

PABLO: If you'd like to see pictures of the "Prince of Clean" as he was cleaning our studios, visit our website at www.thepabloshow.org.

PART VII   Achievement Test

MARISOL: I'm going to the store. We need to buy some boxes, and I plan on getting some extra tape too. Are you interested in going with me?

THEO: Why do you want to buy boxes? We can get them for free at the grocery store.

MARISOL: Yeah, but then they won't be all the same size. I used to use free boxes, but I couldn't stack them very easily. Besides, grocery store boxes are too dirty.

THEO: Not having boxes that are all the same size is no problem. We can just pack them well. I don't think we should buy boxes because I don't want to waste money. We can get them for free!

MARISOL: But it's easy for the boxes to fall and for things to get damaged if they don't stack well in the truck. Believe me, I used grocery store boxes in order to save money once, but then I spent money to replace the things that got broken.

THEO: OK . . . let's go see how much they cost.

PART VIII   Diagnostic Test

LISA: Hello?

MELISSA: Hi Lisa! It's Melissa. How are things going?

LISA: OK. I have to go to a picnic for my co-workers and their families this afternoon. I'm supposed to help with the kids' activities.

MELISSA: When do you have to leave?

LISA: I was supposed to leave 20 minutes ago, but I lost my keys.

MELISSA: They've got to be there somewhere. Or maybe your son has them.

LISA: I'm not sure. Actually, now that I think about it, he must have them. They can't be in this house. I've looked everywhere!

MELISSA: Do you think he'll be back soon?

LISA: I hope so! He wasn't supposed to be gone for very long. In fact, he was going to be back by 3:00, but it's already 4:00 now!

MELISSA: Do you need a ride?

LISA: That would be great if it's not too much trouble. But my son might get back before you get here. If he does, I'll call your cell phone.

MELISSA: OK.

Unit 33   Achievement Test

AGENT: Thank you for calling ABC Realty. How can I help you?

ARLENE: Well, my husband and I are looking for a place to rent. We'd prefer a house to an apartment. Also, we'd rather not spend more than $800 a month.

AGENT: Well, there are some nice houses for rent in the West End.

ARLENE: Actually, we prefer to live on the North Side—closer to our jobs at the university.

AGENT: OK. There are some good one- and two-bedroom places available there.

ARLENE: We'd rather have two bedrooms.

AGENT: All right. I know of a nice house around there for $750 a month. Would you be interested in seeing it?

ARLENE: Sure. But I prefer to see places with my husband. Oh, are pets allowed there?

AGENT: I'm sorry, but the landlord would rather not rent to people with pets.

ARLENE: That's too bad. We have a cat, so that won't work. What else do you have?

AGENT: Well, there's an apartment on Center Street. It's very close to the university. And there's another house that's a little bigger, but it's further away from campus.

ARLENE: Well, my husband would rather walk to work than drive. But I'd rather rent a big house than get a small apartment. So I guess we should see both.

AGENT: Great. How about taking a look at them tonight? I'd rather not wait because places in that neighborhood are going fast.

ARLENE: OK. Sounds good.

Unit 34 Achievement Test

KIRSTEN: Clifton General Hospital. This is Kirsten. How can I help you?

TERESA: Hi, I'm calling about the nursing position advertised in the Sunday paper. Can you give me some more information about the application process?

KIRSTEN: Sure. Go to our website. It's www.cliftongeneralhospital.com. There's an application form there. You have to complete it and send it back to us.

TERESA: OK. Do I have to send my résumé with it too? I've had to do that for some other jobs I've applied for.

KIRSTEN: Yes. In fact, you've got to read the application instructions carefully and send everything we need. We have to receive all the information together to evaluate your application.

TERESA: All right. And do I have to e-mail all the information?

KIRSTEN: You can, but you can use regular mail too, or you can fax it. But we must receive it by May 31st. It can't be late. If we receive your application after the deadline, we can't accept it.

TERESA: OK. Where do I have to send the completed application?

KIRSTEN: The e-mail address, street address, and fax number are all on the website.

TERESA: Great. Thanks for your help.

KIRSTEN: You're welcome.

Unit 35 Achievement Test

LUISA: What did you do last night for New Year's Eve?

JAVIER: Nothing. A friend and I were going to go to a party, but he couldn't come pick me up. I went to bed just before midnight.

LUISA: What? Everyone is supposed to stay up until midnight, at least! You're supposed to count the seconds until midnight and then make a lot of noise.

JAVIER: I know. I was going to stay up, but I was really tired. How about you? What did you do?

LUISA: Well, there were supposed to be fireworks downtown. Some friends and I were going to go, but then it started raining. So we decided to stay home and celebrate there. It's too bad, though, because it was supposed to be a great show.

JAVIER: Yeah, I heard last night that they weren't going to have the show since the weather was so bad. I guess they weren't supposed to light the fireworks in the rain. But they also said that they're supposed to set the fireworks off another night instead.

LUISA: Really? Cool. If the weather's good, then I'll go. I don't care if it's actually New Year's Eve or not.

Unit 36 Achievement Test

RAQUEL: Tomorrow is the first presidential debate between candidates Senator Jackson from Connecticut and Governor Crowley from Texas. Political analyst Will Pelton joins us now to talk about what might happen at tomorrow's debate. Welcome, Will.

WILL: Thank you, Raquel.

RAQUEL: Will, Senator Jackson has been ahead in the polls for the past month. Is it possible that Governor Crowley will change his position in the polls tomorrow?

WILL: He might. Some voters are still not sure of how they'll vote. Now, will all those undecided votes go to Governor Crowley? They could, but they probably won't.

RAQUEL: Do you think Governor Crowley will announce anything new?

WILL: He may, but he probably won't change his message.

RAQUEL: What about Senator Jackson?

WILL: Senator Jackson could say something new. His message has continued to develop over time. Some people have said that he may not win the election with this strategy. But you never know. He may be the next president.

RAQUEL: And of course everyone is talking about Governor Crowley and the budget. Is he going to announce a plan to balance it?

WILL: He may. However, if he's planning that, it's not official.

RAQUEL: How about Senator Jackson?

WILL: He might mention the budget tomorrow as well. But again, we're not sure.

RAQUEL: Thank you, Will.

WILL: You're welcome, Raquel.

Unit 37 Achievement Test

VERONICA: That new TV show *Mysteries* is on in a few minutes. It might be good. Do you want to watch it?

COLLEEN: *Mysteries*? That sounds like it might be interesting. What's it about?

VERONICA: UFOs. You know, unidentified flying objects—the space ships that aliens travel in.

COLLEEN: What?! Those things can't be real. I mean, there's no proof that they really exist.

VERONICA: They've got to be real! Just think of all the people who say they've seen them! Could all of them be wrong?

COLLEEN: Well, they must be. Their stories can't be true.

VERONICA: They could be. You don't know. Would you believe in UFOs if you saw proof of their existence?

COLLEEN: I might, I guess. I don't really know.

VERONICA: Well, people see strange things in the sky all the time. If they're not UFOs, then what could they be?

COLLEEN: I don't know. They might be airplanes or something.

VERONICA: All right, the show's starting. Let's watch it, and you'll see!

PART VIII Achievement Test

MATEO: Hey, Leonard! My wife sent me to borrow some salt. Do you have any?

LEONARD: Sure . . . here you go.

MATEO: Are you OK?

LEONARD: I'm fine, but I have to take my son to basketball practice. I was supposed to leave 15 minutes ago, but my daughter has our truck.

MATEO: Oh, no. How frustrating.

LEONARD: Yeah. I was supposed to get there early to help the coach with a few things. He must be wondering if I'm going to show up.

MATEO: Could your daughter be on her way home now?

LEONARD: I don't know. She's not answering her cell phone. She might be home soon, but I'm not sure. She wasn't supposed to take the truck without telling me.

MATEO: Well, she can't be too far. Do you think you'll wait for her to get back?

LEONARD: I guess I don't have much choice. I was going to call her friend's house and see if she's there, but I can't find the number.

MATEO: Well, I'd be happy to give you both a ride if you like.

LEONARD: Do you have to go out anyway? If it's not too much trouble, that'd be great. Let me just leave a note for my daughter.

MATEO: OK.

Answer Key

PART I Diagnostic Test

1 | LISTENING: GOING OUT

A.
1. are you going `U1, U8`
2. who are you going `U8`
3. What's `U8`
4. as soon as `U7`

B.
1. met `U3`
2. is going `U6`
3. hand `U2`
4. used to live `U5`
5. Let `U2`

2 | AFTER THE LECTURE

1. like `U1`
2. showed `U3`
3. explained `U3`
4. used to be `U3, U5`
5. speak `U1`
6. don't have `U1`
7. meet `U6`
8. going to be `U7`
9. won't be `U6`
10. work `U1`
11. going to go `U6`
12. before `U7`
13. 'll call `U6, U7`
14. 's raining `U1`
15. 'll give `U6`

3 | AFTER THE FIRST DATE

1. What happened `U8`
2. Who is `U8`
3. what did he talk `U8`
4. He lectured `U3`
5. tell me `U2`
6. used to live `U5`
7. she knows `U1`
8. We're / We are going to go `U6`
9. We leave / We're leaving `U6`
10. we'll / we will probably have `U6`
11. You never used to have `U5`
12. let me know `U2`

4 | GETTING READY

Note: Both contracted and noncontracted forms are acceptable.
1. 'll be / 'll get / 'm getting / 'm going to get / 'm going to be `U6, U7`
2. 'm getting `U1`
3. are going / are going to go `U6`
4. 're going to be / 'll be `U6`
5. have `U7`
6. saw `U3`
7. took / got `U4`
8. gave `U3`
9. thought / think `U3`
10. was telling / told `U4`

11. loved / loves `U3`
12. wants `U1`

5 | EDITING: ON THE HIKE

SHEILA: I think it's ~~being~~ amazing how much we have in common!

RAY: Me too. I was ~~being~~ `U4` glad that you wanted to go to the lecture with me yesterday. I *thought* `U3` ~~thinked~~ it was interesting.

SHEILA: I did too. It was a very nice evening, and I *had* `U4` ~~was having~~ a great time! I told my roommate all about the lecture when I *got* `U3` ~~getted~~ home.

RAY: Oh, good. Hey, I brought some sandwiches. Would you like one?

SHEILA: Sure, I'm getting hungry. When you called this afternoon , `U4` I was eating lunch. But that was four hours ago . . . Mmm. Thanks for the sandwich. It's *tastes* `U1` ~~tasting~~ good.

RAY: This place *reminds* `U1` ~~is reminding~~ me a little bit of Manakara in Madagascar. Were you ever there?

SHEILA: No, I *was never* `U3` ~~never was~~ there. I *spent* `U3` ~~spended~~ most of my time in Antananarivo. Do you want to see my pictures sometime?

RAY: Sure.

SHEILA: OK. I'll *bring* `U6` ~~bringing~~ them when ~~we'll~~ *we* `U7` see each other next.

RAY: And I'll ~~X~~ `U6` show you my pictures, too.

SHEILA: That sounds great!

Unit 1 Achievement Test

1 | LISTENING: QUINTUPLETS

A.
1. is doing `N1`
2. looks `N5`
3. want `N3`
4. 's resting `N1`

B.

Present progressive	Simple present
1. are watching `N1`	1. appreciate `N2`
2. is preparing `N1`	2. believe `N5`
	3. need `N2`

2 | AT HOME WITH THE GRIFFITHS

1. is feeding **N1**
2. always want **N4**
3. makes **N2**
4. nowadays **N3**
5. feels **N5**
6. come **N2**
7. is working **N1**
8. works **N2**
9. hurries **N2**

3 | A YEAR LATER

1. are sleeping **N3**
2. cry **N2**
3. understand **N5**
4. live **N5**
5. leaves **N2**
6. arrives **N2**
7. is working **N1**
8. is testing **N1**

4 | EDITING: BEDTIME

    It's nighttime, and Mary Griffith ~~gets~~ *is getting* ready for bed. She can hardly believe that the house is so quiet. At the moment, all five babies ~~sleep~~ *are sleeping* **N1**, and she wants to sleep too. All five babies rarely ~~are sleeping~~ *sleep* **N2** at the same time. ~~There usually is~~ *There is usually* **N4** at least one baby up or crying. She looks in their room to make sure they are all OK. They are all sleeping, and they ~~are looking~~ *look* **N5** beautiful.

Unit 2 Achievement Test

1 | LISTENING: EXERCISE

A.
1. stay **N1**
2. Don't bend **N1**
3. Relax **N1**
4. don't hold **N1**

B.
1. come **N1**
2. Breathe **N1**
3. Concentrate **N1**
4. stand **N1**
5. Exhale **N1**

2 | WHO'S SAYING WHAT?

1. a driving instructor **N1**
2. a robber **N1**
3. a telephone operator **N1**
4. a receptionist **N1**
5. a boss **N1**
6. an employment specialist **N1**
7. a librarian **N1**
8. an airport security officer **N1**
9. a financial advisor **N1**

3 | EDITING: RECIPE FOR CHICKEN CASSEROLE

~~You preheat~~ *Preheat* the oven to 400° F or 200° C. ~~Spraying~~ *Spray* **N1** a casserole pan with cooking spray. ~~No~~ *Don't* **N1** use butter because butter will burn.

~~You are heating~~ *Heat* **N3** the oil in a large pan until hot. ~~Cooks~~ *Cook* **N1** the onion and garlic for a few minutes. Add the corn, bell peppers, ½ cup of the chicken broth, black pepper, and thyme. ~~Continued~~ *Continue* **N1** cooking until the bell pepper becomes soft. Stir in the other ½ cup of broth, the sour cream, mustard, and cooked rice. ~~To add~~ *Add* **N1** the chicken. When the chicken is cooked, ~~removes~~ *remove* **N1** the pan from heat, and mix until everything is well combined. ~~Stirring~~ *Stir* **N1** in ¼ cup of the mozzarella cheese and all the parsley. ~~You transfer~~ *Transfer* **N3** the mixture to the casserole dish. ~~Spreads~~ *Spread* **N1** the mixture evenly. Sprinkle the rest of the mozzarella cheese on top and ~~you~~ *(—)* **N3** bake for about 25 minutes. ~~Overcook not~~ *Don't overcook* **N1**. The casserole is ready when it is hot all the way through.

Unit 3 Achievement Test

1 | LISTENING: CONVERSATION BETWEEN CO-WORKERS

A.
1. did you come **N4**
2. we worked **N3**
3. did you become **N4**
4. Did I hear **N4**

B.
1. a **N2, N4**
2. d **N2, N4**
3. e **N2, N4**
4. f **N2, N3**
5. g **N2, N4**

2 | ROBERTO AND MARCELA'S ANNIVERSARY

1. went **N4**
2. had **N4**
3. went **N4**
4. didn't hike **N3**
5. returned **N3**
6. didn't watch **N3**

3 | MARCELA'S BIOGRAPHY

1. made **N4**
2. moved **N3**
3. felt **N4**
4. found / got **N4**
5. worked **N3**
6. met **N4**
7. got / were **N4**
8. had **N4**
9. enrolled **N3**

4 | EDITING: SATURDAY

    Roberto and Marcela ~~did have~~ *had* a good Saturday. In the afternoon, they ~~eated~~ *ate* **N4** at one of their favorite Mexican restaurants. They saw some of their friends there. Their friends were happy to see the new baby. After lunch, they ~~goed~~ *went* **N4** shopping. They needed to buy food for the week. After shopping

returned **N3**

they ~~return~~ home and put their food away. Then

did **N4**   *gave* **N4**

Marcela ~~do~~ laundry while Roberto ~~give~~ the baby a bath. In the evening, they invited their neighbors

played **N3**

over and they ~~play~~ a board game.

Unit 4 Achievement Test

| **1** | **LISTENING: QUESTIONS ABOUT THE ROBBERY** |

A.
1. were you doing **N1**
2. Were you talking **N1**
3. Were you listening **N1**
4. was moving **N3**
5. were working **N3**
6. was entering **N1**

B.
1. were (you) doing **N3**
2. was sitting **N3**
3. was listening **N3**
4. were (you) listening **N3**

| **2** | **EARTHQUAKE** |

1. were getting . . . **N2** began **N2**
2. were watching . . . **N2** went **N2**
3. stopped . . . **N5** told **N5**
4. got . . . **N5** turned **N5**
5. were driving . . . **N2** heard **N2**
6. heard . . . **N5** got **N5**
7. got . . . **N2** were standing **N2**
8. entered . . . **N5** discovered **N5**

| **3** | **EDITING: GRACE REMEMBERS THE EARTHQUAKE** |

GRACE: Do you remember that big earthquake in 1989?

CHERYL: Of course. How could I forget? What

were you

~~you were~~ doing that day?

N4

GRACE: Well, when the earthquake hit‸I was working at the stadium at Candlestick Park.

were you **N1**

CHERYL: Really? What ~~you were~~ doing when you first felt it?

was selling **N1**   *shaking* **N3**

GRACE: I ~~sold~~ soda. While the stadium was ~~shake~~, the sodas were jumping out of my box like popcorn! I was OK, but they spilled all over the customers. No one was angry, though—everyone was too scared. I remember it took a long time to get home that night!

Unit 5 Achievement Test

| **1** | **LISTENING: TEENAGERS AND FASHION** |

A.
1. Did you use to sit **N4**
2. to wearing **N5**
3. Now **N2**
4. anymore **N2**

B.
1. (never) used to do **N3**
2. used to buy **N1**
3. did (we) use to do **N4**
4. used to get **N1**

| **2** | **FASHION, THEN AND NOW** |

1. c **N3**   2. d **N3**   3. c **N1**   4. d **N1**
5. b **N1**

| **3** | **TIMES HAVE CHANGED** |

1. didn't use to consider **N3**
2. used to write **N1**
3. used to walk **N1**
4. used to listen **N1**
5. used to braid **N1**
6. used to use **N1**
7. used to love **N1**
8. used to be **N1**
9. used to watch **N1**
10. used to listen **N1**

| **4** | **EDITING: BARRY** |

Leslie's husband, Barry, ✗ used to be really different. He used to have long hair, but now it's

used **N5**

short. Leslie liked his long hair, but she got ~~use~~ to

wear **N1**

the new style. Barry used to ~~wore~~ colorful clothes, but now he usually wears a business suit. He

's / is **N5**

didn't like wearing ties at first, but now he‸used to it. He used to have a beard, but now he is clean

use **N1, N3**

shaven. Barry didn't ~~used~~ to read the paper, but he does now. He used to listen to rock, but now he

play **N1**

listens to classical music. He used to ~~playing~~ his guitar a lot, but now he doesn't have time because

used to **N1**

he works full-time. He ~~uses~~ stay up past midnight, but now he goes to bed at 10:30. He used to

go **N1**

~~going~~ dancing, but he doesn't anymore.

Unit 6 Achievement Test

| **1** | **LISTENING: THE NEW MALL** |

A.
1. going to be **N2**
2. won't need **N2**
3. not going to **N2**
4. 'll look **N3**

B. Items checked:
1 **N2** , 2 **N2** , 4 **N3** , 5 **N4** , 7 **N2**

2 | PROTESTING THE NEW MALL

1. b `N2` 2. c `N2` 3. a `N2` 4. d `N2`
5. a `N4`

3 | ADVANTAGES OF THE NEW MALL

1. 'll be / will be `N2`
2. is going to have `N3`
3. 'll be / will be `N2`
4. going to open `N3`
5. 'll be / will be `N2`
6. will be able `N3`
7. will create `N2`
8. 'll contribute / will contribute `N2`
9. going to be `N3`
10. is going to have `N3`
11. 'll be / will be `N2`
12. is going to attract `N2`

4 | EDITING: A JOB AT THE MALL

I just got a job at the mall, and I'm so excited!
I'm
~~I~~ going to work in the food court. Finally, I'll be
able to make my own money and pay for my own

to `N2`
clothes! I'm going ∧ visit all the stores and find
not going `N3`
some great clothes for myself! Dad's ~~going not~~ to
like it. He's against the mall. But he should be
happy that he won't have to give me money all
`N2`
the time. I'll ✗ tell him tonight. I looked for a job
for a long time, so hopefully he'll understand. I
start `N4`
~~starts~~ on Monday!

Unit 7 Achievement Test

1 | LISTENING: JOBS ARE US

A.
1. will you do `N1`   3. will be `N1`
2. we'll look `N1`   4. you'll realize `N1`

B.
1. when you graduate `N2`
2. As soon as you give us some basic
   information, `N2`
3. Before you know it, `N2`
4. After you sign up with us, `N2`

2 | AFTER GRADUATION

1. c `N1` 2. c `N1` 3. a `N1` 4. b `N2`

3 | PREDICTIONS ABOUT THE FUTURE

1. after `N2`
2. You're going to move to a larger
   apartment `N1`
3. Calvin gets a raise `N1`
4. As soon as / After `N2`
5. (a month) before `N2`
6. while `N2`
7. your child is five `N1`
8. will graduate from medical school `N1`
9. Calvin will begin his medical practice `N1`
10. he graduates `N1`
11. until `N2`
12. Calvin works for two years `N1`
13. while `N2`

4 | EDITING: PLANS FOR WORKING AT HOME

is
After summer ~~will be~~ over, Clint will start
school again. I can't believe that he'll be in second
grade already! I want to start working from home
starts `N1`   *as* `N2, N1`
when Clint ~~will start~~ school this year. As soon ∧ he
`N1`
does, I'll ✗ have more time than I have now. Right
now he's home all the time, and he needs attention.
I think I'll work only part-time so that I'll finish
`N1`
working ∧ before Clint comes home from school. I'll
until `N2`
need a faster computer, but I won't buy one ~~after~~ I
find one on sale.

Unit 8 Achievement Test

1 | LISTENING: THE ACTING INTERVIEW

A.
1. did you perform `N6`
2. Whom did you play `N5`
3. whose scripts `N4`
4. What did he write `N4`

B.

Question about subjects	Questions about objects
1. Who wrote the review? `N2`	1. How many performances did you have? `N4`
2. What happened in May? `N2`	2. Which kinds of characters do you prefer to play? `N4`

2 | WHO GETS THE PART?

1. a `N4` 2. e `N2` 3. b `N2` 4. g `N5`

3 | QUESTIONS FOR AN ACTRESS

1. Which movies did you like `N4`
2. When did you start `N6`

3. Who taught you **N2**
4. Which methods did she use **N4**
5. Why did you start **N6**
6. How many people contacted **N2**
7. Who directed **N2**
8. Whose music did they use **N4**
9. How many people saw **N2**
10. How much (money) did they pay **N4**
11. How long was **N6**

SCOTT: How ~did~ your interview ~~went~~ *go*?
KATHY: It was great! I got a part in a commercial!
SCOTT: You did? Congratulations! How much
~~they are~~ *are they* **N2** going to pay you?
KATHY: A lot. More than I hoped for.
SCOTT: Awesome! ~~Whom~~ *Who* **N3** interviewed you?
KATHY: The owner of the agency.
SCOTT: Which company ~~the commercial's~~ *is the commercial* **N4** for?
KATHY: Boston Global.
SCOTT: Oh yeah? Which product ~are~ you going to **N4** advertise?
KATHY: Their imported furniture.
SCOTT: Which part will you ✗ have? **N3**
KATHY: I'm going to play a wife who wants to decorate her home.
SCOTT: Who ~~the director is~~ *is the director* **N3** of the commercial?
KATHY: His name is Hal Malloy.
SCOTT: When ~do / will~ you start filming? **N6**
KATHY: In two weeks.

PART I Achievement Test

A.
1. are you eating **U8**
2. who are you going **U8**
3. What's **U8**
4. as soon as **U7**

B.
1. is going to eat **U6**
2. met **U3**
3. give **U2**
4. used to live **U5**
5. Let **U2**

1. enjoy **U1**
2. disappeared **U3**
3. reappeared **U3**
4. dressed **U3**
5. don't speak **U1**
6. 're coming **U6**
7. teach **U1**
8. won't be **U6**
9. going to be **U6**
10. are **U7**
11. going to go **U6**
12. before **U7**
13. 'll call **U7**
14. 's getting **U6**
15. 'll drive **U1**

1. What happened **U8**
2. Who is **U8**
3. He performed **U3**
4. tell me **U2**
5. used to live **U5**
6. she knows **U1**
7. We're / We are going to go **U6**
8. You never used to have **U5**
9. What time are you leaving **U1, U8**
10. opens **U1, U6**
11. we'll / we will leave **U6**
12. let me know **U2**

1. 'll be / 'll get **U6**
2. 'm getting / 'm going to get **U1**
3. are leaving / are going to leave / leave **U6**
4. 'm going to be / 'll be **U6**
5. know **U7, U1**
6. go **U3**
7. drove **U3**
8. opened **U3**
9. thought / think **U3**
10. was telling / told **U4**
11. enjoyed **U3, U4**
12. hopes **U1**

SHARON: The river is ~~being~~ really pretty.

REGGIE: I know. I love the water. I was ~~being~~ glad **U4** that we went to the magician last night. I
~~thinked~~ *thought* **U3** he was really good.
SHARON: Me too. It was a wonderful evening, and
I ~~was having~~ *had* **U4** a great time! I told my roommate
all about the magician when I ~~getted~~ *got* **U3** home.
REGGIE: Oh, good. Hey, I brought some crackers. Would you like some?
SHARON: Sure, I'm getting hungry. Before you
picked me up, I ate breakfast. But that **U4** was hours ago. Oh, I like these crackers.
They ~~'re reminding~~ *remind* **U1** me of when I was a kid.
REGGIE: This river ~~is looking~~ *looks* **U1** a lot like the Cagayan River in the Philippines. Did you ever go there?
SHARON: No, I ~~never was~~ *was never* **U1** there. I ~~spended~~ *spent* **U3** most of my time in Manila. I think it would be fun to go back. Maybe I could go this summer.
REGGIE: I think there are some good deals on tickets on the Internet right now.

SHARON: Really? I'll ~~X~~ look online when I ~~will~~ get
    send **U7**
                  U6
    home. I'll ~~sending~~ a postcard if I go.
REGGIE: That sounds good.

PART II Diagnostic Test

1	LISTENING: SHARING AN APARTMENT

A.
1. figuring out **U10**
2. yourself **U9**
3. myself **U9**
4. finding out **U10**
5. yourself **U9**
6. himself **U9**
7. each other **U9**
8. yourself **U9**

B.
1. T **U9**
2. F **U9**
3. F **U9**
4. F **U9**
5. T **U9**
6. T **U9**

2	NEW ROOMMATES

1. out **U10**
2. each other's **U9**
3. off **U10**
4. up **U10**
5. up **U10**
6. out **U10**
7. called up **U10**
8. up **U10**
9. out **U10**
10. out **U10**

3	EXERCISING

1. yourself **U9**
2. yourself **U9**
3. himself **U9**
4. each other **U9**
5. himself **U9**
6. himself **U9**
7. myself **U9**
8. ourselves / each other **U9**

4	STAYING FIT

1. yourself **U9**
2. yourself **U9**
3. yourself **U9**
4. myself **U9**
5. each other / one another **U9**
6. themselves **U9**

5	A TRIP TO THE LIBRARY

1. up **U10**
2. into **U10**
3. out **U10**
4. up **U10**
5. out **U10**
6. by **U10**
7. up **U10**
8. out **U10**
9. out **U10**
10. up **U10**
11. out **U10**

6	EDITING: TALK BETWEEN ROOMMATES

BOB: What time do you wake ^*up* in the morning?

JUAN: Well, I figured ~~up~~ I need about nine hours of
          out **U10**
    sleep. So I get up around 9:00 or sometimes
    10:00. Why do you ask?

          myself **U9**
BOB: I get ~~me~~ out of bed by 6:00 every day so
    that I can go running before class. And I like
    to play music in the morning. But I can turn
    down / off **U10**
    it ^ if it's too loud for you.

JUAN: 6:00?! I know some people who can't get
    themselves **U9**
    ~~them~~ out of bed until noon. But don't worry
    about the music. I can sleep through anything.

BOB: That's great. A friend of mine who went
    on **U10**
    ~~out~~ to win lots of races told me that he
    listened to music before running. I thought it
    might help me.

                             yourself **U9**
JUAN: Whatever you need to do to keep ~~your~~
                me **U9**
    energetic is fine with ~~myself~~. I like to play
    music at night while I study. Will that bother
    you?

BOB: Usually I can study with music. But if I'm
                  myself **U10**
    working on math, I need to be by ~~me~~ in a
    room with no distractions.

                          by **U9**
JUAN: I understand. I had a friend who lived ^
    himself and still needed to go to the library
    because his neighbors were noisy. Don't worry.
                  out **U9**
    This kind of problem is easy to work ~~in~~. I'll be
    sure to tell you before I play music.

BOB: Sounds good. It's great that we can discuss
          each other **U9**
    things with ~~you and me~~.

Unit 9 Achievement Test

1	LISTENING: AN OPTIMISTIC PERSON

1. itself **N3**
2. herself **N1**
3. yourself **N1**
4. myself **N1**
5. one another **N5**
6. each other **N5**

2	HELP YOUR CHILD BE OPTIMISTIC

1. themselves **N1**
2. each other **N5**
3. itself **N3**
4. herself **N1**
5. himself **N1**
6. each other **N5**
7. himself **N1**
8. one another **N5**
9. themselves **N1**
10. themselves **N1**

3	WHO IS OPTIMISTIC?

1. himself **N1**
2. himself **N1**
3. ourselves **N1**

4 | OPTIMISM AND YOUR HEALTH

1. each other / one another **N5**
2. themselves **N1**
3. each other / one another **N5**
4. yourself **N1**
5. yourself **N1**
6. yourself **N1**
7. myself **N1**

5 | EDITING: BE AN OPTIMISTIC PERSON ALL THE TIME!

The true measure of being healthy is how

optimistic you are about ~~myself~~ *yourself* and your life. You can learn how to control your thinking so that you feel good about almost any situation. First, instead of looking at a problem as permanent, ~~yourself~~ *you* **N1**, as an optimistic person, can see it as a temporary problem that has a solution. You may see the problem as a challenging situation that you can resolve alone or with another person. Optimistic

people rely on each *other* **N5** to discover solutions together. Secondly, when something goes wrong, don't take it personally. Once you learn that you can't control

everything by ~~himself~~ *yourself* **N4**, you are on the road to becoming an optimistic person. You can believe in

yourself **N1** ~~you~~ and the world around you.

Unit 10 Achievement Test

1 | LISTENING: MOVIE PLANS

A.
1. figure out **N3**
2. look over **N3**
3. pick out **N3**
4. drop off **N3**
5. look up **N3**
6. get back **N4**

B.
1. hand (it) in **N3**
2. get by **N4**
3. pass (that movie) up **N3**
4. find out **N3**

2 | HOMEMADE TORTILLAS

1. wake up **N4**
2. figured out **N3**
3. set up **N3**
4. go on **N4**
5. pass up **N3**
6. drop off **N3**

3 | LIFE IN MEXICO

1. out **N3**
2. on **N3**
3. up **N3**
4. out **N3**
5. on **N4**
6. up **N4**

4 | EDITING: DINNER PLANS

PABLO: I only have $10 for dinner.

CARMEN: I have $20. Do you think we can ~~get out~~ *get by* with only $30?

PABLO: Well, I can use my credit card. I can help ~~out you~~ *you out* **N3** if you order something expensive. Let's go to the restaurant, look ~~on~~ *over / at* **N3** a menu, and then decide.

CARMEN: OK, but first I need to take ~~down~~ *off* **N3** these shoes and put ~~out~~ *on* **N3** my sneakers. They're more comfortable.

PABLO: Where I was brought ~~on~~ *up* **N3**, women never wore sneakers out to dinner.

CARMEN: Oh, really? Where I grew *up* **N4** in California, everyone wore sneakers everywhere.

PABLO: My dad always points *out* **N3** how different things are here in the United States.

CARMEN: Hmmm. Do you want to think ~~over this~~ *this over* **N3**?

PABLO: What do you mean?

CARMEN: I thought you might be embarrassed to eat dinner with a woman wearing sneakers.

PABLO: Ha-ha. Very funny. Let's go.

PART II Achievement Test

1 | LISTENING: JOB OPPORTUNITY

A.
1. signed up **U10**
2. yourself **U9**
3. is setting out **U10**
4. carry out **U10**
5. by himself **U9**
6. themselves **U9**
7. each other **U9**
8. yourself **U9**

B.
1. T **U9**
2. F **U9**
3. F **U9**
4. F **U9**
5. F **U9**
6. F **U9**
7. T **U9**
8. F **U9**

2 | AT BILL AND JOHN'S APARTMENT

1. pick out **U10**
2. got back **U10**
3. figure out **U10**
4. clean up **U10**
5. get by **U10**
6. got back **U10**
7. turning into **U10**
8. look up **U10**
9. Turn down **U10**

3 | TIME TO REGISTER FOR CLASSES

1. talk over **U10**
2. found out **U10**
3. set up **U10**
4. pick up **U10**
5. pick out **U10**

4 | WAITING IN LINE

1. c U9
2. b U9
3. d U9
4. a U9
5. b U9
6. d U9
7. a U9
8. b U9
9. d U9

5 | NEED A JOB?

Reflexive pronouns
1. ourselves U9
2. yourself U9

Reciprocal pronouns
1. each other U9
2. one another U9

6 | THE JOB SEARCH

1. up U10
2. up U10
3. itself U9
4. myself U9
5. over U10
6. each other / one another U9

7 | EDITING: LISA'S FIRST DAY OF WORK

BILL: So, Lisa found ~~her~~ *herself* a job.

JOHN: Yes, but she called ~~up me~~ *me up* U10 last night and told me her first day of work as a waitress was miserable. She says she thought it ~~up~~ *over* U10 and she has no confidence in ~~her~~ *herself* U9.

BILL: Sounds like her first day turned into a disaster. What happened?

JOHN: Well, she figured ~~up~~ *out* U9 that she can't carry a tray.

BILL: Don't tell me. Did she spill food on ~~her~~ *herself* U10?

JOHN: Worse! She spilled on some customers! She picked ^*up* U10 the tray, and it was too heavy. A few plates of food fell on them.

BILL: Then what happened?

JOHN: Well, the customers were angry. They left the table. Lisa just sat ~~out~~ *down* U9 and started crying.

BILL: That sounds horrible. Did they leave the restaurant?

JOHN: No, they cleaned ~~them~~ *themselves* U9 up in the bathroom. But they didn't want Lisa to be their waitress after that. They weren't very happy with ~~herself~~ *her* U10.

BILL: I don't understand. Lisa told me she grew ^*up* U10 working in her family's restaurant.

JOHN: Yes, that's true. But she worked in the kitchen with the cooks. She helped ~~out them~~ *them out* U10 by preparing the vegetables. So she has no experience serving customers.

BILL: Well, she'll have to find a way to keep herself optimistic.

JOHN: I agree, but sometimes it's hard to keep yourself optimistic when you're dropping food on your customers.

PART III Diagnostic Test

1 | LISTENING: THE BIG IDEA

A.
1. Can we make U11
2. Should we build U14
3. May we build U12
4. won't be able to U11
5. Could we please build U12
6. can hold U11
7. couldn't U11

B.

Advice	Ability	Request	Suggestion
1. You should build it in the tree on the side of the house. U14	1. We can convince him. U11	1. Could you please shut the door? U13	1. Let's go ask Dad. U15

2 | GATHERING THE MATERIALS

1. can't U11
2. Why don't U15
3. go U13
4. help U13
5. to wear U14
6. 'd better U14
7. closing U13
8. why not U15
9. Would U13

3 | BUILDING THE TREEHOUSE

1. a U15
2. b U13
3. b U11
4. a U12
5. c U12
6. b U12
7. c U15
8. a U11
9. c U14

4 | SHOWING THE TREEHOUSE

1. couldn't / wasn't able to U11
2. Will . . . be able to U11
3. can U11
4. can / will be able to / are able to U11
5. may / can U12
6. can't / may not U12
7. Can / Could / Will / Would U13
8. wasn't able to / couldn't U11
9. will U13
10. may not / can't U12

---

236 | ANSWER KEY

5 | TALKING ABOUT THE BOYS

1. Maybe we could get **U15**
2. the boys should build **U14**
3. I ought to ask **U14**
4. They had / They'd better go **U14**
5. How about taking **U15**
6. we shouldn't make **U14**
7. Let's talk **U15**

6 | EDITING: SHOPPING FOR MORE MATERIALS

ANDY: Can we ~~looking~~ *look* at the wood for the roof now?

U15
DAD: Let's ~~X~~ get the wood last so we don't have

buy **U14**
to carry it around the store. We should ~~buying~~

please get some / get some, please **U13**
more nails. Taylor, can you ~~get please some~~? They're over there.

TAYLOR: Sure, no problem.

ANDY: Why don't we put a refrigerator in the

buy **U13**
treehouse? Could we ~~buying~~ one, Dad?

DAD: No, I don't think so.

get **U15**
TAYLOR: Why not ~~getting~~ just a small one?

DAD: You can't use a refrigerator without electricity.

TAYLOR: Oh, right. Too bad. A refrigerator would be pretty cool.

U14
ANDY: Well, we'd better ~~X~~ think of something else to get.

DAD: Andy, my hands are getting full. Would you mind holding these tools?

Not at all. / No problem. **U13**
ANDY: ~~Sure.~~ Give them to me. Hey, how about having a pole to slide down like a firefighter?

DAD: That sounds like fun.

should we **U14**
TAYLOR: When ~~had we better~~ buy the pole? Right now?

to **U14**
DAD: Well, I think you ought ∧ wait until you have more practice with building things. That might be a little complicated.

can't **U11**
TAYLOR: I ~~couldn't~~ wait for you to teach us more about building stuff. By the time you teach us

'll be able to **U11**
everything you know, we ~~can~~ make lots of improvements on the treehouse.

if **U12**
ANDY: Dad, do you mind ∧ we look around a little? We might get some good ideas for improvements.

shouldn't / can't **U14**
DAD: That's fine. But we ~~ought not~~ take too long. Mom needs to use the car today too, and she

go **U11**
can't ~~going~~ anywhere until we get home.

Unit 11 Achievement Test

1 | LISTENING: AN INTERVIEW

A.
1. can work **N6**
2. Are you able to dance **N6**
3. Can you play **N3**
4. Are you able to do **N6**

B.
1. can't sing **N1**
2. can dance **N3**
3. can do **N3**
4. couldn't come **N5**

2 | GREG'S E-MAIL

1. a **N5**   2. d **N6**   3. d **N3**   4. b **N4**

3 | ENRIQUE CRUZ

Note: Both contracted and noncontracted forms are acceptable.

1. was able to learn **N6**
2. is able to / can act **N3**
3. is able to / can play **N3**
4. is able to / can speak **N3**
5. weren't able to / couldn't tell **N5**
6. is able to / can sing **N1**
7. is going to / will be able to perform **N4**
8. to be able to play **N6**
9. was able to / could dance **N5**
10. isn't able to / can't dance **N3**
11. was able to perform **N5**
12. isn't able to / can't do **N3**
13. will be able to / can go **N6**

4 | EDITING: ESTELLA'S JOURNAL

July 14

was
I ~~am~~ finally able to have my interview with Greg Rollins yesterday. I was able to tell him all about my talents as an actor. Then today he called and asked me to audition for a role on a new TV

wait **N1**
show. The audition is tomorrow. I can't ~~waiting~~! It's so exciting! And here's the best part: I'll be

to **N4**
able ∧ meet Enrique Cruz, who's going to be on the show! He's my favorite actor! I could never wait for his movies to come out when I was

was able to **N5**
young. One day last summer, I ~~could~~ catch a glimpse of him at a studio, but I didn't actually

N4
meet him. Anyway, I can ~~X~~ go to the studio tomorrow for my audition. Greg sent me a script to read at the audition. I'm going to study it all

'll / will be able to **N4**
night. By tomorrow I ~~can~~ say my lines really well. I hope I get this job!

Unit 12 Achievement Test

1 | LISTENING: AT THE COMPANY PICNIC

A.
1. Yes, of course you can **N3**
2. could I ask **N1**
3. you can use **N3**
4. Can I please go **N2**

B.
1. F **N3**
2. T **N4**
3. F **N4**
4. F **N3**

2 | LOOKING FOR THE TENNIS COURTS

1. May we please **N2**
2. sorry **N3**
3. ask **N4**
4. Can we take **N1**

3 | QUESTIONS AND ANSWERS AT SCHOOL

1. Do you mind if I call you tonight **N4**
2. Not at all / No, I don't / Go right ahead / No problem **N4**
3. Can I please borrow $5 / Can I please borrow $5 from you / Can I borrow $5, please / Can I borrow $5 from you, please **N2**
4. Sure / Yes / Yes, of course you can / Yes, you can / Yes, you may / Of course / Certainly / OK / No problem **N3**
5. May I check out this book / May I check this book out **N1**
6. No / No, you may not / No, you can't / I'm sorry, no / I'm sorry / No, I'm sorry **N3**
7. Could I turn in my paper tomorrow / Could I turn my paper in tomorrow **N1**
8. Can I give you my homework after class / Can I give my homework to you after class / Can I give you it after class / Can I give it to you after class **N1**
9. Could I use your dictionary **N1**
10. I'm sorry / No, you can't / I'm sorry, no / No, I'm sorry **N3**
11. Can I borrow your blue pen **N1**
12. May I go to the bathroom **N1**
13. May I get a book from my locker **N1**

4 | EDITING: AT THE LIBRARY

LIBRARIAN: Can I ~~X~~ help you?
CAROLYN: Yes, I'm returning an overdue library book. Can I pay the fine now?
      can / may **N3**
LIBRARIAN: Yes, you ~~could~~.
CAROLYN: And I also want to check out these books.
      see **N1**
LIBRARIAN: OK. May I ~~saw~~ your library card, please?
      Sorry, / I'm sorry **N3**
CAROLYN: ~~I sorry~~, but I left it at home. Can I get the books without it?
LIBRARIAN: Sure. I just need another form of identification, and then you can pay the

please see / see . . . license, please **N2**
fine. Can I ~~see please~~ your driver's license?
CAROLYN: Uh-oh. I don't have any identification
      if **N4**
with me. Do you mind ˄ I just pay the fine later?
Librarian: That's fine, but you can't check out any books until you pay the fine.
CAROLYN: OK. Thank you for your help.

Unit 13 Achievement Test

1 | LISTENING: PHONE CONVERSATION

A.
1. Could you water **N1**
2. Would you please let **N2**
3. Would you e-mail **N1**
4. can you buy **N1**
5. would you mind stopping **N4**
6. Can you please rent **N2**

B.

Responses: Will do what the person requests	Response: Will not do what the person requests
1. No problem. **N3**	1. I'm sorry, I can't today. **N3**
2. Not at all. **N4**	
3. Of course. **N3**	

2 | CLEANING THE HOUSE

1. c **N3**
2. b **N4**
3. c **N4**
4. b **N2**
5. c **N2**
6. a **N3**
7. c **N2**
8. b **N4**
9. b **N1**
10. a **N1**
11. c **N2**
12. a **N1**
13. b **N2**
14. a **N1**
15. c **N2**

3 | EDITING: IN THE EVENING

GABE: Can you ~~X~~ put on some music?
      turning **N4**
JACKIE: Sure. Would you mind ~~to turn~~ on the lights?
      make **N1**
GABE: Not at all. Then could you ~~makes~~ us some hot chocolate?
      can't **N3**
JACKIE: Sorry, I ~~couldn't~~. We don't have any. Do you want tea instead?
GABE: That sounds good. But can you buy some more hot chocolate the next time you go to the store?
JACKIE: Certainly. Is this music OK?
      please turn up / turn up the volume, please **N2**
GABE: Yes. But will you ~~turn up please~~ the volume?
Sure. / Sure I will. / Certainly. / Yes, I will. / Of course. / Of course I will. / No problem. **N3**
JACKIE: ~~Not at all~~. Is this better?
GABE: Perfect. Thanks.

Unit 14 Achievement Test

1 | LISTENING: *MONEY MATTERS*

A.
1. you ought to do N1
2. When should I call N3
3. you'd better write N2
4. you should get N1
5. had better pay N2

B.

Statements of advice	Questions asking for advice
1. You had better call as soon as you realize your wallet is missing. N2	1. Should I cancel my credit cards right away? N3
2. You ought to do that right after you call the police. N1	2. When should I get new ID cards? N3

C.
1. T N2   2. F N1   3. T N1   4. T N1

2 | HOW CAN I PROTECT MYSELF?

1. Should I write them down N3
2. Yes, you should N1
3. Should I give it to them N3
4. No, you shouldn't N1
5. Should I shop online only at secure websites N3
6. Yes, you should N1

3 | EDITING: HOW TO AVOID IDENTITY THEFT

0. You should ~~leaving~~ *leave* any ID cards that you don't use often in a safe place at home.

1. You ought *to* N1 ‸sign your credit cards as soon as you get them, and you should cancel any cards you don't use.

2. You should not ~~carrying~~ *carry* N1 your birth certificate with you. Keep it in a safe place.

3. You should not ~~wrote~~ *write* N1 your PIN numbers on your cards.

4. You had better ✗ N2 shred any documents that have personal information on them.

5. You should ~~checks~~ *check* N1 your credit card accounts regularly to look for any unusual activity.

6. If you don't receive a credit card statement, you ought ‸ *to* N1 contact the company.

---

7. You ~~shoulds~~ *should* N1 change the passwords and PIN numbers for your bank accounts frequently.

8. You ~~ought to not~~ *shouldn't* N1 give your bank account information over the phone or online.

9. You ought to ~~using~~ *use* N1 passwords that are difficult for people to guess.

10. You should ~~putting~~ *put* N1 outgoing mail in a secure post office box, and you ought to remove your mail from your mailbox soon after it is delivered. N1

11. You ~~are~~ should protect your computer with anti-virus software.

Unit 15 Achievement Test

1 | LISTENING: WEEKEND PLANS

A.
1. Why don't we get N1
2. Let's not spend N2
3. Why not buy N1
4. How about having N1

B.
1. F N1
2. F N1
3. T N1
4. F N1

2 | WHAT SHOULD WE DO TODAY?

1. Maybe we could N1
2. Why don't N1
3. Why not N1
4. How about N1
5. Let's N2
6. Maybe we could N1
7. Let's N1
8. Let's not N1
9. meet N3
10. Why not N1
11. How about N1

3 | GETTING READY FOR THE BARBECUE

1. set up the chairs. N4
2. put on some music? N4
3. open the windows. N4
4. play some games? N4
5. making some iced tea? N4

4 | EDITING: DURING THE BARBECUE

TAYLOR: Why ~~we don't~~ *don't we* get the food out? Or maybe people could start with drinks.

GABRIELLA: Yes, that sounds good. How about ~~to bring~~ *bringing* N3 out the lemonade first?

TAYLOR: You've been busy all day. Why ~~you don't~~ *don't you* **N1**
sit down and relax? I can get the lemonade.

GABRIELLA: OK. Thanks!

(A little while later)

GABRIELLA: Look, there are Matt and Anita.

They're all by themselves. Let's ✗ *introduce* **N3**

them to some people. Maybe they could ✗ **N1**
meet a few new friends.

TAYLOR: We could ~~introducing~~ *introduce* **N3** them to Joshua and
Kate.

GABRIELLA: Yeah. Maybe we could all play a game
together. That will start a conversation.

TAYLOR: OK, but let's ~~don't~~ *not* **N1** play anything too
hard. I want to have fun!

PART III Achievement Test

1 | LISTENING: THE PROJECT

A.
1. Can we do **U11**
2. can come **U11**
3. Should we ask **U14**
4. can we please talk **U12**
5. couldn't understand **U11**
6. you'll be able to **U11**
7. may we come **U12**

B.

Advice	Ability	Request	Suggestion
1. (I think) you should wait until tomorrow. **U14**	1. You can get a good grade on this project. **U11**	1. Could you please tell us more about the project? **U13**	1. Let's go. **U15**

2 | FINDING THE MATERIALS

1. looking **U13**
2. couldn't **U11**
3. Why don't **U15**
4. go **U13**
5. have **U13**
6. to talk **U14**
7. 'd better **U14**
8. Would **U13**
9. Why not **U15**

3 | STARTING THE BOTTLE ROCKET

1. c **U15**
2. a **U13**
3. b **U11**
4. b **U12**
5. c **U12**
6. a **U12**
7. c **U15**
8. b **U11**
9. c **U14**

4 | THE PRACTICE LAUNCH

1. Will . . . be able to **U11**
2. Can **U11**
3. can **U11**
4. may / can **U12**
5. can't / may not **U12**
6. can / will / could / would **U13**
7. couldn't / wasn't able to **U11**
8. will **U13**
9. couldn't / wasn't able to **U11**
10. you can't / you may not **U12**

5 | TALKING ABOUT AMBER

1. How about encouraging **U15**
2. She should do **U14**
3. maybe she could pick out **U15**
4. we had better ask **U14**
5. we should make **U14**
6. we ought to help **U14**
7. Let's talk **U15**

6 | EDITING: A MORNING OF ERRANDS

AMBER: Hey, Dad, can I ✗ show you the rocket
kits that I want?

DAD: Sure. Let's ✗ compare them. **U15**

AMBER: Well, I like both of these. Can ~~please I~~ *I please / I get two, please* **U12** get
two?

DAD: Certainly. But you should ~~remembering~~ *remember* **U14** that
you're paying for part of them.

AMBER: I know. I want them. They're really cool.

Hmmm . . . I ~~couldn't~~ *can't / 'm not able to* **U11** imagine how to make a
rocket with these.

DAD: Why not ~~asking~~ *ask* **U15** someone? Excuse me, sir.

Could you ~~helps~~ *help* **U13** us with these rocket kits?

CLERK: Of course. Would you mind waiting for
just a few minutes?

DAD: ~~Sure.~~ *No problem. / Not at all.* **U13** We're not in a hurry.

AMBER: We'd better ✗ **U14** get Mom a new battery for
her cell phone while we're shopping today. She

can't even ~~having~~ *have* **U11** it on a whole day without the
battery going dead. Should we get that here?

DAD: No, we ~~ought not.~~ *shouldn't* **U14** It's too expensive. Do you

mind ∧ *if* **U12** we stop by the electronics store on the
way home?

AMBER: No, I don't.

DAD: They have a new battery for her phone.

be able to (U11)

After we buy her that, she will ~~can~~ use her phone several days without charging the battery.

should we (U14)

AMBER: Great! When ~~had we better~~ give it to her? How about her birthday?

to (U14)

DAD: Well, I think we ought ⌃give it to her right away. She needs it now.

PART IV Diagnostic Test

1 | LISTENING: OLD FRIENDS

1. haven't changed (U16)
2. 've been living (U20)
3. lived (U19)
4. 've recently moved (U18)
5. wanted (U19)
6. 've worked (U16)
7. opened (U19)
8. 've recently opened (U18)
9. heard (U19)
10. 've been writing (U20)
11. 've recently finished (U18)
12. haven't had (U16)

2 | BEAUTY SALON OF BOSTON

1. a (U20)
2. c (U16)
3. c (U16)
4. b (U17)
5. a (U16)
6. c (U18)
7. a (U19)
8. b (U19)
9. b (U18)
10. a (U20)

3 | CONVERSATION OVER COFFEE

1. Have you enjoyed (U16)
2. Yes, I have (U16)
3. 've worked (U18)
4. 've managed (U18)
5. 've processed (U20)
6. Have you found (U16)
7. 've applied (U18)
8. Have you . . . considered (U18)
9. 've never thought (U18)

4 | CONNIE'S BLOG

1. 's lived (U20)
2. 's owned (U16)
3. 've already seen (U17)
4. has never been (U19)
5. has recently quit (U18)
6. 's been looking (U20)
7. 's called (U20)
8. haven't finished (U19)

5 | CONNIE'S MOVE TO BOSTON

1. lived (U19)
2. 's recently quit / recently quit (U18)
3. 's already found / already found (U17)
4. 's been looking for (U20)
5. hasn't accepted / didn't accept (U17)
6. has asked / asked (U20)
7. haven't met / didn't meet (U20)
8. hasn't told / didn't tell (U17)
9. has continued (U16)
10. 's received / received (U16)
11. 's met / met (U19)
12. hasn't made / didn't make (U16)

6 | EDITING: CONNIE'S BLOG, PART 2

decided

Well, last month I've ~~decided~~ to accept Donna's offer to be the new accountant for her salons. I've

for (U16)   *been enjoying / enjoyed* (U19)

been there ~~since~~ three weeks now, and I've ~~enjoy~~

has been (U16)

every minute of it. Donna ~~was~~ really nice to work

needed (U19)

with so far. Last week I've ~~need~~ to catch up on some work that the old accountant didn't do.

finished (U17)

There was a lot of work, but I've already ~~finish~~ it all. I've never enjoyed a job as much as I'm

already had (U20)

enjoying this one. I've ~~already been having~~ my hair

I've (U20)

cut, and ~~I'm~~ met a lot of the people who work in

recently had (U18)

the salons. They're all very nice. I've ~~had recently~~ a couple of the girls over for dinner. Donna and

come (U17)

her husband have already ~~came~~ over twice. I've been hoping to have a large dinner party for everyone sometime soon.

Unit 16 Achievement Test

1 | LISTENING: COMPUTER TALK

1. 've done (N4)
2. 've built (N4)
3. since (N2)
4. have you studied (N4)
5. For (N3)
6. 's created (N4)
7. since (N2)
8. 's made (N4)

2 | WE MEET AGAIN

1. since (N2)
2. for (N2)
3. since (N2)
4. for (N3)
5. since (N2)
6. for (N3)
7. since (N2)
8. since (N2)
9. since (N2)

3 | QUESTIONS FOR A PRO

Note: Both contracted and noncontracted forms are acceptable.

1. 've done **N4**
2. for **N3**
3. 've created **N4**
4. since **N2**
5. Have you received **N4**
6. 've won **N4**
7. since **N2**
8. Have you earned **N4**
9. since **N2**
10. 've made **N4**

4 | EDITING: SCOTT'S WEBSITE

<u>About me:</u> I'm Scott Johnson, and ~~I~~ *I've* been a web

designer and a computer science major ~~since~~ *for* **N3** two

years. ~~For~~ *Since* **N2** I started studying computer science,

I've ~~help~~ *helped* **N4** some friends build their websites. I'd be happy to help you with your Web design needs. Contact me at sjohnson@uua.edu.

Unit 17 Achievement Test

1 | LISTENING: HARD TO PLEASE

1. yet **N5**
2. 've read **N1**
3. Have you seen **N5**
4. already **N2**
5. haven't done **N5**
6. haven't taken **N3**

2 | WHAT HAS DAVID DONE?

Note: Both contracted and noncontracted forms are acceptable.

1. has already drunk **N1**
2. hasn't drunk . . . yet **N3**
3. has already read **N1**
4. hasn't read . . . yet **N3**
5. has already eaten **N1**
6. hasn't eaten . . . yet **N3**
7. has already taken **N1**
8. hasn't taken . . . yet **N3**

3 | BACK IN THE OFFICE

1. b **N5**
2. a **N1, N2**
3. c **N5**
4. b **N3**
5. c **N1, N2**
6. a **N3**
7. c **N1, N2**
8. b **N1, N2**
9. a **N5**
10. a **N1, N2**

4 | EDITING: NURSE'S NOTES

David's already ~~be~~ *been* here twice this winter with cold symptoms. He's had his present cold for four

days ~~yet~~ *already* **N1**, and he's now starting to feel somewhat

better. He's ~~received already~~ *already received* **N2** his flu shot, and he has

already ~~have~~ *had* **N1** a complete physical. David usually

gets allergies in the spring, and he ~~have~~ *has* **N1** already

bought his allergy medication, but he hasn't ~~start~~ *started* **N3** to use it yet. He went to his allergist for more

testing, but the results haven't come back ~~already~~ *yet* **N3**.

Unit 18 Achievement Test

1 | LISTENING: MOTHER'S DAY

A.
1. 've often written **N2**
2. several times **N2**
3. twice **N2**
4. ever forgotten **N3**

B.
1. b **N1**
2. c **N2**
3. c **N2**
4. a **N2**
5. b **N3**

2 | MOTHER'S DAY PLANS

Note: Both contracted and noncontracted forms are acceptable.

1. Have we ever made her **N3**
2. we've never made her **N3**
3. Have we ever bought her **N3**
4. we've never bought her **N3**
5. Have we ever forgotten **N3**
6. we've never forgotten **N3**
7. Has Mom ever complained **N3**
8. Mom has / She's never complained **N3**

3 | CLEANING HOUSE

1. has vacuumed **N1**
2. has washed **N1**
3. has dusted **N1**
4. has swept **N2**
5. 've / have made **N1**
6. has straightened **N1**
7. has planted **N1**
8. has mowed **N1**
9. 've / have just watered the plants **N4**
10. has cleaned **N1**

4 | EDITING: THE CLEAN HOUSE

I've ~~have~~ *had* a nice Mother's Day. Howard and Leanne are such sweethearts. The house ~~have~~ *has* **N1** been a mess because I've been ~~lately so busy~~ *so busy lately* **N4**. I haven't had time to clean when I get home from work. I just eat and go to bed. But they've just ~~clean~~ *cleaned* **N4** everything! It's like I'm in a new house! What a great Mother's Day gift.

Unit 19 Achievement Test

1 | LISTENING: BARRY'S COOKIES

1. bought **N2**
2. haven't eaten **N1**
3. ate **N3**
4. I've had **N3**
5. has done **N2**
6. happened **N1**
7. 's disappeared **N2**
8. thought **N1**

2 | FACTORY TOUR

1. worked **N2**
2. saved **N2**
3. started **N2**
4. has grown **N3**
5. made **N3**
6. 've improved **N1**
7. 've produced **N1**
8. has worked **N1**
9. has developed **N2**
10. has been **N3**

3 | CHANGES

1. In the 1970s Barry was skinny. **N3**
2. Since then, he has gained weight. **N1**
3. In the 1970s Barry was unsuccessful in school. **N3**
4. Since then, he has become a successful businessman. **N1**
5. In the 1970s Barry worked as a bakery assistant. **N3**
6. Since then, he has learned how to manage a company. **N1**
7. In the 1970s Barry was single. **N3**
8. Since then, he has gotten married. **N1**

4 | EDITING: BARRY'S COOKIES IN THE NEWS

Over the past 10 years, Barry's Cookies ~~became~~ *has become* the leading cookie company in the United States. The value of the company ~~climbed~~ *has climbed* **N3** steadily since it first opened in 1979. The company has opened markets in 12 foreign countries—last year, it ~~has opened~~ *opened* **N3** its first store in Mexico. Since the mid-1990s, the company ~~sold~~ *has sold* **N1** billions of dollars' worth of cookies.

What does Barry say about his success? "I have always wanted to make people happy. I guess I've done that. And I'm glad that people ~~started~~ *have started* **N2** to think of Barry's as America's favorite cookie."

Unit 20 Achievement Test

1 | LISTENING: WORLD MUSICIAN

A.
1. 's been putting **N1**
2. has been **N1**
3. lived **N2**
4. has been playing **N2**

B.

Present perfect progressive	Present perfect
1. 's been writing **N1**	1. 's studied **N3**
2. 's been living **N3**	2. 's picked up **N2**

2 | DANIEL MEYERS'S WEBSITE

1. finished **N1**
2. used **N2**
3. been touring **N2**
4. been making **N2**
5. been having **N2**
6. been planning **N1**

3 | INTERVIEW WITH DANIEL MEYERS

1. How long have you been making music? **N2**
   I've been making music for twenty years. **N2**
2. How many awards have you received over the past year? **N2**
   I've received three awards. **N2**
3. Where have you been touring this month? **N2**
   I've been touring (in) Australia. **N1**
4. How many times have you toured Asia? **N2**
   I've toured Asia six times. **N2**
5. What has been your inspiration for your recent album? **N2**
   My daughter has been my inspiration. **N1**
6. Has your daughter been listening to the album a lot these days? **N1**
   Yes. She's been listening to it a lot. **N1**

4 | EDITING: WEB REVIEW

I've been ~~listen~~ *listening* to Meyers's new CD, *The Cradle of Sound*, for the past week, and I ~~has~~ *have* **N1** been struggling to find the words to describe this album. He's changed his sound many times, and in this album his sound changes with every song. Some songs are danceable and some are like lullabies, yet Meyers has been ~~being~~ **N1** able to create an album in which all the songs work together. In my opinion, Meyers ~~has been creating~~ *has created* **N1** another masterpiece in music. Dan Meyers, you've done **N2**

~~been doing~~ great work on all of your previous albums. You have now given us pure genius.

My rating: ★★★★★

PART IV Achievement Test

1 | LISTENING: OLD FRIENDS

1. 's been **U18**
2. have you moved **U16**
3. since **U16**
4. 've just moved **U18**
5. studied **U19**
6. completed **U19**
7. started **U19**
8. 've already opened **U17**
9. 've been working **U20**
10. 've been teaching **U20**
11. Have you eaten **U18**
12. had **U18**

2 | CALIFORNIA PRIVATE INVESTIGATIONS

1. b **U18**
2. a **U20**
3. c **U16**
4. a **U16**
5. a **U18**
6. c **U16**
7. b **U18**
8. a **U19**
9. c **U20**
10. c **U20**

3 | AT DINNER

Note: Both contracted and noncontracted forms are acceptable where contracted forms are given.

1. 've been **U16**
2. 've come **U18**
3. have . . . worked **U18**
4. 've written **U16**
5. 've reported **U20**
6. Have . . . found **U16**
7. 've applied **U18**
8. haven't started **U17**
9. have **U16**

4 | CARLOS'S E-MAIL

1. saw **U19**
2. 's been **U20**
3. 've already seen **U17**
4. has been **U19**
5. 's had **U19**
6. 's been looking **U20**
7. 's called **U16**
8. yet **U17**

5 | CARLOS'S MOVE TO LOS ANGELES

1. lived **U19**
2. 's just quit / just quit **U18**
3. 's already moved / already moved **U17**
4. 's been trying **U20**
5. hasn't had **U16**
6. 's called / called **U20**
7. has invited / invited **U20**
8. has told / told **U16**
9. visited **U19**
10. 's watched / watched **U19**
11. 's observed / observed **U18**
12. hasn't done **U16**

6 | EDITING: ANOTHER E-MAIL

Hey, Travis,

        decided
Last month I've ~~decided~~ to accept Doug's job

       for **U16**   *already* **U17**
offer. I've been there ~~since~~ two weeks, and I've ~~yet~~

       has been **U19**
learned a lot. Doug ~~was~~ really good to work with

       needed **U16**
so far. I've ~~need~~ to learn a lot of things, but I've

made **U18**
~~maked~~ progress. I've started to really like the

       has already **U17**
work, and Doug ~~already has~~ put me in charge of

       I've **U20**
a small case. ~~I'm~~ met some interesting people. I've

had **U20**
~~have~~ some of them over for dinner. One guy has

come **U19**
~~came~~ over a couple of times, and he's told me lots of useful things. I haven't gotten a big case yet, but I think I will soon.

See you later,
Carlos

PART V Diagnostic Test

1 | LISTENING: SPORTS HISTORY

1. much **U21**
2. enough **U21**
3. a lot of **U21**
4. a lot of **U21**
5. enough **U21**
6. some **U21, U22**
7. a few **U21**

2 | BASEBALL: REPORT ON THE WORLD SERIES

1. b **U21**
2. c **U21, U22**
3. b **U22**
4. b **U21**
5. d **U22**
6. c **U21**
7. d **U21**

3 | SOCCER: THE FIFA WORLD CUP

1. A lot `U21`	6. Several `U21`
2. several `U21`	7. a few `U21`
3. a few `U21`	8. Ø `U22`
4. any `U21`	9. many `U21`
5. many `U21`	10. the `U22`

4 | TENNIS: THE FRENCH OPEN

1. Ø `U21`	8. a `U22`
2. the `U21, U22`	9. the `U21, U22`
3. Ø `U22`	10. a `U22`
4. The `U22`	11. the `U22`
5. the `U22`	12. Ø `U22`
6. a `U22`	13. The `U22`
7. an `U22`	14. the `U22`

5 | TENNIS: WIMBLEDON

1. the `U22`	9. a `U22`
2. the `U22`	10. an `U22`
3. the `U22`	11. Ø `U22`
4. a `U22`	12. the `U22`
5. Ø `U22`	13. an `U22`
6. the `U22`	14. a `U22`
7. the `U22`	15. the `U22`
8. The `U21, U22`	

6 | EDITING: DIARY

October 12th

    Today I gave my presentation about ~~a~~ *the* history
of the World Series. I didn't have ~~some~~ *any* `U21` problems
giving my speech, and I wasn't nervous at all. My
teacher is ~~the~~ *a* `U22` baseball fan, and she said she enjoyed
it. She and my classmates asked a lot of ~~question~~ *questions* `U21`,
and I was able to answer several of them. Scott,
another student who also loves ~~the~~ `U22` baseball, has
an `U22` amazing memory, and he was able to answer
many of the questions / many questions `U22`
~~many of questions~~ I didn't know the answers to.
It was actually ~~the~~ *a* `U22` very enjoyable class!

Unit 21 Achievement Test

1 | LISTENING: 2004 NOBEL PEACE PRIZE WINNER

A.

1. the winner `N3`	4. courage `N4`
2. movement `N3`	5. a member `N3`
3. the country `N3`	6. the program `N3`

B.

Proper nouns	Non-count nouns	Count nouns
1. Nobel Peace Prize `N1`	1. environment `N4`	1. dictator `N3`
2. Kenya `N1`	2. peace `N4`	2. woman `N3`
	3. intelligence `N4`	3. region `N3`
	4. democracy `N4`	

2 | ALFRED B. NOBEL

1. c `N2, N3`	5. a `N5`	8. a `N6`
2. b `N5`	6. b `N6`	9. b `N5`
3. c `N4`	7. d `N5`	10. a `N2, N4`
4. d `N6`		

3 | EDITING: THE NOBEL MUSEUM

May 31st

    What a great trip! Today I arrived in Stockholm,
Sweden, and so far I haven't had any ~~troubles~~ *trouble*.

    I just got back from the ~~nobel~~ *Nobel* `N1` Museum. They
have a new exhibition about Albert Einstein. The
exhibition focuses on his younger years, from
1905–1925. I didn't know ~~many~~ *much / a lot of / any* `N6` history about
Einstein, and I found the museum quite interesting.
I spent a lot of ~~times~~ *time* `N4` there learning about this part
of Einstein's life. He did ~~a great many of~~ *a great deal of / a lot of / much* `N6` work in
his 20s and 30s, and he received the Nobel Prize
in physics when he was 42 years old.

    I bought a few ~~postcard~~ *postcards* `N3` at the museum, and I
got a book about Albert Einstein too. Now that
I've been to the museum, I'm really interested to
learn even more about him.

Unit 22 Achievement Test

1 | LISTENING: DINNER PLANS

A.

1. the store `N4`	4. an excellent `N5`
2. a good idea `N3`	5. the world `N4`
3. A friend `N3`	

B.

Phrases with definite articles	Phrases with indefinite articles
1. the supermarket `N4`	1. a dish `N3`
2. the ingredients `N4`	2. an Indian dish `N3`
	3. an amazing curry `N3`
	4. a chicken curry `N3`
	5. a beef curry `N3`
	6. a great international market `N3`

2 | PLANS FOR TOMORROW NIGHT

1. a **N3**
2. the **N4**
3. the **N4**
4. Ø **N3**
5. an **N3**
6. the **N4**
7. an **N3**
8. the **N4**
9. the **N4**
10. Ø **N3**
11. the **N4**
12. Ø **N3**

3 | EDITING: VACATION PLANS

Shari,

Hi! Thanks again for inviting me to ˄*the* lake next

week! It will be nice to have ˄*a* **N3** vacation from work.

the / some / Ø **N4**
I'm really looking forward to ~~a~~ peace and quiet,

a **N3**
and I'll bring ~~the~~ good book to read.

the **N4**
When you have a minute, can you send me ~~a~~

phone number of your house there? I'd like to give
it to my parents so they can reach me.

an **N3**
I can't wait. You're ~~a~~ awesome friend! See you
next week!

Ashley

PART V Achievement Test

1 | LISTENING: CULTURAL STUDIES

1. much **U21**
2. many **U21**
3. a lot of **U21**
4. any **U21**
5. some **U21, U22**
6. a few **U21**
7. a little **U21**

2 | JAPANESE CHOPSTICKS

1. c **U21, U22**
2. d **U21, U22**
3. c **U21**
4. b **U21**
5. d **U21**
6. a **U21**
7. d **U21**

3 | TEX-MEX FOOD

1. some **U21, U22**
2. some **U21, U22**
3. a great deal of **U21**
4. a lot of **U21**
5. the **U22**
6. several **U21**
7. the **U22**
8. many **U21**
9. a lot of **U21**
10. enough **U21**

4 | MISS MANNERS: TABLE MANNERS

1. some **U21**
2. a **U22**
3. the **U22**
4. the **U22**
5. a **U22**
6. an **U22**
7. the **U22**
8. a **U22**
9. an **U22**
10. the **U22**
11. a **U22**
12. an **U22**
13. a **U22**
14. Ø **U22**

5 | MISS MANNERS: ANSWER

1. A **U22**
2. the **U22**
3. The **U22**
4. the **U22**
5. The **U22**
6. the **U22**
7. the **U22**
8. the **U22**
9. the **U22**
10. the **U22**
11. Ø **U22**
12. the **U22**
13. the **U22**
14. an **U22**
15. Ø **U22**

6 | EDITING: SOUTH AFRICA OYSTER FESTIVAL

July 5

a lot of
My trip to South Africa has been ~~many~~ fun so
far! This is a great place. The past few days I've been

many / a lot of **U21**   *the* **U21, U22**
participating in ~~much~~ activities at ˄Oyster Festival.

an **U22**
The festival is ˄amazing celebration. It's ~~the~~ ten-day

a **U22**
party! I've eaten several kinds of oysters, and I

any **U21**
didn't eat ~~some~~ kinds I didn't like! I've had so

U22
many wonderful things, but I still haven't tried ~~a~~

few **U21**
enough food. I'm glad I have a ~~little~~ more days left.

PART VI Diagnostic Test

1 | LISTENING: JOB FAIR

A.
1. the longest **U26**
2. as well as **U26**
3. unhappy **U23**
4. more happily **U26**

B.
1. ADV **U26**
2. ADV **U26**
3. ADJ **U25**
4. ADJ **U25**

2 | JOB DISSATISFACTION

Adjectives
1. boring **U23**
2. interested **U23**

Adverbs
1. slowly **U23**
2. well **U23**

Comparative adjectives
1. more pleasant **U24**
2. more content **U24**

Superlative adjectives
1. the worst **U25**
2. the most satisfying **U25**
3. the most rewarding **U25**

3 | JOB FAIR ATTRACTS HUNDREDS

1. suddenly **U23**
2. as lively as **U24**
3. the liveliest **U25**
4. great **U23**
5. general **U23**
6. amazing **U23**
7. better **U24**
8. as efficient as **U24**
9. fast **U23**

4 | COMPARING COMPANIES

1. seriously **U23**
2. big **U23**
3. risky **U23**
4. long **U23**
5. useful **U23**
6. usually **U23**
7. nice **U23**
8. well **U23**

5 | COMPARING JOBS

1. newer than **U24**
2. the biggest **U25**
3. smaller than **U24**
4. harder than **U26**
5. as frequently as **U26**
6. more difficult **U24**
7. as quietly as / more quietly than **U26**
8. richest **U25**
9. more skillfully **U26**
10. the coolest **U25**
11. higher than **U24**
12. better **U26**
13. as successful as / more successful than **U24**
14. the most relaxed **U25**
15. less formally than **U26**
16. more knowledgeable than **U24**
17. more professionally than **U26**

6 | EDITING: WADE'S NEW JOB

Hi Kerem,

    I wanted to catch up a little. I just started a

new

~~newly~~ job at Epicenter Group! I have a ~~quiets~~ *quiet* **U23** office,

nice **U23**   *more* **U24**

and everything is very ~~nicer~~. It's a lot _^interesting than

of **U25**

my last job. Epicenter is one _^the best employers

than **U24**

in the state. I think it will be better here ~~that~~ at Agicor, which is another company that offered me a job. I applied for both jobs at the local job fair,

me pretty quickly **U23**

and both companies called ~~pretty quickly me~~ after

most **U25**

that. The ~~mostest~~ enjoyable part of my new job is that I feel like I've accomplished something at the

efficiently **U26**

end of the day. I use my time much more ~~efficient~~ here than I did at my other job, and my new

me more frequently **U26**

co-workers encourage ~~more frequently me~~. So I think I chose the right job.

Talk to you later!
Wade

Unit 23 Achievement Test

1 | LISTENING: UPCOMING CONCERT

A.
1. favorite **N1**
2. enjoyable **N1**
3. hardly **N5**

B.
1. ADJ **N4**
2. ADV **N6**
3. ADJ **N1**
4. ADJ **N7**
5. ADV **N3**

2 | THE CONCERT

1. old ones **N1**
2. lovely song **N4**
3. beautifully **N2**
4. great **N1**
5. never sings **N6**
6. wonderful shows **N1**
7. well **N5**
8. perfect **N1**
9. large **N1**
10. fascinated **N7**
11. happily **N2**
12. energetically **N2**

3 | HISTORY OF THE BAND

1. amazed **N7, N1**
2. quickly **N2**
3. serious **N1**
4. regularly **N6**
5. first **N1**
6. fast **N5**

4 | EDITING: ALBUM REVIEW

boring

    Music has been a little ~~bored~~ for me this year. Most bands aren't coming up with new ideas. A lot of what I hear is disappointing. But I've just

excellent **N1**

discovered an ~~excellently~~ album, Dot Matrix's

recently **N2**

This Way to Freedom. I bought the album ~~recent~~, and I haven't stopped listening to it. The album

good **N5**   *hard* **N5**

isn't just ~~well~~, it's great! It's ~~hardly~~ to compare to any other music. The band has many different influences, from classic rock and roll to rhythm and blues. You should definitely check it out!

Unit 24 Achievement Test

1 | LISTENING: THE COUNTRY INN

A.
1. more expensive than **N2, N3**
2. as delicious as **N1**
3. as fresh as **N1**
4. harder and harder **N6, N3**

B.
1. F **N1**
2. F **N2, N6**
3. T **N2**
4. F **N1, N3**

2 | WHAT'S THE DIFFERENCE?

1. higher **N3**
2. more nutritious **N3**
3. the faster **N7**
4. less time **N6**
5. as expensive as **N1**

3 | FACTS ABOUT RICE

1. lighter **N3**
2. more typical **N3**
3. stickier **N2**
4. better **N2**
5. more common **N3**
6. more known **N6**
7. as easy as **N1**
8. The longer **N7, N3**
9. the softer **N7, N3**
10. worse **N3**
11. richer **N3**
12. as healthy as **N1**

4 | EDITING: RICE PUDDING

RUSS: What do you recommend for dessert—the ice cream or the rice pudding?

WAITER: It depends on what you're looking for.

 colder
The ice cream is ~~more cold~~, of course. And it's

 than **N2**
also sweeter ~~that~~ the rice pudding.

 as **N1**
RUSS: Hmmm. I see that the ice cream is just ^ expensive as the rice pudding.

WAITER: Well, yes, all of our desserts are the same price. We added rice pudding to our menu

 popular **N1**
last month, so it's not as ~~popularer~~ as the ice

 and **N6**
cream yet, but it's becoming more ~~than~~ more popular.

RUSS: I want to try the rice pudding, but I usually like sweeter desserts. Is there anything on the rice pudding?

WAITER: If you'd like, I can make the rice pudding

 livelier / more lively **N3**
~~more livelier~~ by adding some whipped cream. Some customers think it tastes more flavorful that way.

RUSS: OK, I'll try that.

Unit 25 Achievement Test

1 | LISTENING: PHONE MESSAGES ON VALENTINE'S DAY

A.
1. the most interesting **N2, N3**
2. the most beautiful **N2, N3**
3. the most wonderful **N2**
4. one of the greatest **N3**

B.
1. the kindest **N2**
2. the most intelligent **N2**
3. the most amazing **N2**
4. the happiest **N2**

2 | AD FOR A CHOCOLATE STORE

1. the most delicious **N2**
2. the second largest **N3**
3. in **N3**
4. you've ever tasted **N2**

3 | VALENTINE'S DAY CARDS

1. the greatest **N3, N2**
2. the most fantastic **N2**
3. the funniest **N2, N3**
4. the most expensive **N2, N3**
5. the newest **N2, N3**
6. the most inexpensive **N2**

7. cheapest **N2, N3**
8. the most romantic **N2, N3**
9. the most gorgeous **N2**
10. the worst **N3, N2**
11. the smallest **N2, N3**
12. the fanciest **N2**
13. the loveliest / the most lovely **N2, N3**

4 | EDITING: MARLENE'S DIARY

I love Valentine's Day. It's the best day of the

 nicest
year! Paul left the ~~most nice~~ messages on my answering machine today. He said so many wonderful things. We went out to dinner tonight,

 prettiest **N2** *'ve* **N3**
and he gave me the ~~most pretty~~ card that I ^ ever

 N2
seen. He also gave me the ~~most~~ biggest box of chocolates. They're very fancy, and they taste

 in **N3**
delicious. They're definitely the best chocolates ^ town! It was the most fabulous night of my life.

 special **N2**
Paul is so great. He's the most ~~specialest~~ guy I know. I'm the luckiest girl in the world!

Unit 26 Achievement Test

1 | LISTENING: CHOOSING A NEW MANAGER

A.
1. the hardest **N5**
2. the faster **N9**
3. as highly as **N1**
4. than **N2**

B.
1. F **N2, N5**
2. F **N1**
3. F **N5**
4. T **N3**

2 | THE COMPANY

1. more steadily **N2, N5**
2. The longer **N9**
3. as well as **N1**
4. the most effectively **N5**
5. more highly **N2**

3 | COMPARING THE CANDIDATES

1. the longest **N4, N5**
2. the fastest **N4, N5**
3. the most cooperatively **N4, N5**
4. as respectfully as **N1**
5. less often than **N2, N5**
6. the most regularly **N3, N5**
7. more frequently than **N2, N5**
8. more often **N8**
9. the most skillfully **N4, N5**
10. more slowly than **N5, N2**
11. more accurately than **N2, N5**
12. the more quickly **N9**

4 | EDITING: THE NEW MANAGER

OLIVIA: So, what do you think?

DENISE: Well, honestly, I think Marty is the best

one for the position. He's simply more ~~higher~~ *highly*
qualified than the others.

OLIVIA: I agree. He scored better on his quality
evaluations than they did. And although he's
a little slower than the others with certain
tasks, he's been learning things more and more
~~quick~~ as time passes. *quickly* **N8**

DENISE: Yes. He also works more ~~carefuller~~ than *carefully* **N5**
Sidney and Albert, so he doesn't have to redo
his work. And he has worked more aggressively
than the others to improve his sales record. No
one has worked as hard ^ he has. That really *as* **N1**
impressed me.

OLIVIA: Me too. I also thought that Marty
answered ~~more professionally my questions~~ *my questions more professionally* **N7**
during the interview.

DENISE: Well, all the candidates were quite
professional during their interviews with me.
But I think Marty will be able to perform the
duties of general manager more ~~effective~~ than *effectively* **N5**
anyone else could.

PART VI Achievement Test

1 | LISTENING: HOMES FOR SALE

A.
1. as well as **U26**
2. more comfortably **U26**
3. beautiful **U23**
4. the most consistently **U26**

B.
1. ADJ **U25**
2. ADV **U26**
3. ADV **U26**
4. ADJ **U25**

2 | SOPHIA'S HOUSE

Adjectives
1. old **U23**
2. nice **U23**

Adverbs
1. surprisingly **U23**
2. happily **U23**

Comparative adjectives
1. more aggressive **U24**
2. more likely **U24**

Superlative adjectives
1. (one of) the biggest **U25**
2. the most expensive **U25**
3. the most wonderful **U25**

3 | HOME EXPO A SUCCESS

1. quickly **U23**
2. as lively as **U24**
3. the liveliest **U25**
4. large **U23**
5. wonderful **U23**
6. gorgeous **U23**
7. better **U24**
8. as good as **U24**
9. easily **U23**

4 | COMPARING HOUSES

1. big **U23**
2. unusual **U23**
3. lovely **U23**
4. well **U23**
5. friendly **U23**
6. close **U23**
7. usually **U23**
8. quickly **U23**

5 | COMPARING HOUSES AND NEIGHBORHOODS

1. the most incredible **U25**
2. smaller than **U24**
3. cheaper than **U24**
4. more expensive than **U24**
5. the prettiest **U25**
6. more beautiful than **U24**
7. more professionally **U26**
8. the most attractive **U25**
9. more conveniently than **U26**
10. newer than **U24**
11. largest **U25**
12. fast as **U26**
13. longer **U26**
14. more quietly **U26**
15. good as **U24**
16. carefully as **U26**
17. more seriously **U26**

6 | EDITING: SOPHIA'S NEW HOUSE

Hi Naomi,

We finally moved in to our ~~newly~~ house! *new*
I'm sitting in our living room looking out the
~~larges~~ windows at the beautiful garden. The *large* **U23**
neighborhood is very ~~calmer~~ here. It's a lot ^ *calm* **U23** *more* **U24**
peaceful than my old house. This is one ^ the best *of* **U25**
neighborhoods in the city. I think I'll be ^ happier
here ~~that~~ at my old house. The grass here grows *than* **U24**
~~more tall~~ than at my other house, and I'm *taller* **U26**
~~more skillfully working in the garden~~ than ever *working more skillfully in the garden / working in the garden more skillfully* **U26**
before. This house doesn't have the most
convenient location, but everything else is perfect.
I saw many wonderful houses at the Red Sky
Home Expo, but I decided this one was the best.
I liked ~~immediately this house~~. The ~~mostest~~ *this house immediately* **U23** *most* **U25**
wonderful part is that we have more room for all
our things. Finally, we have a place we will be
happy in for a long time!

Come visit!
Sophia

PART VII Diagnostic Test

1 | LISTENING: THRIFT STORES

A.
1. used to U28
2. too poor U31
3. because U30
4. in order to U30

B.

Gerunds
1. coming U32
2. Not having U27

Infinitives
1. To save U30
2. to think U31

2 | MACHIKO'S BLOG

1. to come / to go U29
2. Shopping / To shop U27, U32
3. going U27
4. to shop / shopping U32
5. to stay U32
6. seeing U28
7. to get U29
8. feeling U32
9. to watch / watching / to see / seeing U32
10. buying / getting U32

3 | SHOPAHOLISM

1. to spending U28
2. shopping U27
3. too expensive to afford U31
4. easy enough to overspend U31
5. to watching U28
6. frustrated enough U31
7. to fulfill U30
8. to prove U30
9. Spending U27
10. getting U32
11. too difficult U31

4 | TAMARA'S BLOG

1. to go U29
2. going U32
3. Shopping U27
4. walking / going U32
5. to be U32
6. going / walking U27
7. insisting U28
8. seeing U28
9. to buy / to get U29
10. looking / shopping U32

5 | MALE SHOPPERS

1. marketing U27, U32
2. shopping / to shop U27
3. to attract U29
4. to find U29
5. to understand U29
6. to go U29
7. buying U32
8. to look U32
9. targeting U28
10. to help U32
11. marketing U28

6 | EDITING: SMART SHOPPERS

Are you a smart shopper? When is the last
time you went to the mall in order ^*to* buy a sweater,
look for gifts, or ~~eating~~ *eat* U30 lunch? If you do these
things regularly, you're wasting your money. Smart
shoppers prefer ~~to not~~ *not to* U29 spend more money than
necessary. I quit ~~to go~~ *going* U27 to malls because the stores
there charge way too much. Besides, I got sick
of ~~to spend~~ *spending* U28 a lot of money on something, and
then hearing my roommate say that she found
something similar at a thrift store for only a
dollar or two. I've learned that it's OK to check
thrift stores first in order ~~to not~~ *not to* U30 pay more money
than necessary. I believe ~~on~~ *in* U28 looking nice and
fashionable, but not if I have to spend all my
money to do it. For instance, I needed ~~buying~~ *to buy* U32 a
dress, and I found one for $70 at the mall. I
regretted ~~to buy~~ *buying* U27 it the very next day when I found
an even nicer dress at a thrift store for $10. If
you are ~~enough rich~~ *rich enough* U31 to buy things without going
into debt, go right ahead. After all, smart shoppers
like us need you ^*to* U29 buy things at full price so that we
can have them later for much less money.

Unit 27 Achievement Test

1 | LISTENING: TIME TO PRACTICE

A.
1. Playing N2
2. letting N3
3. asking N3
4. losing N3

B.

Subject gerund
1. Quitting N2

Object gerunds
1. practicing N3
2. skateboarding N4
3. hanging (out) N3

2 | PHILLIP'S REQUEST FOR ADVICE

1. telling **N3**
2. skateboarding **N3**
3. being **N1**
4. staying / being **N2**
5. doing **N3**
6. making **N3**

3 | GREG'S ADVICE

1. staying **N3**
2. arguing **N3**
3. exploring **N3**
4. figuring **N3**
5. Watching **N2**
6. watching **N3**
7. Finding **N2**

4 | EDITING: NO MORE TV!

   Last month, the newspaper printed Greg's response to my letter for help. He had a great

idea. He suggested ~~to watch~~ *watching* less TV so that I could have more time to skateboard. I admit

~~feel~~ *feeling* **N3** at first like he was wrong. I denied ~~waste~~ *wasting* **N3** my

time. I considered ~~to watch~~ *watching* **N3** TV an important time for me to relax before starting my homework.

But Greg was right! I always avoided ~~start~~ *starting* **N3** my homework until after I watched *two hours* of TV!

At first, I missed ~~watches~~ *watching* **N3** my favorite shows. But

I made it a goal to finish ~~do~~ *doing* **N3** my homework at the

school library before coming home. Now, ~~think~~ *thinking* **N2** about how much time I used to waste on TV

makes me sick! ~~Practice~~ *Practicing* **N2** the violin is still not great

fun, but ~~no~~ *not* **N1** practicing was worse because it made my mom mad, and it made me feel guilty!

Unit 28 Achievement Test

1 | LISTENING: APPLYING TO THE UNIVERSITY

A.
1. afraid of being **N2**
2. to living **N3**
3. to be **N3**

B.
1. to finding **N1**
2. for taking **N1**
3. before making **N1**
4. in studying **N1**
5. about getting **N1**
6. about hearing **N1**

2 | WAITING

1. about receiving **N2**
2. not getting **N1**
3. of waiting **N1**
4. to waiting **N3**
5. to work **N3**
6. to calling **N1**
7. of waiting **N1**
8. on getting **N1**

3 | GOOD NEWS!

1. being **N1**
2. getting **N1**
3. starting **N2**
4. having **N1**
5. to know **N3**
6. understanding **N1**
7. to studying **N3**
8. listening **N1**
9. sitting **N1**

4 | EDITING: E-MAIL TO A PROFESSOR

Dear Professor Hunt:
   I will be a new student at Greendale in the

fall, and I'm interested ~~to observe~~ *in observing* some of your

classes. I am from Mexico, and I used ‸*to* study in an **N3** English language program. If you are not opposed

~~to have~~ *having* **N1** an observer, I would like to come to your

classes so that I can get used to ~~listen~~ *listening* **N3** to classroom lectures before I start school in the fall. I look

forward to ~~hear~~ *hearing* **N1** from you.

Sincerely,
Luz Maria Lerma

Unit 29 Achievement Test

1 | LISTENING: RADIO CALL-IN SHOW

A.
1. not to go **N1**
2. want to know **N5**
3. invited **N4**
4. try to help **N3**

B.

Verb + infinitive	Verb + object + infinitive
1. refuses to bring **N3**	1. encourage her to bring **N4**
2. decides to go **N3**	
3. need to take **N5**	

2 | TINA'S ANSWER

1. not to bring **N1**
2. to introduce **N4**
3. fails to bring **N3**
4. need to allow **N5**
5. to meet **N5**
6. learn to trust **N3**
7. choose to **N5**

3 | IN SUMMARY

1. promised to call (his mother) / agreed to call (his mother) **N3**
2. agreed to clean / promised to clean **N3**
3. volunteered to help / volunteered to **N5**
4. reminded her daughter to take / reminded her daughter not to forget (to take) **N4**
5. chose to have / asked to have **N5**
6. forgot to lock **N3**
7. advised his daughter to finish **N4**

8. is planning to go / planned to go / plans to go `N3`

9. asked to borrow `N5`

4 | EDITING: PLANNING A PARTY AT HOME

My mom seems ^*to* be relaxing about my friends. I think she trusts me more these days. I told her today that I wanted to have some friends over for a party this weekend. She said, "OK, that's fine." I thought she'd be much more excited. Anyway, she's going to help me ~~to cleaning~~ *clean / to clean* `N5` the house. I also asked ^*her* `N5` to make her famous homemade ice cream. I hope to ~~invites~~ *invite* `N3` a lot of people. I managed to ~~talked to~~ *talk to* `N3` about 10 people so far. I persuaded Mark ^*to* `N4` come. He's so cute! And I also told Bridget to ~~bringing~~ *bring* `N4` her CDs because she has a fabulous CD collection.

Unit 30 Achievement Test

1 | LISTENING: INTERNET USE

A.

1. to sell `N1`
2. because `N3`
3. To read `N1`
4. To play `N1`

B.

Affirmative infinitives of purpose	Negative infinitive of purpose
1. to purchase `N1`	1. not to lose `N3`
2. to e-mail `N1`	
3. to find `N1`	

2 | HOW PEOPLE USE THE INTERNET

1. to look `N1`
2. to teach `N1`
3. to study `N1`
4. to do `N1`
5. in order not to `N3`
6. to find `N1`
7. make `N1`
8. because `N3`

3 | MESSAGE BOARD

1. to find `N1`
2. to give `N2`
3. to get `N1`
4. to read `N1`
5. to look up `N1`
6. to order `N1`
7. to check `N1`
8. to e-mail `N1`
9. not to pay `N3`

4 | EDITING: STUDENT ERRANDS

PHILLIP: I just went to the bookstore in order to ~~bought~~ *buy* my books, but the line was so long!

GREG: I know. I went online ^*to* `N1` buy my books a couple of days ago. I usually buy my books online ~~not in order~~ *in order not* `N3` to stand in line at the bookstore and ~~cause~~ *because* `N3` the prices are usually better than in the bookstore.

PHILLIP: That's a good idea. Hey, I need to go out again to eat lunch, get a newspaper, and ~~sending~~ *send* `N1` a letter. Do you want to come?

GREG: Thanks, but I can't. I need to read this article now ^*in* `N2` order to finish it before class.

Unit 31 Achievement Test

1 | LISTENING: TOO BUSY

A.

1. too busy `N5`
2. angry enough `N2`
3. short enough `N5`

B.

Too + adjective / adverb infinitive	Adjective + enough + infinitive
1. too few to remember `N1`	1. long enough to do `N2`
2. too tense to relax `N1`	2. mad enough to scream `N2`
3. too tightly to do `N1`	

2 | FASTER IS NOT ALWAYS BETTER

1. too busy to do `N1`
2. too hard to be `N1`
3. too full to allow `N1`
4. good enough to make `N2`
5. too late to make `N1`
6. too fast to be `N1`
7. rare enough to count `N2`
8. relaxed enough to sleep `N2`
9. long enough to spend `N2`
10. productive enough to get `N2`
11. well enough to stay `N2`
12. too long to have time `N1`
13. too stressed to be `N1`

3 | DR. PACKARD'S NOTES

1. stressful enough to make `N2`
2. too early to feel `N1`
3. too late to eat `N1`
4. tired enough to sleep `N2`

4 | EDITING: A NEW LIFE

I've decided to simplify my life! I quit my job because I was too anxious ^*to* be valuable to the company anymore. After meeting with Dr. Packard,

I felt that my happiness was ~~enough important~~ *important enough* **N3** to fight for. I was getting too frustrated to ~~handling~~ *handle* **N1** the stress. Now I have a new job. It pays less, but it's too relaxing *for* **N4** me to complain about the money. Besides, the salary is ~~enough high~~ *high enough* **N3** to pay the bills. Before, my time at home was ~~to~~ *too* **N1** short to play with my kids. Now I have the time to play with them, and it's wonderful!

Unit 32 Achievement Test

1 | LISTENING: THE "PRINCE OF CLEAN"

A.
1. to find **N6**
2. spending **N1**
3. to do **N4**
4. to see **N2**

B.

Phrases with gerunds
1. thank you for being **N5**
2. appreciated being **N1**

Phrases with infinitives
1. plan to spend **N2**
2. it's easier to keep **N6**

2 | WHAT'S YOUR CLEANING PERSONALITY?

1. scrubbing **N1**
2. having **N1**
3. to clean **N3**
4. washing **N1**
5. to hire **N2**
6. to clean **N2**
7. to keep **N2**
8. cleaning **N1**
9. to put **N4**
10. to throw **N4**
11. cleaning **N5**
12. cleaning **N5**

3 | *THE PABLO SHOW* WEBSITE

1. to vacuum / vacuuming **N3**
2. buying **N1**
3. to have **N2**
4. to empty **N4**
5. dusting **N5**
6. knowing **N1**
7. to visit **N2**

4 | EDITING: E-MAIL TO NICK POLITZ

Dear Nick,

I usually avoid ~~to clean~~ *cleaning* at all costs, but I realized that I can't postpone ~~to do~~ *doing* **N1** housework all my life. This year, I've promised myself ~~being~~ *to be* **N2** better about cleaning, but it's hard for me ~~making~~ *to make* **N6** the change. Can you recommend anything for people like me?

Sincerely,
Kara Peterson

PART VII Achievement Test

1 | LISTENING: MOVING

A.
1. used to use **U28**
2. too dirty **U31**
3. because **U30**
4. in order to **U30**

B.

Gerunds
1. going **U32**
2. Not having **U27**

Infinitives
1. to get **U31**
2. to replace **U30**

2 | MARISOL'S JOURNAL

1. to buy / to get **U29**
2. spending **U27**
3. to get / getting **U28**
4. to spend **U27, U32**
5. moving **U32**
6. to let **U29**
7. to go **U29**
8. being **U32**
9. to watch / watching **U32**
10. getting / buying **U32**

3 | TOO FRUGAL

1. to saving **U28**
2. shopping **U27**
3. too frugal **U31**
4. too expensive **U31**
5. to spending **U28**
6. frustrated enough **U31**
7. to fulfill **U30**
8. to prove **U30**
9. Walking **U27**
10. getting **U32**
11. too hard **U31**

4 | THEO'S JOURNAL

1. to go **U29**
2. buying **U32**
3. wasting / spending **U27, U32**
4. helping **U32**
5. to work **U32**
6. admitting **U27**
7. insisting / asking **U28**
8. spending / wasting **U28**
9. to buy / to get **U29**
10. going **U32**

5 | NOMADS

1. to sleep **U30, U32**
2. Moving **U27, U32**
3. owning **U27, U32**
4. to make **U29**
5. to learn **U29**
6. to discover **U29**
7. learning **U28**
8. buying **U27, U32**
9. to consider **U29**
10. to share **U32**
11. reading **U28**

6 | EDITING: SMART MOVERS

Are you a smart mover? The last time you needed *to* move, did you take the time to ask for help, tell others you were packing, or ~~talking~~ *talk* **U30** to

professional movers? Smart movers prefer ~~to not~~ *not to* (U32)
do it alone. I used to move alone because I thought

it was my own responsibility. But I quit ~~to try~~ to *trying* (U27)

move all by myself because I got sick of ~~to spend~~ *spending* (U28)
so much time and energy, and other people were
happy to help. I've learned that it's OK to ask

people to help in order ~~to not~~ waste my time and *not to* (U30)

energy. I believe ~~on~~ helping other people, so why *in* (U28)
shouldn't I let them help me? For instance, I needed

~~putting~~ my refrigerator onto a moving truck. I did *to put* (U32)

it by myself, but I later realized ~~to do~~ that was a *doing* (U27)
mistake. I was so sore the next day that I couldn't

get out of bed! If you are ~~enough strong~~ to move a *strong enough* (U31)
refrigerator by yourself, feel free. But smart movers

like me need people like you‸help us sometimes! *to* (U29)

PART VIII Diagnostic Test

1 | LISTENING: LATE FOR THE PICNIC

A.
1. do you have to (U34)
2. 've got to be (U37)
3. Do you think (U36)
4. was going to be (U35)

B.
1. T (U35)
2. T (U37)
3. F (U35)
4. F (U36)

2 | TRAFFIC JAM

Expresses a preference
1. 'd rather not walk (U33)
2. 'd rather take (U33)

Expresses a necessity
1. have to take (U34)
2. have got to change (U34)
3. must get (U34)

Expresses prohibition
1. can't turn (U34)

Expresses a past expectation
1. were going to finish (U35)
2. was going to get (U35)

Expresses a possibility
1. Do you think (U36)
2. could try (U36)

Expresses a conclusion
1. 's got to be (U37)

3 | LOOKING FOR THE PICNIC

1. a (U36)
2. c (U33)
3. c (U33)
4. b (U36)
5. a (U34)
6. c (U34)
7. a (U34)
8. d (U36)
9. a (U37)
10. d (U37)
11. a (U37)
12. c (U36)

4 | AT THE PICNIC

Note: Both contracted and noncontracted forms are acceptable where contracted forms are given.
1. had to (U34)
2. could (U36)
3. 'd rather (U33)
4. is supposed to / has to (U35)
5. can't (U34)
6. 'd rather (U33)
7. have to / 'm supposed to (U34)
8. could / might / may (U37)
9. could / might / may (U37)
10. 'd rather (U33)
11. 'm supposed to / have to (U35)

5 | HOW TO BARBECUE

1. than (U33)
2. might / may (U37)
3. has / has got (U37)
4. don't (U34)
5. got (U34)
6. supposed (U35)
7. prefer (U33)
8. must (U34)
9. not (U34)
10. may / might (U36)

6 | EDITING: BACK HOME

LISA: I was going‸take the car today, but I *to*
couldn't find the keys. Do you have them?
NELSON: Oh, sorry. I guess I took them by
accident.

LISA: You must ~~X~~ remember to leave them by the (U34)
door. And I prefer ~~know~~ when you're going to *knowing / to know* (U33)
be home.

NELSON: I know. Hey, I was going‸use the car *to* (U35)
tomorrow at 2:30. Is that OK?
LISA: Sorry, but I need it then. I have an
appointment at 3:00.
NELSON: But I have an appointment too. And I
can't ~~X~~ miss it. It's a job interview at Fiamont. (U34)
LISA: Oh! That's ~~suppose~~ to be a good company. *supposed* (U35)
You must ~~being~~ really excited. *be* (U37)
NELSON: I am!
LISA: Well, I can try to change my appointment,
but I ~~mayn't~~ be able to. Or, I ~~maybe~~ able to *may not* (U36) *may be* (U36)
take the bus. I would rather take the bus than
make you miss this opportunity. I'll go check
the bus schedule.
NELSON: Thanks a lot, Mom. I appreciate it.

Unit 33 Achievement Test

1 | LISTENING: HOUSE HUNTING

A.
1. We'd rather have **N1**
2. would rather not rent **N3**
3. than get **N5**
4. I'd rather not wait **N3**

B.
1. prefer to live **N2**
2. prefer to see **N1**
3. would rather walk (to work than drive) **N5**
4. 'd rather rent **N1**

2 | MOVING IN

1. 'd rather **N1**
2. prefer **N2**
3. to **N4**
4. 'd rather **N3**
5. to keep **N2**
6. not put **N3**
7. to **N4**
8. cook **N5**

3 | WHERE DOES IT GO?

1. rather **N1**
2. rather not **N3**
3. rather **N1**
4. prefer **N1**
5. prefer **N2**
6. rather not **N3**
7. prefer **N1**
8. to **N4**
9. to **N4**
10. than **N5**

4 | EDITING: HOUSEWARMING PARTY

ARLENE: We should have a party so our friends can come see how the house looks.

TJ: Great idea. Would you rather ~~sending~~ *send* invitations or just call people?

ARLENE: I ~~rather would~~ *would rather* **N1** call people.

TJ: I agree. I'd rather not ✗ **N3** send invitations because it's too much work. When would you prefer to have the party, on a Saturday or a Sunday?

ARLENE: Well, I generally ~~would~~ **N1** prefer parties on Saturday evenings. But if we want people to see the house during the day, then a Sunday afternoon would be nice. So I guess I would rather have it on a Sunday afternoon.

TJ: Sounds good. We could do it this weekend or next weekend.

ARLENE: I'd prefer next weekend ~~than~~ *to* **N4** this one.

Unit 34 Achievement Test

1 | LISTENING: THE APPLICATION PROCESS

A.
1. have to receive **N1**
2. do I have to e-mail **N3**
3. must receive **N1**
4. do I have to send **N3**

B.

Phrases that express necessity	Phrases that express prohibition
1. 've had to do **N2**	1. can't be **N4**
2. 've got to read **N1**	2. can't accept **N4**

2 | REQUIREMENTS AND RESPONSIBILITIES

1. a **N2**
2. c **N4**
3. d **N1**
4. a **N1**
5. b **N1**
6. c **N4**
7. d **N1**
8. a **N4**
9. b **N1**
10. b **N4**

3 | HOSPITAL RULES FOR VISITORS

1. have to / have got to / will have to / must **N2**
2. must / have to / have got to / will have to **N1**
3. can't / must not **N4**
4. don't have to **N4**
5. can't / must not **N4**
6. have to / have got to / must / will have to **N1**
7. can't / must not **N4**
8. have to / have got to / must / will have to **N1**
9. have to / have got to / will have to / must **N2**

4 | EDITING: E-MAIL TO SARAH

Hi Sarah,
   I can't believe that I've been out of nursing school for a month already! I have *to* get a job soon! I'm applying for a position at Clifton General Hospital. Yesterday I ~~have~~ *had* **N2** to fill out an application. I must ✗ **N1** send it in today because the deadline is tomorrow.
   What have you been up to? We have to get together soon so we can catch up on everything.
   Well, I just wanted to say hi. I've got ^*to* **N1** go mail my application. Wish me luck!

Love,
Teresa

Unit 35 Achievement Test

1 LISTENING: NEW YEAR'S EVE

A.
1. was going to stay N2
2. were supposed to be N1
3. weren't going to have N2
4. 're supposed to set N1

B.
1. 're supposed to count N1
2. were going to go N2
3. was supposed to be N1
4. weren't supposed to light N1

2 JAVIER'S JOURNAL

1. 'm N1
2. was supposed N1
3. were N2
4. was supposed N1
5. going to send N2
6. was N2
7. to spend N1

3 NEW YEAR'S CELEBRATIONS AND CUSTOMS IN JAPAN

1. are supposed to eat N1
2. are supposed to receive N1
3. are supposed to spend N1
4. were supposed to be N1
5. is supposed to come N1
6. was going to try N2
7. aren't supposed to celebrate N1
8. was going to send N2
9. was going to visit N2

4 EDITING: AT THE NEW YEAR'S EVE PARTY

GEORGE: Sorry I'm late. I know I was supposed ^to get here a while ago. I had car trouble.

COLLIN: No problem. But where's Javier? You were ~~supposing~~ *supposed* N1 to pick him up, right?

GEORGE: Yeah, we ~~are~~ *were* N2 going to come together, but since my car wouldn't start, I took a taxi instead. I *was* N2 ^going to call him and tell him to take a taxi too, but I didn't. I feel bad. I was supposed to pick him up an hour ago.

COLLIN: That's OK. I'll call him right now.

HARU: Hey, George! Did you just get here?

GEORGE: Yeah, just now. I was going *to* N2 ^be here earlier, but I had car trouble.

HARU: Well, get something to eat. And don't forget the pork and cabbage.

GEORGE: Why? Are they traditional New Year's foods?

HARU: Well, Collin said we ^*'re* N1 supposed to eat them. They're supposed to bring good luck and money through the year.

GEORGE: I've heard that you're supposed to ~~eating~~ *eat* N1 something round so you'll live through the year.

HARU: Yeah, I think I've heard that too.

Unit 36 Achievement Test

1 LISTENING: PRESIDENTIAL CANDIDATES TO DEBATE

A.
1. He may N3
2. may not win N2
3. Is he going to N3
4. He might N3

B.

Verb phrases that express future possibility	Short answers to questions about possibility
1. could say N1	1. He might. N3
2. may be N1	2. He may. N3

2 WHAT WILL THEY SAY?

1. might discuss N1
2. may N1
3. might N1
4. could say N1
5. may talk N1
6. might not speak N2
7. may tell N1
8. might N1
9. could N1
10. may not N2
11. could mention N1
12. might not N2
13. might say N1

3 PLANS FOR THE EVENING

1. might not go N2
2. could go N1
3. might record N1
4. may do N1

4 EDITING: DEBATES FOCUS ON BUDGET

This presidential race is very close, and either candidate could ~~winning~~ *win* . Here's a look at their positions on one issue:

Senator Jackson may ~~raises~~ *raise* N1 taxes. He says he doesn't want to, but it ~~maybe~~ *may be* N1 necessary. He could expand education programs with that extra money. He says, "The government could X spend N1 more on education. We have to make it a priority."

Governor Crowley, on the other hand, says he won't raise taxes. However, according to his plans, *might not* **N2**

there ~~mightn't~~ be enough money in the budget to increase education spending. Parents and educators may not like that idea very much, so

N1

Governor Crowley might ~~✗~~ need to find additional support from other groups of voters.

Unit 37 Achievement Test

1 | LISTENING: MYSTERIES

A.
1. can't be **N4**
2. must be **N6**
3. I might **N6**
4. could they be **N5**

B.
1. T **N2**
2. T **N4**
3. F **N3**
4. F **N3**

2 | UFOS

1. must be **N2**
2. have to exist **N2**
3. have got to exist **N2**
4. must be **N2**
5. may not be **N4**
6. might not provide **N4**
7. might not come **N4**
8. may be **N3**
9. might be **N3**
10. could be **N3**

3 | PEOPLE'S THOUGHTS ON UFOS AND ALIENS

1. must / have to / have got to create **N2**
2. might / may / could know **N3**
3. must / has to / has got to be **N2**
4. might / may / could see **N3**
5. might / may / could fly **N3**
6. can't / couldn't travel **N4**
7. must / have to / have got to exist **N2**
8. may not / might not want **N4**
9. must / have to / have got to live **N2**

4 | EDITING: AFTER THE SHOW

VERONICA: So what do you think now? Do you believe in UFOs?

can't

COLLEEN: Not at all! I strongly feel they ~~may not~~ exist. Do you still believe in them?

VERONICA: Absolutely. I could be wrong, but I just think that so many people have seen them that

N2

they must ~~✗~~ be real.

could / couldn't / can't **N5**

COLLEEN: But ~~may~~ some people be mistaken?

be **N6**

VERONICA: A few of them might, but not all of them. Some of them have to be telling the truth.

COLLEEN: Well, maybe they're just unsure about what they saw.

PART VIII Achievement Test

1 | LISTENING: LATE FOR PRACTICE

A.
1. must be **U37**
2. Do you think **U36**
3. was going to call **U35**
4. Do you have to go **U34**

B.
1. T **U35**
2. F **U36**
3. F **U35**
4. T **U37**

2 | STUCK IN TRAFFIC

Expresses a preference	Expresses a necessity	Expresses prohibition
1. 'd rather take **U33**	1. have to change **U34**	1. can't turn **U34**
2. would rather not stay **U33**	2. must use **U34**	
	3. have to be **U34**	

Expresses a past expectation	Expresses a possibility	Expresses a conclusion
1. were going to do **U35**	1. could take **U36**	1. has got to be **U37**
2. was going to take **U35**	2. Is it possible **U36**	

3 | LOOKING FOR THE GYM

1. c **U33**
2. b **U33**
3. d **U34**
4. c **U34**
5. b **U34**
6. c **U36**
7. c **U36**
8. a **U37**
9. c **U37**
10. b **U37**
11. d **U36**
12. c **U37**

4 | AT THE GYM

1. had to **U34**
2. might / may / could / must / has to **U37**
3. have to / are supposed to **U34**
4. can't **U34**
5. are supposed to / have to **U35**
6. were supposed to **U35**
7. can't **U37**
8. could / might / may **U36**
9. 'd rather / would rather / prefer to **U33**
10. 'd rather / would rather **U33**
11. prefer **U33**

5 | NEWSLETTER TO THE PARENTS

1. than **U33**
2. might / may **U37**
3. have / have got **U34**
4. can't **U34**
5. don't **U34**
6. supposed **U35**
7. got **U37**
8. must **U34**
9. prefer **U33**
10. might / may **U36**

ANSWER KEY | **257**

LEONARD: I was going ^to^ use the truck to take your brother to basketball practice this afternoon.

You must ~~X~~ talk to me before taking it. [U34] If you'd rather not discuss your plans with me, then you can take the bus.

NELLY: No! I prefer ~~drive~~ *driving / to drive* [U33]. Let's talk about our schedules. I was ~~go~~ *going* [U35] to use the truck tomorrow. It's my first day of volleyball practice.

LEONARD: Oh, that's right. You must ~~being~~ *be* [U37] excited. But you can't have the truck. I need it.

NELLY: Dad, I can't ~~missing~~ *miss* [U34] the first practice! If I'm not there, I'll get in trouble.

LEONARD: Look, I might ~~am~~ *be* [U36] able to drop you off, but I ~~maybe not~~ *may not be* [U36] able to pick you up. Can you find a ride home?

NELLY: Yeah, I'm sure I can. Everyone on the team is ~~suppose~~ *supposed* [U35] to help each other out.

Test Generating CD-ROM

General Information

The test generating CD-ROM (TestGen®) that accompanies the *Focus on Grammar Assessment Pack* provides you with the TestGen software program and a testbank of hundreds of items per level. You can use the software program to create and customize tests. With TestGen, you can:

- create tests quickly using the TestGen Wizard
- select questions by part, unit, or grammar topic
- edit questions
- add your own questions
- create multiple versions of a test

Because the items in the TestGen testbank are different from those in the printed tests, you can use TestGen to create additional tests, review quizzes, or practice exercises.

Organization of Items in the *Focus on Grammar* TestGen CD-ROM

The *Focus on Grammar* TestGen CD-ROM includes five testbanks, one for each level of *Focus on Grammar*. Within each testbank, the items are divided by part of the Student Book.

Each *Focus on Grammar* test item is labeled for easy sorting. You can sort by grammar point or unit. See "How to Create a Test" for an example of a test with items sorted by grammar point.

How to Create a Test

There are two ways to create a test using the TestGen software. You can create a test manually, or you can use the TestGen Wizard.

Using the TestGen Wizard to Create a Test
The TestGen Wizard is the easiest, fastest way to create a customized test. Follow these easy steps to create a test.

STEP 1
Select a **Testbank** from the **Testbank Library** window.

STEP 2
Click on **Use the TestGen Wizard to create a new paper test** icon.

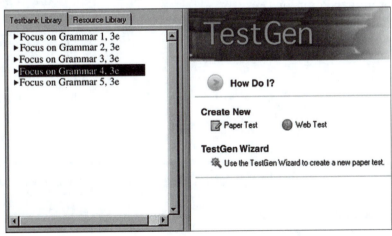

STEP 3

When the **TestGen Wizard** launches, you will be prompted to enter a name for your test. After assigning a name to your test, click the **Next** button to proceed.

STEP 4

Select the part or parts you want to include in your test.

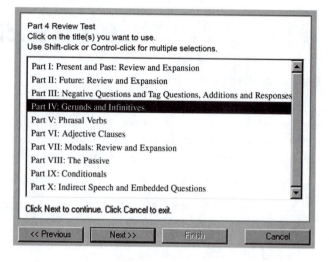

STEP 5

On the next screen, you will choose "Select questions randomly" or "Select specific questions from a list." Choose **Select questions randomly** and click the **Next** button.

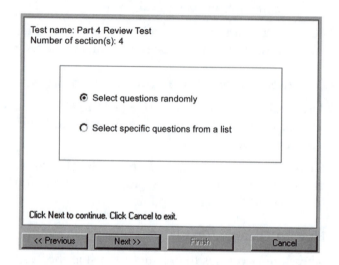

STEP 6

Use the drop-down list to choose questions randomly by Question Type, Section,* Grammar Point, or Unit.

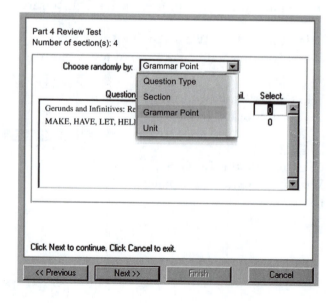

---

* "Section" refers to *Focus on Grammar* parts. Each level has 8 to 10 parts.

STEP 7

Under the "Select" column, choose the number of items you want in the test. Click the **Next** button to continue to the **Test Summary**.

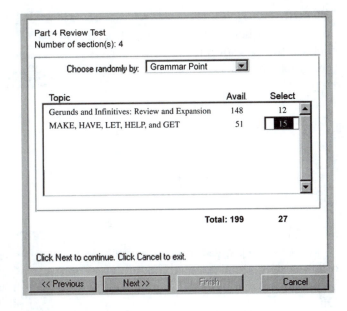

STEP 8

The **Test Summary** window will display the name of your test, the number of sections (parts) you selected, the selection method, and the total number of questions on the test. Click **Finish** to build the test.

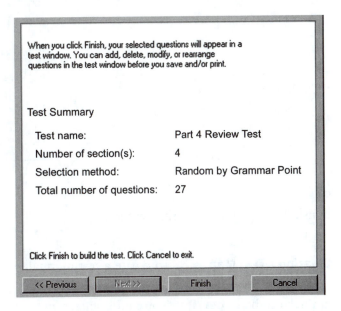

STEP 9

The **TestGen Wizard** will close, and a **Test Window** will open with your selected questions.

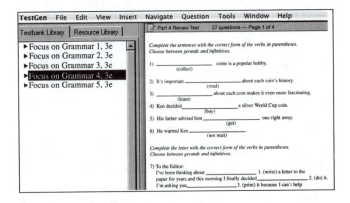

STEP 10

To put your questions in the correct order, click on the **Question** menu at the top of the screen and select **Sort**.

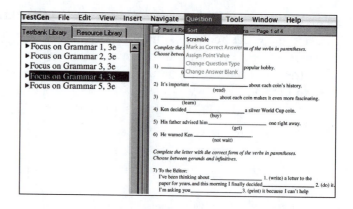

STEP 11

Next, click **Keep questions in the same order as they are in the testbank** under **SmartSort by test bank order** and click **OK**.

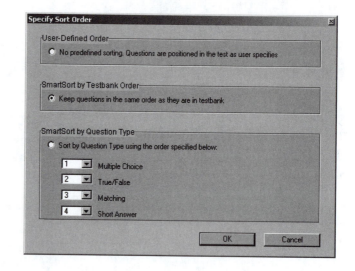

STEP 12

Finish by saving and/or printing the test.

Creating a Test Manually To create a test manually:

1. Open the TestGen software and select a **Testbank** from the **Testbank Library** window.
2. Click on the **Paper Test** icon in the startup pane. A new blank test appears.
3. Click on the arrows in the **Testbank Library** window to expand the outline and see the testbank questions.
4. Drag and drop each question you want to include into the **Test** window.

For more information, see the User's Guide located on the TestGen CD-ROM in the "Resources" folder.

How to Create New Questions

To add a new question to your test:

1. Click the place in the **Test window** where you want to add a new question.
2. In the menu bar, click **Insert > Question.**
3. Choose a **Question Type** from the drop down menu.
4. Double-click on the new question in the **Test** window.
5. Type the question and answer into the appropriate fields.

How to Edit Questions

To edit a question in your test:

1. Click on the **Tools** menu at the top of the screen and select **Preferences > Test Options.**
2. Click on the **Descriptors** tab.
3. Check **Correct Answer** to display the answers in the Test window.
4. Return to the test window and double-click on the question you want to edit.
5. Make any changes you want to both the question and answer.

How to Change the Order of Questions

If you want to move a question to a specific location in the test:

1. Click on the **Tools** menu and select **Sort.**
2. Click **User-defined order.**
3. Click **OK.**
4. Now you can drag the question to any location you want in the test.

Other TestGen Features

You can modify your TestGen test in many ways. You can change the display, create questions with graphics, edit direction lines, and much, much more. To learn more about the features that the TestGen software offers, go to the *Focus on Grammar* Companion Website (www.longman.com/focusongrammar) and click on the **TestGen** link.

TestGen 7.2 System Requirements

Windows®

Operating System:	Microsoft® Windows NT®, Windows 2000 or Windows XP	
Processor	233MHz or faster Pentium-compatible processor	
Random access memory (RAM)	128 MB	
Available hard disk space	20 MB (varies depending on testbank size)	
Web browser*	Windows NT®	Internet Explorer 5.5 or Netscape® Navigator 6.2.3
	Windows 2000	Internet Explorer 5.5, 6.0 or Netscape Navigator 6.2.3
	Windows XP	Internet Explorer 6.0 or Netscape Navigator 7.0

Macintosh®

Operating System:	Mac OS X v 10.2, 10.3, 10.4**
Processor	PowerPC G3, G4, or G5 processor
Random access memory (RAM)	128 MB
Available hard disk space	20 MB (varies depending on testbank size)
Web browser*	Internet Explorer 5.2 or Netscape Navigator 7.0

*Required only for viewing TestGen tests on the Web with TestGen Plug-in and for viewing TestGen Help.

**The TestGen application is supported on Mac OS X v 10.3 and 10.4. The TestGen Plug-in is not currently supported on this platform.

Installing TestGen

Windows Computers

- Insert the TestGen CD into your computer's CD drive.
- Open **My Computer**. Then double click on the CD drive icon.
- Double-click on "tgesetup.exe."
- Follow the directions on the screen to complete the installation. Once the installation is complete the program will begin automatically.

Macintosh Computers

- Insert the TestGen CD into your computer's CD drive.
- Double-click on "TestGen 7 Setup."
- Follow the directions on the screen to complete the installation. Once the installation is complete the program will begin automatically.

Note:

If you have existing versions of TestGen on your computer, you will receive a message providing you with the option to remove earlier versions of the program. Click *Yes* to remove the older TestGen versions and continue (recommended).

Removing older versions of the TestGen program does not delete or otherwise compromise tests and testbanks created with earlier versions of the program located on your computer. You can convert older tests and testbanks simply by opening them in the TestGen 7.2 program.

Product Support

The *User's Guide* can be found on the TestGen CD in the "Resources" folder (see TG7UserGuide.pdf). It provides detailed instructions about how to use all of TestGen's tools and features. Once TestGen has been installed, the *User's Guide* is also available by clicking "Help" in the TestGen menu at the top of the screen. To view the *User's Guide*, Adobe® Acrobat® Reader® is required. This free software can be installed from the Internet at the following address: www.adobe.com/acrobat.

For further technical assistance:

- Call Pearson's toll-free product support line: 1-800-677-6337
- Send an email to media.support@pearsoned.com
- Fill out a web form at: http://247.pearsoned.com/mediaform

Our technical staff will need to know certain things about your system in order to help us solve your problems more quickly and efficiently. If possible, please be at your computer when you call for support. You should have the following information ready:

- Product title and product ISBN
- Computer make and model
- RAM available
- Hard disk space available
- Graphics card type
- Printer make and model (if applicable)
- Detailed description of the problem, including the exact wording of any error messages.